GUILDWARS 2®

FEASTS OF TYRIA

GUILD WARS 2®

FEASTS OF TYRIA

Recipes from Kryta to Elona

Victoria Rosenthal & Erin Kwong

SAN RAFAEL · LOS ANGELES · LONDON

CONTENTS

Foreword 7

Introduction 9

APPETIZERS 10
Bowl of Hummus 13
Saffron Stuffed Mushrooms 14
Chili Pepper Popper 17
Cup of Lotus Fries 18
Red-Lentil Saobosa 21
Lake Doric Mussels 22
Spicy Moa Wings 25
Mint-Pear Cured Meat Flatbread 26
Zephyrite Fish Jerky 29
Koi Cake 30
Crispy Fish Pancakes 33

BREADS 34
Cheesy Cassava Roll 36
Flatbread 39
Rosemary Bread 40
Zucchini Bread 43
Cinnamon Toast 44

SALADS 46
Salad à la Consortium 49
Ascalonian Salad 50
Feast of Coleslaw 53
Feast of Bean Salad 54
Fruit Salad with Mint Garnish 57

SOUPS AND STEWS 58
Poultry Stock 60
Red Meat Stock 63
Vegetable Stock 64
Fancy Creamy Mushroom Soup 67
Potato and Leek Soup 68
Tomato Soup 71
Butternut Squash Soup 72
Kimchi Tofu Stew 75
Valravn Stew 76
Carne Khan Chili 79
Savory Spinach and Poultry Soup 80

SIDES 82
Mushroom and Asparagus Risotto 85
Mashed Potatoes 86
Spiced Mashed Yams 89
Meaty Asparagus Skewer 90
Spicy Marinated Mushrooms 93
Eztlitl Stuffing 94
Grilled Plantains with Passion Fruit 97

ENTRÉES...98

Fishy Rice Bowl...100
Jerk Poultry...103
Lemongrass Mussel Pasta...104
Feast of Meatball Dinner...107
Poultry Piccata...108
Peppercorn-Spiced Coq Au Vin...111
Salsa Eggs Benedict...115
Sugar Rib Roast...116
Filet of Rosemary-Roasted Meat...119
Fancy Veggie Pizza...120
Beef Rendang...124
Meaty Rice Bowl...128

DESSERTS...132

Peach Pie...134
Strawberry Cookies...138
Mint Crème Brûlée...141
Tropical Mousse...142
Spicy Chocolate Cookies...145
Bloodstone Bearclaw Pastry...146
Mandragor Root Cake...149
Delicious Rice Ball...153
Super Mixed Parfait...157
Chocolate Omnomberry Cake...161
Ginger-Lime Ice Cream...165

BEVERAGES...166

Buttered Spirits...168
Avocado Smoothie...171
Bloodstone Coffee...172
Pitcher of Desert-Spiced Coffee...175
Mystery Tonic...176
Celebratory Drink...179
Elixir of Heroes...180
Belcher's Bluff...183

Conclusion...187
Difficulty Index...188
About the Authors...189
Conversion Charts...190

FOREWORD

"Some people eat to live. In this family, we live to eat." My grandfather would shout this while balancing a massive dish in each hand en route to the Sunday communal table. Kids seated at one end, adults at the other. Food. Drink. Family. Friends. A houseful of memories built upon stories and laughter loud enough to wake the dearly departed. The importance of family, community, and food was baked into our DNA.

Decades later, I'd find myself working alongside a new family whose mission was to entertain with stories and adventures. And most importantly for this book—with food.

My colleagues went the extra mile to give these dishes identities that meshed with the cultures of Tyria. To make these culinary delights feel like a part of our fantasy world. To let fellow commanders and grandmaster chefs share their creations by dropping a platter of sandwiches within spitting distance of a raid boss, as if to taunt Deimos and his multitude of grasping hands to try and grab one without losing a limb.

Imagine my delight when I learned that Victoria and Erin were writing this book to celebrate the communal spirit of Guild Wars. These dishes that were lovingly designed, illustrated, and given the lore treatment by teams of developers would now be made real by people who had done justice to so many other works of interactive fantasy. My wife heard me squeal with excitement through the home office door the moment I got the email.

It's been nothing short of a pleasure to peek inside Victoria's process and to read Erin's take on our lore while slipping into Seimur's voice. To ponder the menu before the raid. I'm thrilled for them to share their creations that were inspired by ours and to finally make real the dishes and concoctions that have thus far mostly existed on the screens of tens of millions of players. I can't wait for our squad leaders to share their creations with family, friends, and guildmates.

Because in this guild, we live to eat.

Bobby Stein
Studio Narrative Director, ArenaNet

INTRODUCTION

People have been talking. Chefs, mostly. They're saying that a new wave of culinary superstars are on the rise. Is it true? Are you one of them?

There are plenty of master chefs that would spurn newcomers. Not me! I respect anyone, grandmaster or apprentice, who's got the talent to attain greatness. And I was in your shoes once. You know me today as Seimur Oxbone, sous-chef extraordinaire, bloodstone pioneer, and nomadic recipe artisan. But before I was all that, I was a young norn leaving the Shiverpeaks for the first time, not a recipe to my name. Ready to prove myself! Eager to taste the flavors of the world.

The first thing I did in pursuit of that goal was track down the Durmand Priory, a monastery dedicated to protecting knowledge and history. Of course, I didn't know about all that. All I knew was that some of the best chefs in Tyria came out of the Priory, and I was going to join them! I didn't get the other stuff. Lost Knowledge? Research? What did that have to do with cooking delicious food? Who *cared*?

Well, their leader did. Steward Gixx begrudgingly let me join, but for my first mission he told me to spend a year traveling Tyria and beyond. So, experience could make me strong. And it did! Through hardship and adventure, I learned old and new knowledge that enhanced my cooking. Through camaraderie and solitude, I came to understand how deeply the food we eat is tied to the past. After that year, I returned to the monastery and earned a place as an assistant chef.

It's been a long time since then. I've spent many more years journeying around our wild and wondrous world. Now I've got too much knowledge to know what to do with. So! I'm going to share it with you. This book is chock-full of the recipes and stories I've gathered. Don't think this is a shortcut to mastery—it's a challenge. A mission, like Gixx gave me, to take the information in. To learn from it. To make creations that the bards will sing of! So you can prove yourself, like I did, and spread that knowledge to more of Tyria.

Chop, chop!

APPETIZERS

My year of travel began in the Maguuma Jungle. I was raring to go, ready to jump into danger and find some never-before-seen ingredients. The jungle was the best place to start from the beginning; to whet my appetite for what lay ahead. It was also the place where I first truly understood the worth of the appetizer.

Trekking through thick jungle ferns really works up an appetite—I constantly wanted a snack to tide myself over. And it was always easier to fight off skelks and wurms when you knew you had a full-course meal to look forward to! By the time I left the jungle, I had learned how to turn the mushrooms and berries I scavenged into bite-size delicacies. Whether as an on-the-go snack or as the first course of a lavish dinner, these appetizing recipes are a great place to begin your culinary journey.

BOWL OF HUMMUS

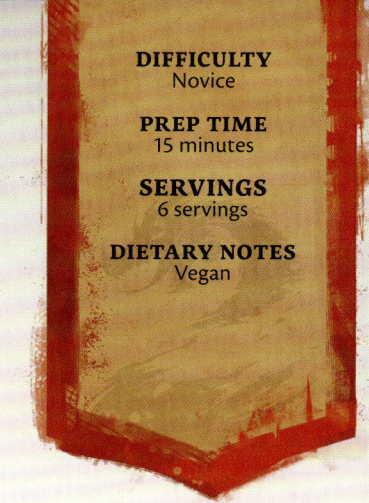

DIFFICULTY
Novice

PREP TIME
15 minutes

SERVINGS
6 servings

DIETARY NOTES
Vegan

You might be wondering: Seimur, why start your cookbook off with a simple bowl of hummus? Why not show off something more difficult, more fantastical? Perhaps bloodstone goulash, or bloodstone pastry, something that really hits you with a bang? Well, the reason is this: Whether you're an apprentice or a grandmaster chef, you've got to know how to make a Bowl of Hummus. It may not be hard to make; my Elonian friends tell me it's one of their easiest recipes. But if you overlook its easy blend of punchy garlic and creamy chickpea, you'll never attain greatness. And who knows? Maybe you could be the one to bring bloodstone hummus to Tyria!

1. In a food processor, pulse the chickpeas, tahini, garlic cloves, lemon juice, water, kosher salt, and cumin until smooth. Slowly pour in the olive oil while running the food processor. Mix until it is all well combined.
Note: If the mixture is too thick to mix, add another teaspoon of water at a time. Transfer to an airtight container and store in the refrigerator. The hummus can be stored for up to 1 week.

2. When ready to serve, garnish with sumac, cilantro, and additional olive oil.

15 ounces cooked chickpeas, drained and rinsed
⅓ cup tahini
2 garlic cloves
3 tablespoons lemon juice
2 tablespoons water
1 teaspoon kosher salt
½ teaspoon ground cumin
2 tablespoons olive oil, plus more as needed
1 tablespoon sumac
2 tablespoons cilantro, chopped

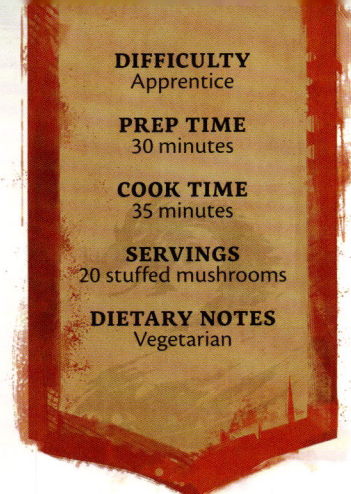

DIFFICULTY
Apprentice

PREP TIME
30 minutes

COOK TIME
35 minutes

SERVINGS
20 stuffed mushrooms

DIETARY NOTES
Vegetarian

SAFFRON STUFFED MUSHROOMS

This dish is popular across Tyria and Elona, but not many know its origin. From my travels and what I've read in ancient texts, I've pieced together its plausible migration. Before the cataclysm, the Orrian royal chef was known to specialize in saffron-spiced delicacies. After the Third Guild War, Orrian refugees brought the recipe to Kryta, where its savory nuance quickly made it a hit. Doesn't really matter to me, though, because it tastes good. The cheese and melted butter enhance the almost meaty taste of the cremini mushrooms, and the way they're stuffed to bursting in the caps makes them irresistible!

---

20 cremini mushrooms
2 tablespoons unsalted butter
Pinch of saffron
1 shallot, chopped
3 garlic cloves, minced
¼ cup panko breadcrumbs
¼ cup Parmesan, grated
4 ounces cream cheese
1 tablespoon parsley, chopped

1. Preheat the oven to 400°F. Remove the mushroom stems and chop them.
2. In a small nonstick pan, melt the butter over medium-high heat. Once melted, add the saffron and cook for 1 minute.
3. Add the chopped mushroom stems and shallots. Cook until softened, 5 to 8 minutes. Add the garlic and cook for another 2 minutes. Finally, add the panko and cook until it absorbs all the liquid and has lightly toasted, 2 to 3 minutes.
4. Transfer to a medium bowl with the Parmesan, cream cheese, and parsley. Mix until well combined.
5. Fill each of the cremini mushroom caps with the filling, making sure to slightly overstuff them. Place on a baking sheet lined with parchment paper.
6. Bake for 20 to 25 minutes, or until the filling is golden brown and the mushrooms are tender.

CHILI PEPPER POPPER

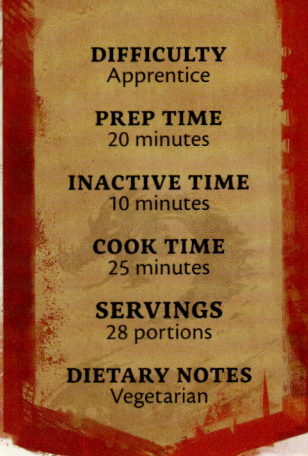

DIFFICULTY
Apprentice

PREP TIME
20 minutes

INACTIVE TIME
10 minutes

COOK TIME
25 minutes

SERVINGS
28 portions

DIETARY NOTES
Vegetarian

No one can deny that the Searing had devastating results. The scorching fires that blazed across Ascalon at the climax of the wars between humans and charr caused irreparable damage to both cultures and their land. Some chefs swear that the fires changed the way that the region's soil affects the taste of crops. I can't say for certain, but I can attest to one thing: There's no pepper better than an Ascalonian chili pepper, especially when stuffed with a mouthwatering blend of delicious cheeses.

1. Preheat the oven to 400°F. In a medium bowl, combine the cream cheese, cheddar, gouda, garlic, salt, and pepper. Mix until well combined and set aside.
2. For the toasted panko breadcrumbs, melt the butter in a small nonstick pan over medium-high heat. Once melted, add the panko and cook until it turns golden brown, 2 to 3 minutes. Remove from the heat and set aside.
3. Place a wire rack over a baking sheet. Take one of the jalapeño halves and slightly overfill with the filling. Place on the wire rack. Repeat until all the jalapeño halves are filled.
4. Top with the toasted panko breadcrumbs. Bake for 18 to 20 minutes, or until golden brown.
5. Allow to cool for 10 minutes before topping with chives and serving.

Filling
8 ounces cream cheese
4 ounces cheddar, shredded
2 ounces gouda, shredded
3 garlic cloves, finely minced
½ teaspoon kosher salt
¼ teaspoon ground black pepper

Toasted Panko Breadcrumbs
2 tablespoons unsalted butter
½ cup panko breadcrumbs

Assembly
14 jalapeños, halved and seeded
2 tablespoons chives, chopped

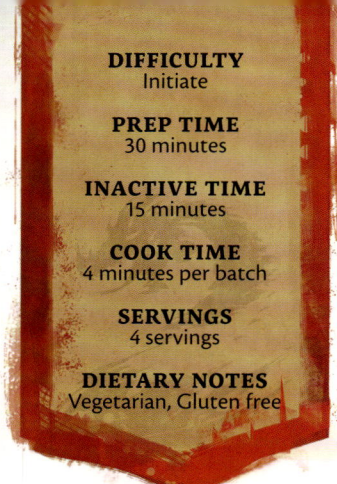

DIFFICULTY
Initiate

PREP TIME
30 minutes

INACTIVE TIME
15 minutes

COOK TIME
4 minutes per batch

SERVINGS
4 servings

DIETARY NOTES
Vegetarian, Gluten free

CUP OF LOTUS FRIES

You can't beat this chip! Simple, crispy, and more nutritious than potato fries, this snack is all the rage in Cantha. In fact, I've heard that Empress Ihn herself requests her chefs make lotus fries when she's frustrated with diplomatic relations or military delays. And even the mention of Elder Dragons has the kitchens whisking gochujang and slicing lotus! I can't blame her—the crunchy texture and light tastiness are irresistible.

Spicy Dip
½ cup sour cream
2 tablespoons gochujang
1 teaspoon garlic powder
1 teaspoon rice vinegar

Lotus Chips
2 cups water
1 teaspoon vinegar
1 lotus root, peeled
Neutral oil, for frying
Kosher salt
Ground black pepper

1. To make the dip: In a small bowl, whisk together all the ingredients. Place in an airtight container and refrigerate until you are ready to serve with the lotus chips.

2. To make the chips: Fill a large bowl with water and vinegar. Slice the lotus root into ⅛-inch-thick rounds. As they are cut, place them in the prepared bowl. Allow them to soak for at least 15 minutes.

3. Fill a deep pot with 2 inches of neutral oil and heat over medium heat to 340°F.

4. Transfer the lotus root to a paper towel and thoroughly dry them off before placing in the oil.
Note: Getting any amount of water in the hot oil can be extremely dangerous. Make sure these are completely dry to avoid any fire hazard.

5. Transfer a small handful of lotus root slices into the pot, making sure not to overcrowd the pot. Fry for 2 minutes, flip and then fry for another 2 minutes or until golden brown. Transfer to a wire rack to allow any excess oil to drain.

6. Season with a generous amount of salt and pepper.

7. Repeat steps 5 and 6 until all the lotus root slices have been fried and seasoned.

RED-LENTIL SAOBOSA

There's an unspoken rule among the chefs of the Durmand Priory—you're not a real cook until you can whip up a pastry that is unequivocally perfect. Well, it turns out this saobosa, packed with red lentils and my unique blend of zesty spices, was my perfected pastry.

DIFFICULTY
Adept

PREP TIME
1 hour

INACTIVE TIME
1 hour

COOK TIME
1 hour

SERVINGS
12 saobosa

DIETARY NOTES
Vegetarian

1. To make the dough: In a medium bowl, combine the flour and salt. Mix in the ghee until it resembles coarse cornmeal. Slowly add the water and work until it forms a firm dough. If the dough is too sticky, add 1 tablespoon of flour at a time. If it is too dry, add 1 tablespoon of water at a time.

2. Form into a ball, place in the bowl, and cover with a kitchen towel. Let rest for 1 hour while you prepare the filling.

3. To make the filling: In a medium pot, cover the potatoes with just enough water to cover them and 1 teaspoon salt and heat over high heat. Bring to a boil and then reduce the heat to a simmer for 15 to 20 minutes, or until the potatoes are tender. Drain and set aside.

4. In a large nonstick pan, heat 1 tablespoon of olive oil over medium-high heat. Add the onions and carrots and cook until softened, 3 to 5 minutes. Add the ginger, garlic, and serrano pepper and stir well. Add the cumin, coriander, garam masala, turmeric, Kashmiri chile, amchur, cinnamon, cardamom, fennel, and 1 teaspoon of salt. Toss until the vegetables are coated in the spices.

5. Add the lentils and water. Bring to a simmer, cover, and cook for 20 minutes or until the liquid has been absorbed and the lentils are cooked through. Add the potatoes and lightly mix together.

6. Remove from the heat. Set aside and allow to cool completely.

7. Split the dough into six equal portions, covering the dough you aren't working with.

8. Place one of the portions on a lightly floured surface. Roll out into a thin circle. Cut in half.

9. Take one of the halves and brush the cut edge with water. Take the corners of the cut edge and fold over one another and press together to form into a cone. Fill the cone with the filling. Lightly wet the edges and pinch together to seal the filling in. Repeat this step with the other half.

10. Repeat steps 8 and 9 until all the dough has been used. Pour 1 inch of neutral oil in a deep pot and heat to 350°F.

11. Once the oil has been heated, place three of the samosas into the oil and fry for 3 minutes. Flip and fry for another 3 minutes, or until both sides are golden brown. Transfer to a plate with a paper towel. Repeat until all the samosas have been fried.

Dough

2 cups all-purpose flour

1 teaspoon kosher salt

5 tablespoons ghee, melted then cooled

⅓ cup water

Filling

1 russet potato, peeled and chopped

2 teaspoons kosher salt, divided

½ onion, chopped

½ carrot, chopped

1-inch piece of ginger, grated

6 garlic cloves, minced

1 serrano pepper, chopped

1 tablespoon ground cumin

1 tablespoon ground coriander

2 teaspoons garam masala

1 teaspoon ground turmeric

1 teaspoon ground Kashmiri chile pepper

1 teaspoon amchur powder

1 teaspoon ground cinnamon

½ teaspoon ground cardamom

½ teaspoon ground fennel

¾ cup red lentils

2 cups water

Neutral oil, for frying

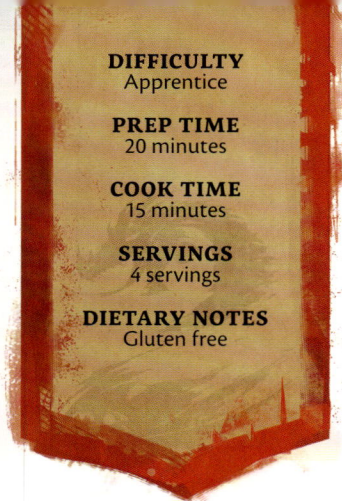

DIFFICULTY
Apprentice

PREP TIME
20 minutes

COOK TIME
15 minutes

SERVINGS
4 servings

DIETARY NOTES
Gluten free

LAKE DORIC MUSSELS

Though this seafood specialty is now considered high-brow, it was once a staple of the prisoners who built the docks of Lake Doric. The prisoners took turns scraping mussels off rocks during their work shifts. They'd steam them while hiding from their captors and divide the mussels among themselves to recover vitality and focus. Of course, my version of the recipe has added pesto, garlic, tomato, and basil for a light, tender seasoning—luxury those poor prisoners couldn't have dreamt of.

Pesto
3 tablespoons pine nuts
2 garlic cloves
3 ounces fresh basil
1 ounce Parmigiano Reggiano
½ ounce Pecorino Romano
2 tablespoons olive oil
Kosher salt
Ground black pepper

Mussels
2 pounds fresh mussels *
1 tablespoon unsalted butter
1 tablespoon olive oil
1 shallot, finely chopped
¾ cup white wine
½ teaspoon ground black pepper
1 teaspoon lemon zest
Juice of 1 lemon
Pesto

1. To make the pesto: In a small stainless-steel pan, toast the pine nuts over medium-high heat until fragrant, 3 to 5 minutes. Transfer to a food processor.

2. Add the garlic and pulse the food processor until it forms a paste. Add the basil and pulse until roughly chopped. Add the cheeses and pulse until combined.

3. Slowly add the olive oil until it forms a nice thick paste. Season with salt and pepper.

4. To make the mussels: In a large pan, heat butter and olive oil over medium-high heat. Once the butter has melted, add the shallots and cook until softened, 3 to 5 minutes.

5. Add the white wine and heat for 1 minute. Season with pepper.

6. If your mussels are sitting in a bowl of water, drain them and then transfer to the pan. Cover and cook until all the mussels have opened, about 3 minutes. Discard any mussels that don't open.

7. Add the lemon zest and juice and pesto and toss until combined. Serve immediately.

*Note: It is vital to clean and check that your mussels are alive before cooking them. If any of them are open, give them a tap with a spoon and discard them if they don't close. To clean them, place them in a large bowl of heavily salted, cold water and let them rest for 15 minutes. Carefully scrub them. Remove any beards on them by pulling them off and discarding.

SPICY MOA WINGS

The best recipes come with at least a little danger, I always say. You'll need to watch out for devourer nests when harvesting the Hatched Chili needed for these wings, as Hatched Chili is grown over the homes of the pesky scorpion monsters! But it's worth it—the fiery kick of the peppers layered over succulent meat will soon have you calling yourself a devourer.

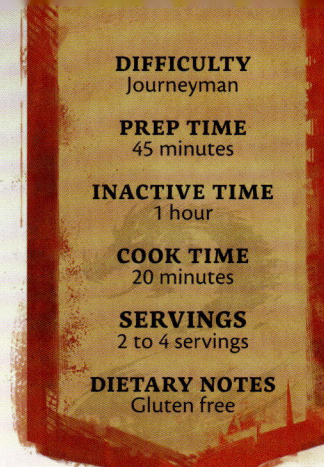

DIFFICULTY
Journeyman

PREP TIME
45 minutes

INACTIVE TIME
1 hour

COOK TIME
20 minutes

SERVINGS
2 to 4 servings

DIETARY NOTES
Gluten free

---

1. Preheat the oven broiler. Place the Hatch chiles, jalapeño, onion, tomatillos, and garlic on a baking sheet. Put the baking sheet under the broiler and cook until the peppers and tomatillos have charred slightly, about 10 minutes.

2. Remove from the oven and allow to cool. Transfer to a food processor. Add the cilantro and lime juice. Pulse the food processor until smooth. Season with salt and pepper if needed. The salsa can be stored in an airtight container in the refrigerator for up to 1 week.
   Note: The salsa will thicken as it sits in the refrigerator. Before tossing the wings, if the salsa is too thick, add a small amount of vegetable broth to loosen it.

3. Place the chicken wings in a bowl with water and let sit for 15 minutes. Lightly rub the wings with your hand, removing any excess blood or gunk. Dry well.

4. In a sealable container, combine the mirin, lime juice, black pepper, and garlic powder. Add the chicken wings and cover in the marinade. Let rest in the refrigerator for at least 30 minutes, up to 2 hours.

5. Transfer the wings to a paper towel–lined baking sheet and pat dry. In a sealable bag, combine the cornstarch and potato starch. Toss the wings in the starch mixture.

6. Fill a deep pot with 2 inches of neutral oil and heat over medium heat to 350°F.

7. Carefully place the wings in the oil and fry for 6 to 8 minutes, flipping halfway through. Make sure not to overcrowd the pot so you don't lower the temperature too rapidly.

8. Transfer to a wire rack with a paper towel–lined baking sheet below it and allow the excess oil to drain.

9. Toss the wings in the Hatched Chili Salsa and serve immediately.

Hatched Chili Salsa
2 green Hatch chiles
1 jalapeño
½ onion
6 tomatillos
4 garlic cloves
1 tablespoon lime juice
½ bunch fresh cilantro
Kosher salt
Ground black pepper

Chicken Wings
1 pound chicken wings
¼ cup mirin
2 tablespoons lime juice
1 teaspoon black pepper
1 teaspoon garlic powder
½ cup cornstarch
¼ cup potato starch
Kosher salt
Neutral oil, for frying

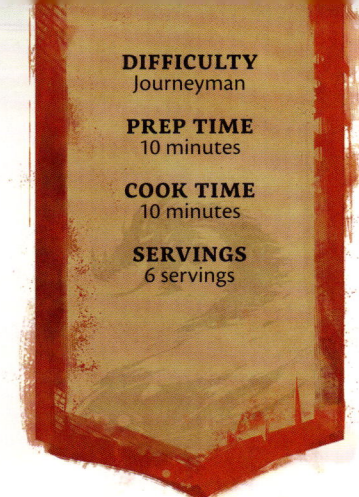

DIFFICULTY
Journeyman

PREP TIME
10 minutes

COOK TIME
10 minutes

SERVINGS
6 servings

MINT-PEAR CURED MEAT FLATBREAD

I've heard a rumor that a particularly renowned Blood Legion warrior looks down on this appetizer—calls it "junk on toast." Well, I don't care if he's got some fancy legendary sword, or if he's part of Destiny's Edge, center, or backside. I can't allow that insult to stand! There's nothing better than a well-bodied flatbread, especially with a balanced curation of toppings. The meat supplies a salty heartiness. The pear offsets that with full, juicy sweetness. And a touch of mint ties it all together. It just goes to show that everyone has a weakness, even if they've defeated the Undead Dragon.

---

8 ounces mascarpone
½ teaspoon garlic powder
4 Flatbreads (page 39)
4 ounces mozzarella, shredded
4 ounces brie, sliced
1 pear, sliced thinly
4 ounces prosciutto
2 ounces arugula
½ ounce mint
Balsamic vinegar glaze

1. Preheat the oven to 400°F. In a small bowl, combine the mascarpone and garlic powder. Place the flatbreads on two baking sheets. Spread the mascarpone over the flatbreads, making sure not to completely go to the edge.

2. Sprinkle the mozzarella on top of the mascarpone. Top each with a one-quarter of the brie, pear, and prosciutto.

3. Place in the oven and bake for 8 to 10 minutes, or until the cheese is melted. Remove from the oven and let cool for 3 minutes before topping with arugula, mint, and balsamic vinegar glaze. Cut into portions to serve.

ZEPHYRITE FISH JERKY

DIFFICULTY
Journeyman

PREP TIME
30 minutes

INACTIVE TIME
24 hours

COOK TIME
5 hours

SERVINGS
12 servings

DIETARY NOTES
Dairy free

One of my friends is a Zephyrite who spends his time roaming the skies in the Zephyr Sanctum! I don't have the patience for their belief system, but to each their own, right? He taught me the recipe for this fish jerky, along with the practice of meditation through tranquil fishing. He swears that any fish caught during meditation will be touched by Aspect magic—magic powered by the Sun, Wind, or Lightning Aspects. Eating the fish is supposed to make tumultuous waters smooth and sailing easy. I've never been a meditative guy, but one bite of the peppery goodness of this toothsome jerky could make me a follower of Glint!

1. In a gallon-size sealable bag, combine the soy sauce, honey, liquid smoke, brown sugar, ginger powder, and pepper. Cut the trout to ⅛ to ¼ inch thick, keeping the skin on. Add the trout to the bag and toss to coat. Place in the refrigerator overnight to marinate, up to 24 hours.
   Note: Make sure your knife is extremely sharp. This will make cutting the trout much easier.

2. Preheat the oven to 175°F. Prepare a baking sheet with aluminum foil and place a wire rack on top. Take the trout out of the marinade and pat dry. Place on the wire rack.

3. Cook in the oven for 4 to 5 hours or until the trout is dry and chewy. Let cool completely. Store in an airtight container in the refrigerator for up to 2 weeks.
   Note: The jerky can be enjoyed with the skin on or you can remove it after it has cooked.

1¼ cups soy sauce
3 tablespoons honey
1 teaspoon liquid smoke
1 tablespoon dark brown sugar
1 tablespoon ginger powder
1 tablespoon ground black pepper
2 pounds steelhead trout, skin on

KOI CAKE

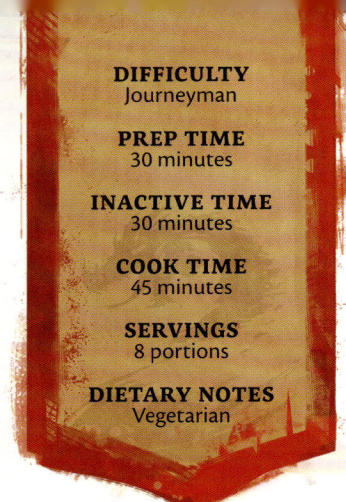

DIFFICULTY Journeyman
PREP TIME 30 minutes
INACTIVE TIME 30 minutes
COOK TIME 45 minutes
SERVINGS 8 portions
DIETARY NOTES Vegetarian

Ah, Dragon Bash! An annual delight, king of all festivals! If you've never had the pleasure of visiting Hoelbrak during the celebration, I can't recommend it enough. From the piñatas to the moa races, there's no better way to celebrate the smashing of the Elder Dragons. And a bash wouldn't be complete without buying this classic pastry from a stall or cooking it up yourself!

- 1¾ pounds russet potatoes, peeled and cut into 1-inch pieces
- 3 tablespoons unsalted butter, room temperature
- 4 scallions, chopped
- 8 ounces ham, diced
- ½ cup sour cream
- 2 teaspoons ground black pepper
- 1 teaspoon kosher salt
- 5 ounces sharp cheddar cheese, shredded
- 3.5 ounces gouda cheese, shredded
- 2 eggs
- ⅓ cup all-purpose flour
- 1¾ cups panko breadcrumbs
- Neutral oil, for frying

1. Place the potatoes in a large pot, add just enough water to cover them, and season with a pinch of salt. Bring to a boil over high heat and then reduce the heat and simmer for 15 to 20 minutes, or until the potatoes are tender. Drain the potatoes. Mash the potatoes in a large bowl and set aside.

2. In a small nonstick pan, heat the butter over medium-high heat. Once melted, add the scallions. Cook until softened, about 3 minutes. Remove from the heat and mix in with the mashed potatoes.

3. Return the pan to the heat and add the ham. Cook until lightly browned, 3 to 5 minutes. Transfer to the bowl with the mashed potatoes.

4. Add the sour cream, pepper, salt, cheddar cheese, and gouda cheese and mix until just combined. Split into eight equally portioned oval patties and place on a tray with parchment paper. Refrigerate, uncovered, for 15 minutes.

5. Prepare three stations for breading the koi cakes. The first station with flour, the second is a bowl with the eggs lightly beaten, and the final station is a plate of panko. Coat each patty in flour, followed by the eggs, and finally in the panko. Place the coated koi cakes back into the refrigerator until the oil has heated up.

6. Place 2 inches of neutral oil in a deep pot and heat to 350°F. Carefully place several of the koi cakes at a time into the heated oil and cook for 2 to 3 minutes, flipping once and until golden. Transfer to a plate lined with paper towels to drain. Repeat until all the koi cakes are cooked.

CRISPY FISH PANCAKES

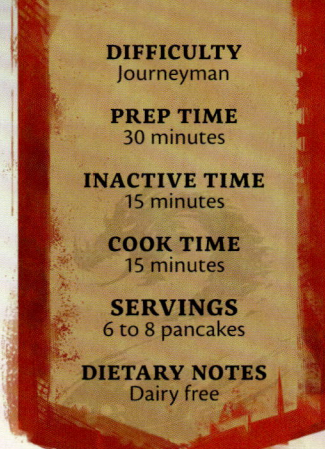

DIFFICULTY
Journeyman

PREP TIME
30 minutes

INACTIVE TIME
15 minutes

COOK TIME
15 minutes

SERVINGS
6 to 8 pancakes

DIETARY NOTES
Dairy free

For all his steady logic and objective, methodical genius, Steward Gixx can hold a grudge. It's not easy to get back in his good graces once you've been cast out of them. For example: Last year, one of my culinary experiments went a bit sideways (the potential of bloodstone is challenging to unlock) and I blew a pretty sizable hole into the wall of the Durmand monastery. Gixx was . . . not happy. But I knew he had a taste for these pancakes. Who could resist the sizzle of sesame oil? The melting tenderness of fillet? The fluff of the mixture holding it all together? I made them for his lunch for a week and was grudgingly forgiven. Now I only experiment when he's out of office.

1. To make the sauce: In a small bowl, whisk together all the ingredients. Transfer and store in an airtight container until you are ready to serve.
2. To make the pancakes: In a medium bowl, combine the flour, potato starch, baking powder, garlic powder, ginger powder, onion powder, and black pepper. In a small bowl, combine the water, fish sauce, and sesame oil. Pour the water into the flour mixture and whisk until smooth. The batter should be thin.
3. Add the scallops, tilapia, tuna, serrano pepper, scallions, bell pepper, and sesame seeds. Mix together with a spatula until it just comes together. Let rest at room temperature for 15 minutes.
4. In a medium nonstick pan, heat 2 tablespoons of canola oil over medium-high heat. Place a large spoonful of the fish-pancake mixture into the pan, forming a 4- to 5-inch-wide pancake. Cook until the bottom has turned golden brown, about 2 minutes. Flip and cook the other side until golden brown, another 2 minutes. Transfer to a paper towel–lined plate to drain any excess oil. Serve immediately.
5. Repeat step 4 with the remaining batter until all of it is cooked.

Sauce

- 2 tablespoons soy sauce
- 1 tablespoon rice vinegar
- ¼ teaspoon sesame oil
- ½ teaspoon sugar
- 1 scallion, white and light green part only, chopped
- 2 teaspoons ginger, grated
- 1 teaspoon toasted white sesame seeds

Pancakes

- ½ cup all-purpose flour
- ½ cup potato starch
- 1 teaspoon baking powder
- ½ teaspoon garlic powder
- 1 teaspoon ginger powder
- ½ teaspoon onion powder
- ½ teaspoon ground black pepper
- ¾ cup water, cold
- 1 tablespoon fish sauce
- 1½ teaspoons sesame oil
- 4 ounces scallops, chopped
- 8 ounces tilapia fillet, chopped
- 4 ounces tuna, chopped
- 1 serrano pepper, chopped
- 4 scallions, chopped
- ½ red bell pepper, chopped
- 1 tablespoon toasted white sesame seeds
- Canola oil, for frying

BREADS

After the jungle, I journeyed into Kryta. I meant to go straight to Divinity's Reach, but while passing through the Township of Claypool, I sniffed out an incredibly tempting smell wafting from one of the inns. The scent of freshly baked bread speaks for itself! As the innkeeper guided me through the mixing, kneading, and baking of the rosemary-infused dough, he called it "the loaf that built Queensdale" and explained why:

Before humans had towns and villages in the area, they had shacks and small fields of wheat. They ground their wheat into flour, baked that flour into bread, and ate that bread so they had the energy to build up their settlements and widen their fields. It was the bedrock of their society! It was inspiring to hear the respect people paid to their food. I kept it in mind as I ate bread to fuel my weeklong vacation training in Claypool.

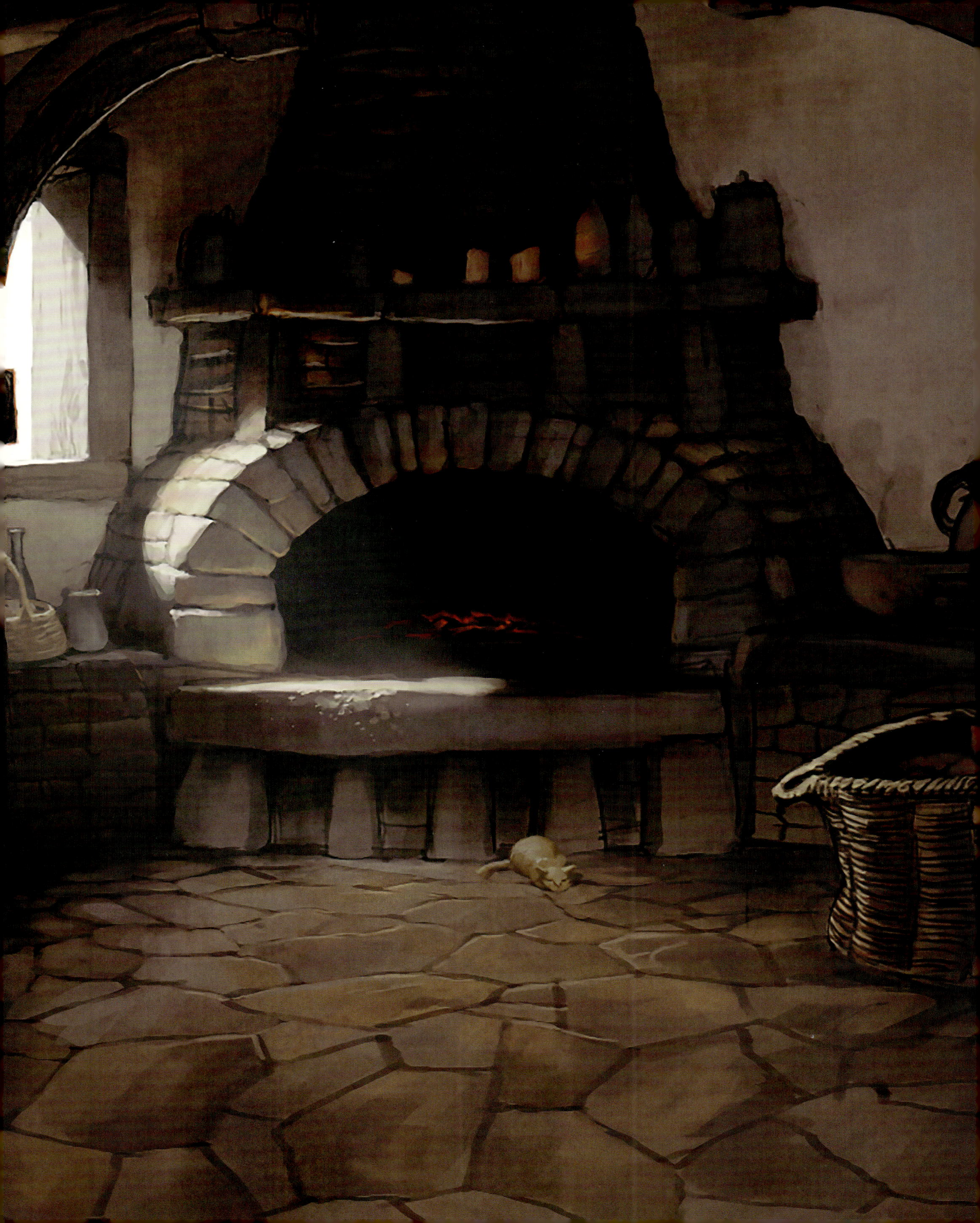

DIFFICULTY
Initiate

PREP TIME
20 minutes

COOK TIME
20 minutes

SERVINGS
12 rolls

DIETARY NOTES
Gluten free

CHEESY CASSAVA ROLL

People seem to have made this cheesy treat since the dawn of Tyria itself. I couldn't track down an origin for it, but what I *did* find was that the recipe for a cheesy cassava roll was fairly unchanged throughout history until recently, when its popularity suddenly exploded. Denizens of Gendarran Fields have come out with their best iterations on the roll, and the fruitful farmland of the area gives them plenty of high-quality ingredients to work with. This recipe is among the most well-known with its novel changes: namely, replacing whole flaxseed with ground ones for a better texture and swapping heavy cream for buttermilk to give it a tangy kick.

- 2¼ cups cassava flour
- 2 tablespoons ground flaxseed
- 2 tablespoons baking powder
- 2 teaspoons kosher salt
- 1 teaspoon sugar
- 2 cups buttermilk
- ¼ cup unsalted butter, melted and cooled
- 2 eggs
- 8 ounces cheddar cheese, finely shredded.
- 2 ounces Parmesan cheese, finely shredded

1. Preheat the oven to 375°F. In a large bowl, combine the cassava flour, flaxseed, baking powder, salt, and sugar. In a small bowl, combine the buttermilk, butter, and eggs.
2. Pour the liquid into the dry mixture and mix together. Add the cheeses and mix until fully incorporated.
3. Place parchment paper on a baking sheet. Split the batter into 12 equal portions onto the baking sheet with a spoon. Bake for 20 minutes or until lightly golden.

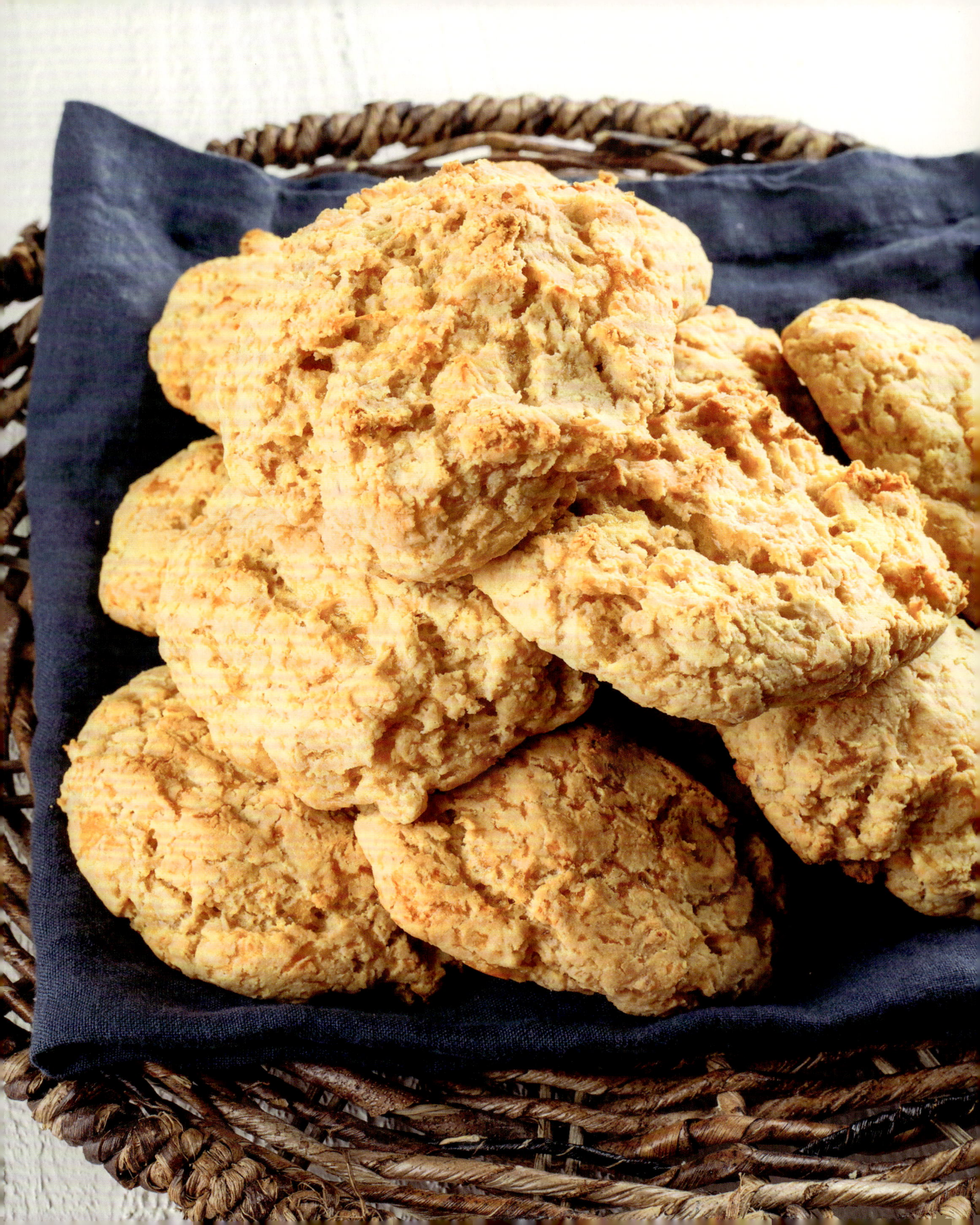

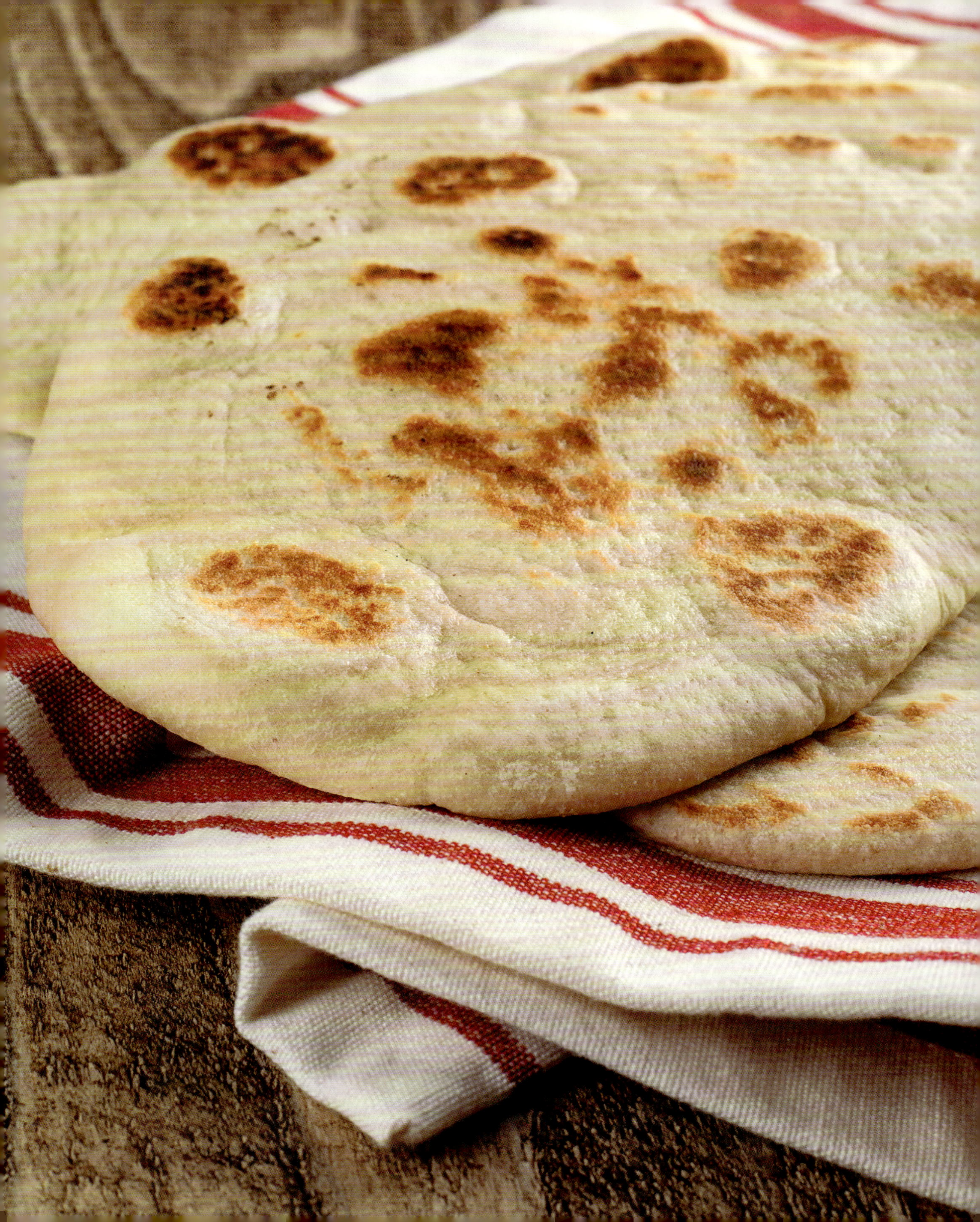

FLATBREAD

DIFFICULTY
Apprentice

PREP TIME
30 minutes

INACTIVE TIME
1½ hours

COOK TIME
35 minutes

SERVINGS
6 flatbreads

DIETARY NOTES
Vegan

It may be odd to describe a bread as dependable, but this one is. When I was a younger norn, I traveled far and wide, picking up skills and experience so I could join the Priory. No matter where I was, flatbread was a constant. In the Shiverpeaks, I was never served a stew without a tear of flatbread to go with it. In the thick jungle of Maguuma, people love to pair it with butternut squash soup. And the high tables of Divinity's Reach always introduced their multicourse meals with a mint-pear cured meat flatbread spread. If there's any food that deserves to be called the foundation of Tyrian cuisine, it's this one.

---

1. In a large bowl, combine the water, olive oil, sugar, and yeast. Mix well and set aside for 10 minutes to allow the yeast to get frothy. In a medium bowl, combine the bread flour, cassava flour, and salt.

2. Add the flour to the wet mixture and mix until well combined. If the dough is too sticky, add 1 tablespoon of bread flour. Transfer the dough to a lightly floured surface. Knead the dough for 5 minutes.

3. Transfer the dough ball into an oiled bowl and toss the dough in the oil until all sides are coated. Cover the bowl with plastic wrap and let the dough rest until it has doubled in size, about 60 to 90 minutes.

4. Lightly flour a work surface and place the dough on the counter. Lightly pat and divide the dough into six equal pieces. Tuck in the sides and form each of the pieces into a ball. Cover the dough with a towel and let rest for 30 minutes.

5. Working on a lightly floured countertop, take a portion and pat down with your hands. With a rolling pin, roll out into an 8½-inch oval.

6. Place a skillet over medium-high heat. Make sure the skillet is hot. Take a rolled-out piece of dough and flip it onto the skillet. Cook until the disk begins to puff up, or the bottom turns golden brown, 2 to 3 minutes. Flip and repeat on the other side, about 2 minutes. Place the cooked flatbread in a kitchen towel and wrap.

7. Repeat steps 5 and 6 with the remaining portions. To store, remove the flatbreads from the towel after they have cooled and place them into a resealable bag. They will remain fresh for up to 4 days.

- ¾ cup plus 1 tablespoon warm water
- 2 tablespoons olive oil, plus more for greasing
- 2 teaspoons sugar
- 1½ teaspoons active dry yeast
- 1½ cups bread flour, plus more for dusting
- ½ cup cassava flour
- 1 teaspoon kosher salt

DIFFICULTY
Journeyman

PREP TIME
1 hour

INACTIVE TIME
24 hours

COOK TIME
50 minutes

SERVINGS
1 loaf

DIETARY NOTES
Vegan

ROSEMARY BREAD

There's a rumor that rosemary bread is not only enjoyed but also required on Aetherblade airships. Upon refueling, each ship of the bloodthirsty pirate crew is allegedly not allowed to take to air unless they've got at least two crates full of the stuff. It sounds strange at first, but I get it—just a few quick kneads of dough and you have an artisan-level result that could inspire any degenerate to keep on pillaging! I'm not endorsing the Aetherblades by any means, but you must admit they've got great taste in bread.

Poolish

½ cup bread flour
⅓ cup plus 1 tablespoon water
Pinch of yeast

Bread

2 cups all-purpose flour, plus more for dusting
1¼ cups bread flour
3 rosemary sprigs, stemmed and leaves roughly chopped
2 teaspoons kosher salt
1½ cups warm water
2 teaspoons active dry yeast
Poolish
2 tablespoons sugar

1. In a tall glass, whisk together the ingredients for the poolish. Loosely cover and allow to rest at room temperature for at least 6 hours, up to 24 hours.

2. In a medium bowl, combine the flours, rosemary leaves, and salt. In a large bowl, combine the warm water, yeast, poolish, and sugar and whisk until the poolish dissolves.

3. Add the flour mixture to the bowl and mix until it just comes together. The dough will be sticky and very loose at this point. Cover with a kitchen cloth and let rest for 30 minutes at room temperature.

4. Wet your hands and take the dough and lightly pull on the edge to the center and pat down. Repeat this around the entire dough. Flip over (smooth-side facing up), cover, and rest for another 30 minutes at room temperature.

5. Once again, wet your hands, pull the edges to the center, and pat down again. Flip, cover again, and rest for 1 hour at room temperature.
   Note: During this stage, the dough will be extremely moist and sticky to work with, which is why your hands should be moist. This will minimize the dough sticking.

6. Generously dust a work surface with flour, transfer the dough on top of it, and shape into a ball. Place on a piece of parchment paper and cover with a kitchen towel for 1 hour.

7. Preheat the oven to 425°F. Place an empty Dutch oven with a lid in the oven to preheat for 30 minutes.

8. Once the dough has risen, cut a slash across the top of the loaf.

9. Transfer the dough with the parchment paper into the preheated Dutch oven. Cover with the lid and bake for 30 minutes. Remove the lid and bake for another 10 to 20 minutes, or until the loaf is cooked. Place on a wire rack to cool completely before cutting.

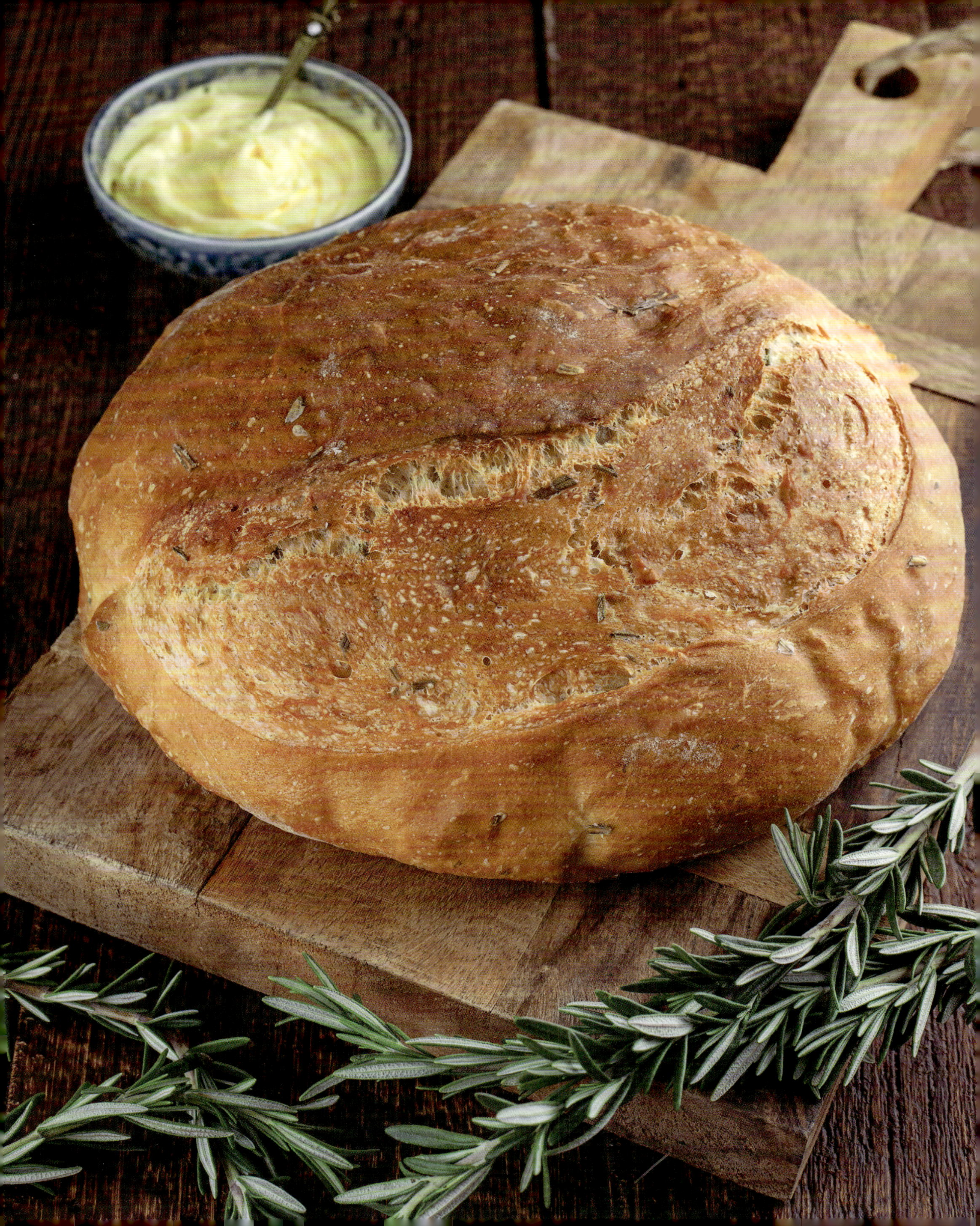

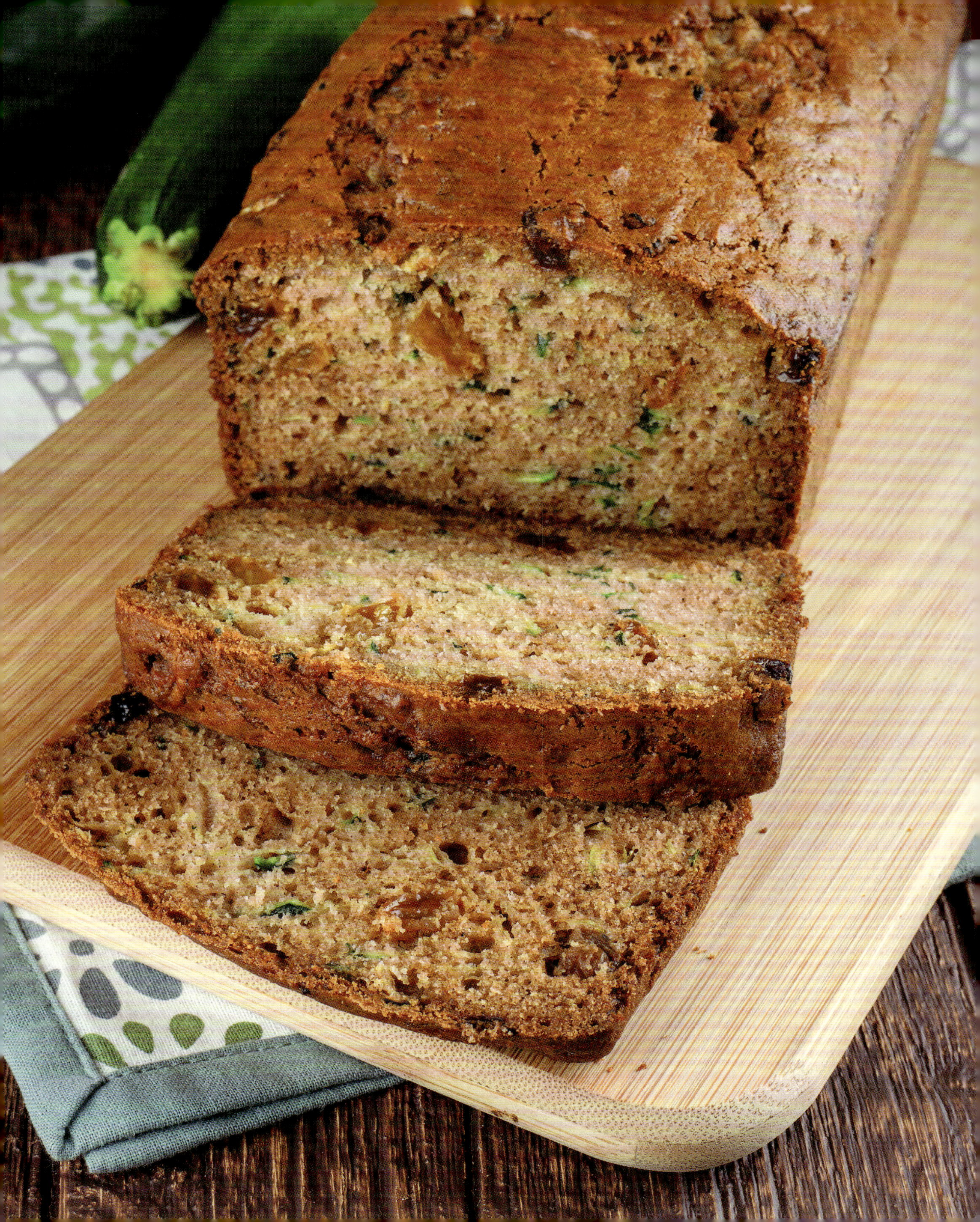

ZUCCHINI BREAD

DIFFICULTY	Initiate
PREP TIME	30 minutes
COOK TIME	1 hour
SERVINGS	1 loaf
DIETARY NOTES	Vegetarian

Zucchini is an unusual ingredient to include in bread, and it didn't occur naturally, either. My old friend Chef Mountainsplitter told me how it came to be. When he was just a young apprentice—a hill cutter, you could say!—his nemesis was the intimidating Dyrfinna, who would sometimes challenge specific culinary customers through such rigorous and demanding tests that they often took their business elsewhere. Well, not my friend Mountainsplitter. After nearly a year of competition, Dyrfinna dared Mountainsplitter to prepare a full-course meal within two hours. In his hurry, he accidentally spilled shredded zucchini into his dough ingredients! There was no time to do it over, so he threw it in the oven with a prayer to the Great Spirits. The result was a bread so moist, with such a light, nuanced sweetness, that even Dyrfinna applauded.

---

1. Preheat the oven to 350°F. Prepare a 9-by-5-inch loaf pan by cutting parchment paper to cover the insides of the pan. Spray the inside of the pan with nonstick spray. Place the parchment paper in the pan, pressing it against the pan until it sticks. Spray the pan again, covering the parchment paper with nonstick spray. Set aside.

2. Place the shredded zucchini in a kitchen towel. Wrap the kitchen towel around the zucchini and squeeze out the excess liquid. Set aside.

3. In a medium bowl, whisk together the flour, cinnamon, allspice, cardamom, nutmeg, baking powder, baking soda, and salt. Set aside.

4. In a large bowl, whisk the eggs until light and fluffy. Add the sugars and whisk until well combined. Whisk in the amaretto and Greek yogurt until just combined.

5. Slowly stream in the olive oil while constantly whisking. Whisk until all the olive oil has been added and the mixture is well combined.

6. Toss the shredded zucchini in the bowl with the flour and break up any clumps that may have formed. Add half of the flour and zucchini mixture to the large bowl and fold in until combined.

7. Add the remaining flour mixture and fold until it just comes together, but do not overwork the batter. Finally, fold in the golden raisins.

8. Transfer the dough into the prepared loaf pan. Place in the preheated oven and bake for 60 to 70 minutes, or until a toothpick comes out clean when testing the loaf.

Nonstick spray
2 cups zucchini, shredded
1½ cups all-purpose flour
1 teaspoon ground cinnamon
¼ teaspoon ground allspice
¼ teaspoon ground cardamom
¼ teaspoon ground nutmeg
1 teaspoon baking powder
1 teaspoon baking soda
1 teaspoon kosher salt
2 eggs
½ cup granulated sugar
⅓ cup light brown sugar
1 tablespoon amaretto
⅓ cup plain Greek yogurt
½ cup olive oil
½ cup golden raisins

DIFFICULTY	Master
PREP TIME	30 minutes
INACTIVE TIME	2 hours
COOK TIME	50 minutes
SERVINGS	1 loaf
DIETARY NOTES	Vegetarian

CINNAMON TOAST

Here's a recipe for all the romantics out there. There's an old tradition in Queensdale: Bake a loaf of Cinnamon Toast with your intended. If the dough and cinnamon swirl well, your love is meant to last. If not, well . . . you may not have a paramour for long, but at least you'll still enjoy this delicious bread. Of course, I don't put much stock in soppy traditions—but if you do, you should be fine if you follow these instructions!

Dough

3 cups bread flour, divided, plus more as needed

1 cup milk, warm, divided

1 tablespoon active dry yeast

1 teaspoon kosher salt

½ teaspoon ground cardamom

⅓ cup sugar

1 egg, room temperature

6 tablespoons unsalted butter, softened

Oil, for greasing

Nonstick spray

Filling

3 tablespoons granulated sugar

1 tablespoon dark brown sugar

1 tablespoon all-purpose flour

1 tablespoon ground cinnamon

1 teaspoon ground cardamom

Pinch of kosher salt

Dough and Filling

Egg Wash

1 egg

2 tablespoons milk

1. In a small nonstick pan, combine ¼ cup of bread flour and ⅓ cup of milk over medium-high heat. Whisk until it comes together, about 1 minute. Remove from the heat, set aside, and allow to cool.

2. In a small bowl, combine the yeast and the remaining ⅔ cup of milk and let it rest for 5 minutes, allowing the yeast to become active and bloom.

3. In the large bowl of a stand mixer, whisk together the remaining 2¾ cups of bread flour, salt, cardamom, and sugar. Add the flour-and-milk mixture, milk-and-yeast mixture, and egg to the bowl and mix until it just comes together.

4. While the dough begins to knead, add 1 tablespoon of butter at a time. Knead the dough for 5 minutes, or until it is smooth. If the dough is too sticky, add 1 tablespoon of flour at a time. If it is too dry, add 1 tablespoon of milk at a time.

5. Transfer to an oiled bowl, cover, and let rest for 1 hour or until it has doubled in size.

6. In a medium bowl, combine all the ingredients for the filling and set aside. In a bowl, combine the egg and milk for the egg wash and set aside.

7. Prepare a 9-by-5-inch loaf pan by cutting parchment paper to cover the insides of the pan. Spray the inside of the pan with nonstick spray. Place the parchment paper in the pan, pressing it against the pan until it sticks. Spray the pan again, covering the parchment paper with nonstick spray. Set aside.

8. Remove the dough from the bowl and punch it down. Roll the dough into a 20-by-9-inch rectangle. Brush the top of the dough with the egg wash. Place the egg wash in the refrigerator until you need it later. Sprinkle the filling evenly over the dough.

9. Tightly roll the dough into a 9-inch log. Pinch the seam together shut. Transfer the log into the prepared loaf pan. Cover and let rest for 1 hour or until it has doubled in size.

10. Preheat the oven to 350°F. Brush the top of the loaf with the egg wash. Place in the oven and bake for 15 minutes. Lightly cover the loaf with aluminum foil to avoid browning too much. Cook for another 25 to 35 minutes, until cooked through.

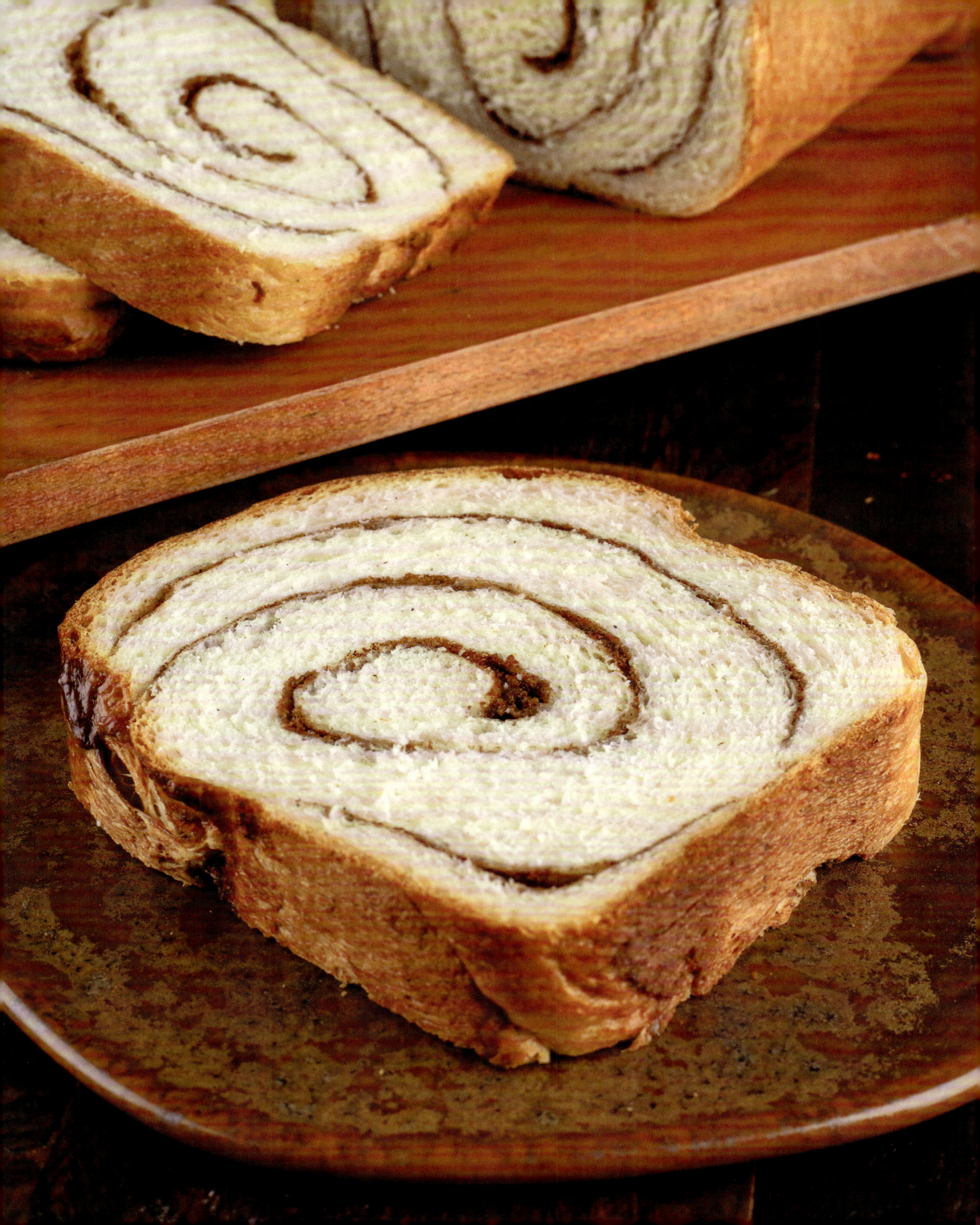

SALADS

I'd hit my nomadic stride by the time I was on my way to the seared lands of Ascalon. I was used to walking and fighting and had no problems with the minor monsters that sometimes attacked on the main roads. I should've seen the signs that Ascalon would be different.

Before I'd even reached the border, three different groups I'd passed had warned me that there were Branded and destroyers ahead, creatures that had been turned dark by their respective Elder Dragon masters. "Bah," I thought. "These people are just weak! I'll be fine." An hour into Ascalon, I was almost killed by a Branded charr. I managed to get away, but when I took a rest, I realized I wasn't carrying anything on me to recover. No medicine, no dinner ingredients, no nothing. I was completely out.

Lucky for me, an uncorrupted warband happened by and took pity on a fellow warrior. They'd eaten all their dried meat rations but served me some of their pre-prepared Ascalonian Salad. Well, leafy greens had never been my favorite, but I would've eaten anything at that point. And thank the Spirits I did! Each ingredient seemed perfectly picked to rejuvenate me after battle and the tastes also worked seamlessly together. Until then, I'd been going where the wind went, jumping in headfirst without much thought. I realized I had to be more thoughtful, more prepared in my adventuring and cooking. It took me a while—preparation was never my strong suit—but I eventually gathered these fantastic salad recipes that show my progress. Nowadays, if any norn tries to ridicule greens, I know how to prove them wrong!

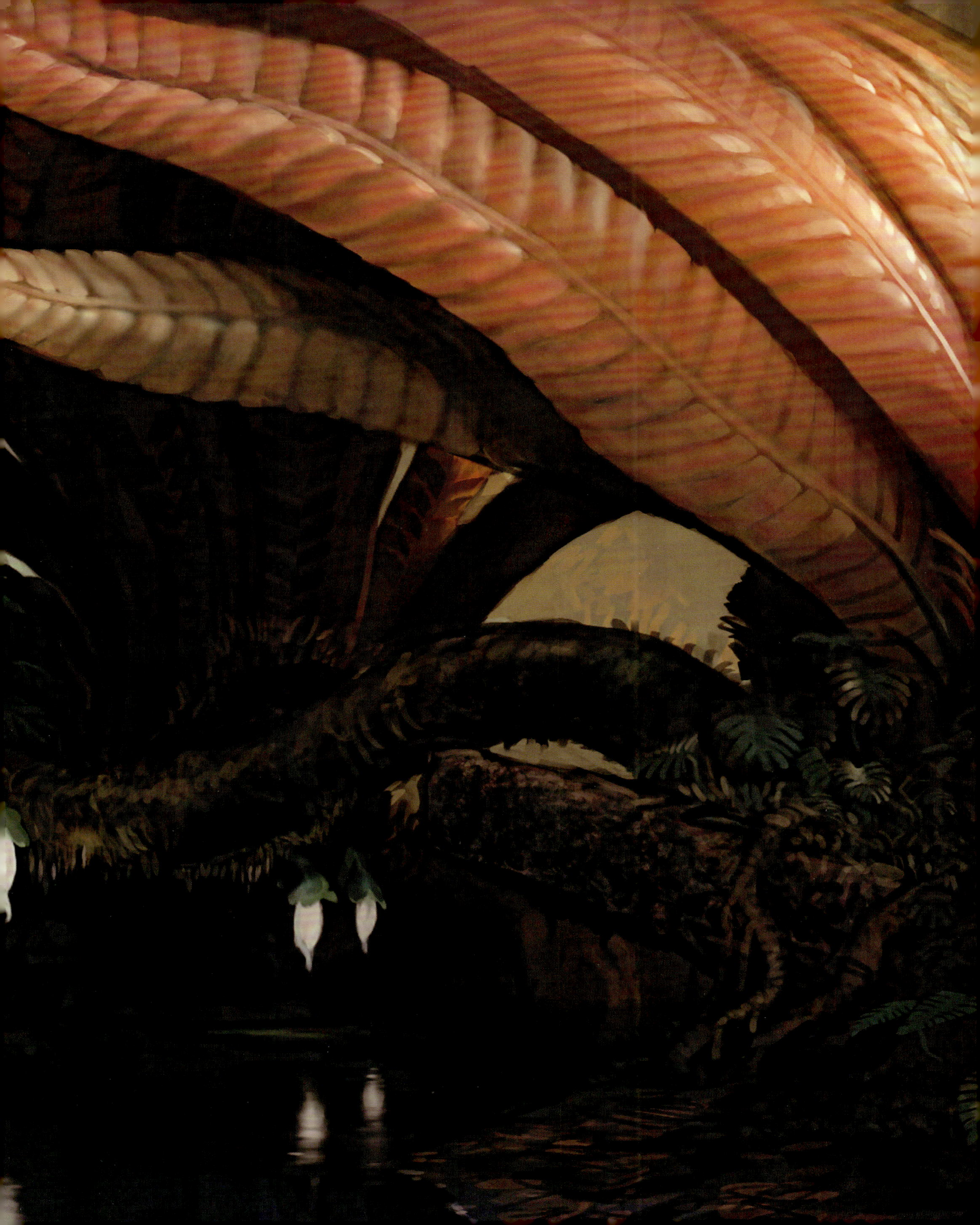

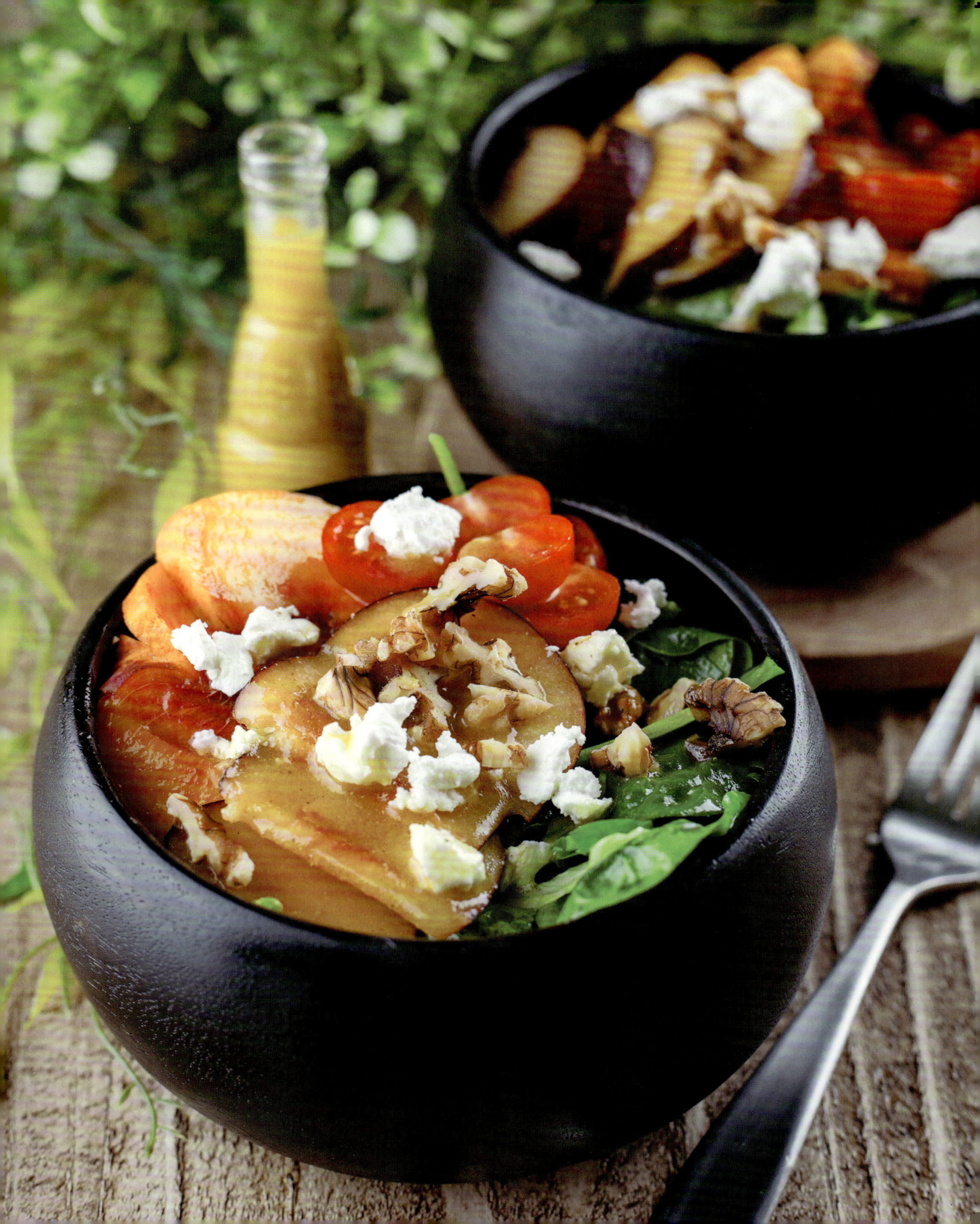

SALAD À LA CONSORTIUM

DIFFICULTY
Apprentice

PREP TIME
25 minutes

SERVINGS
4 portions

DIETARY NOTES
Vegetarian,
Gluten free

Sometimes recipes evolve organically through years of social and global context, and sometimes they're made as tools in corporate marketing rivalry. If you've spent any time in Tyria, you recognize the lion logo that means the Black Lion Trading Company is close by, and you know to look for a Consortium merchant when you see the blue banner. You might not know that the two are locked in a mercantile war! Years ago, as part of their struggle against Evon Gnashblade and the BLTC, the Consortium made a push to sell Consortium-branded dishes. This delightfully tropical salad was the standout. Of course, the Black Lion returned fire with their own set of branded recipes. Ultimately the Consortium backed off, as sending their representatives out to market the dishes was proving to be too pricey for profit. Still, I'd welcome a thousand more mercantile battles if it means we get more dishes like this to enjoy.

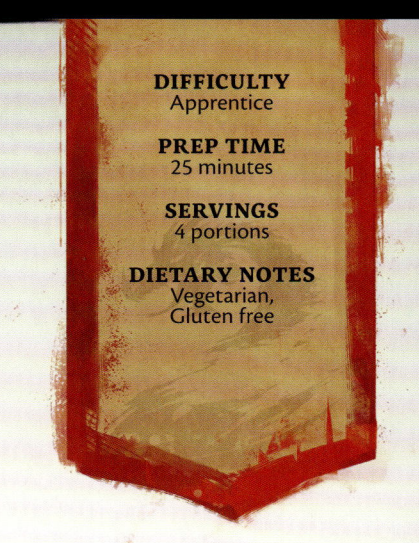

1. In a small bowl, whisk together all the ingredients for the vinaigrette. The vinaigrette can be stored in an airtight container in the refrigerator for up to 5 days.
2. In a large bowl, toss together the spinach and butter lettuce. Pour a small amount of the passion fruit vinaigrette to lightly coat the greens. Split among four serving bowls.
3. Top each with the remaining ingredients and serve with the remaining passion fruit vinaigrette.

Passion Fruit Vinaigrette
½ cup passion fruit juice
⅓ cup olive oil
¼ cup white vinegar
2 teaspoons ginger powder
1 tablespoon Dijon mustard
2 teaspoons honey
Kosher salt
Ground black pepper

Consortium Salad
10 ounces spinach,
  cut into thick slices
3 ounces butter lettuce,
  cut into thick slices
8 ounces peaches, pitted and sliced
4 ounces plums, pitted and sliced
4 ounces cherry tomatoes, halved
3 ounces goat cheese, crumbled
3 ounces walnuts, coarsely chopped

DIFFICULTY
Journeyman

PREP TIME
30 minutes

COOK TIME
1 hour

SERVINGS
4 salads

DIETARY NOTES
Vegetarian

ASCALONIAN SALAD

Ascalon's arid climate makes it the ideal location to grow herbs—besides your homestead garden, of course. The herbs thrived in Ascalon City before its downfall, but when they began to be eaten is a point of contention. Some history books speak of King Adelbern's great-great-something-grandfather as the first to put oregano and basil in a mix together and call it salad, but still older tales make mention of a Khan-Ur eating crushed parsley and thyme over other greens. I try to stay out of the political stuff and just enjoy the food!

Ascalonian Dressing
0.5 ounces parsley
0.88 ounces basil
1 teaspoon dried oregano
½ teaspoon dried thyme
2 garlic cloves
2 teaspoons honey
½ cup olive oil
¼ cup red wine vinegar
Kosher salt
Ground black pepper

Roasted Beets
3 red beets, stemmed
2 tablespoons olive oil, divided
Kosher salt
Ground black pepper
1 tablespoon lemon juice

Salad
5 ounces spring mix greens
5 ounces arugula
1 head of butter lettuce, chopped
2 ounces microgreens
Ascalonian Dressing
Roasted Beets
Parmesan cheese shavings, for serving

1. To make the dressing: In a food processor, pulse all the ingredients until well combined and the parsley and basil has been chopped. Transfer to an airtight container and store in the refrigerator until needed, up to 5 days.

2. To make the beets: Preheat the oven to 400°F. Rub the beets with 1 tablespoon of olive oil. Generously season with salt and pepper. Take one of the beets, place it on a sheet of aluminum foil, and wrap it shut. Repeat with the remaining beets.

3. Place the aluminum-wrapped beets on a baking tray. Transfer to the oven and roast for 45 to 60 minutes, until tender.

4. Allow the beets to cool before peeling and discarding the skin. Thinly slice the beets into ¼ inch (3 mm)–thick pieces. The sliced beets can be stored in an airtight container in the refrigerator for up to 1 week.

5. Before placing on the salad, toss the beets in the remaining 1 tablespoon of olive oil, the lemon juice, salt, and pepper.

6. To make the salad: In a large bowl, combine the spring mix greens, arugula, butter lettuce, and microgreens. Add half of the prepared Ascalonian dressing and toss until well coated. Split the greens among four serving bowls.

7. Top each with the dressed beets and Parmesan cheese. Serve with the remaining dressing.

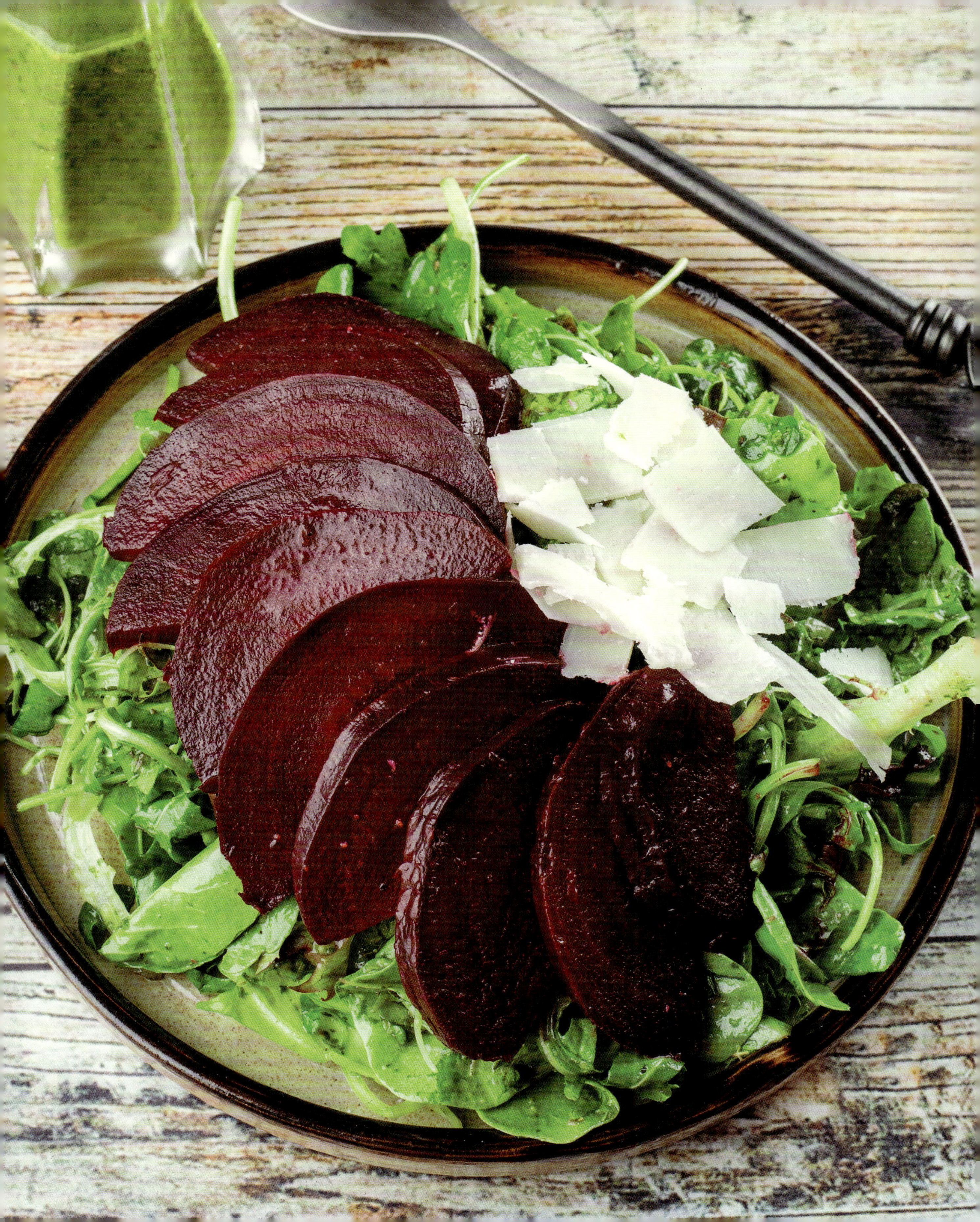

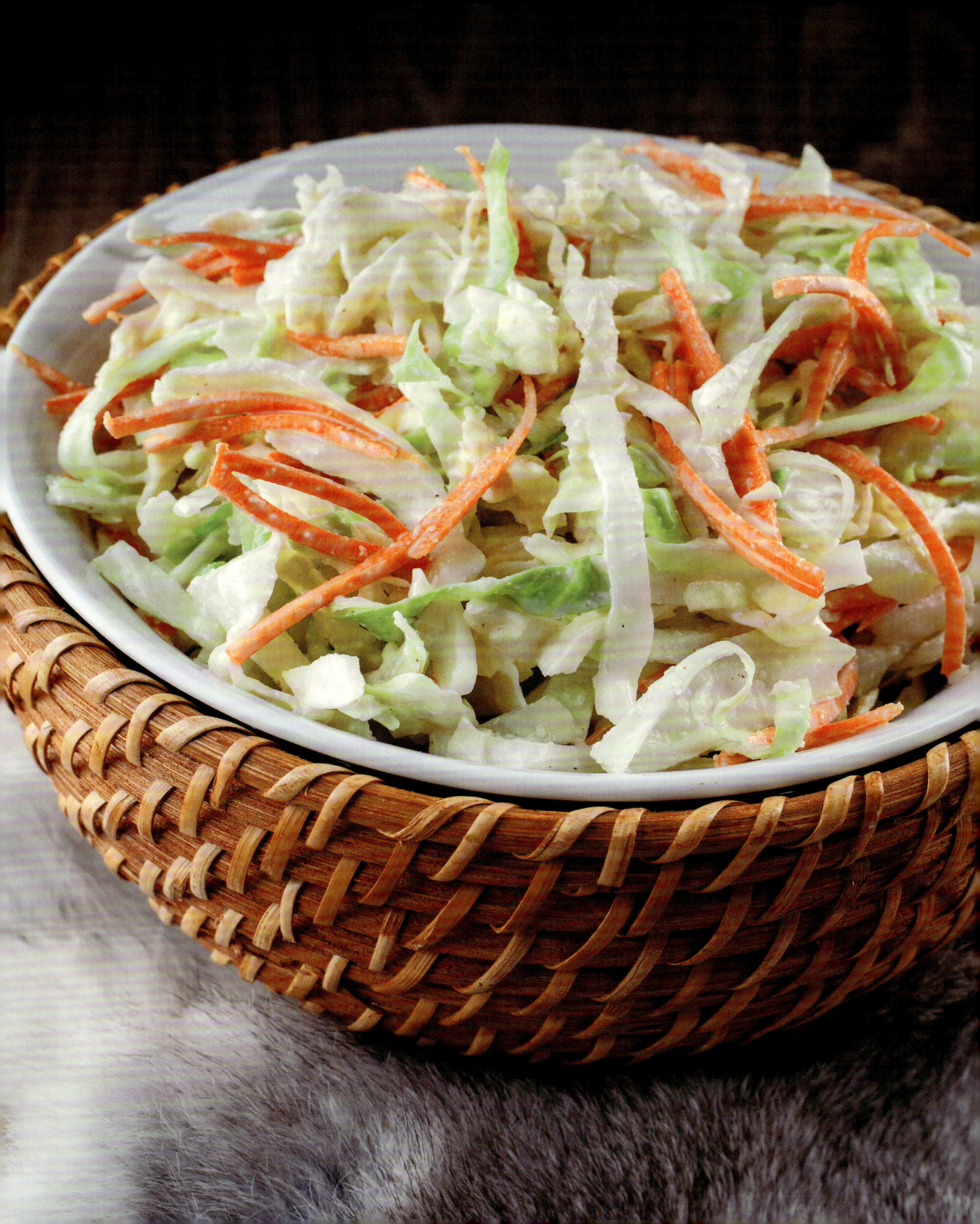

FEAST OF COLESLAW

DIFFICULTY
Initiate

PREP TIME
20 minutes

INACTIVE TIME
12 hours

SERVINGS
4 servings

DIETARY NOTES
Vegetarian

At one point during my trips, I joined a traveling party to cross the Crystal Desert. The days were hot and dry, and it wasn't long till we were sluggishly dragging ourselves across the sands. I had packed a head of lettuce that had somehow, miraculously, stayed crisp, and I traded at various posts for sour cream and other seasonings so I could quickly mix up a huge batch of coleslaw to share. Which was lucky, because as soon as we broke camp, we accidentally strayed too close to a griffon's nest. As we ran to backtrack, with the pounding of their talons hot on our tail, I wasn't the only one who felt like I had rocket boots on! The light but filling coleslaw gave us a huge boost of energy to stay swift on our feet.

---

1. In a small bowl, whisk together the sour cream, mayo, lemon juice, apple cider vinegar, sugar, garlic powder, onion powder, pepper, ginger powder, celery salt, and salt in a small bowl. Combine the cabbage and carrot in a large bowl. Toss in the dressing and fully coat the vegetables. Cover and place in the refrigerator overnight before serving.

½ cup sour cream

¼ cup mayo

2 tablespoons lemon juice

2 tablespoons apple cider vinegar

2 tablespoons sugar

2 teaspoons garlic powder

1 teaspoon onion powder

1 teaspoon ground black pepper

½ teaspoon ginger powder

½ teaspoon celery salt

½ teaspoon kosher salt

16 ounces cabbage, cored and thinly sliced

3 ounces carrots, peeled and julienned

DIFFICULTY
Journeyman

PREP TIME
15 minutes

INACTIVE TIME
30 minutes

SERVINGS
4 servings

DIETARY NOTES
Vegan

FEAST OF BEAN SALAD

Ah, beans! There has been many a time that I've been adventuring and found myself low, just to be saved by this hearty recipe. The earthiness of the black beans combined with the mildness of the kidney beans, enhanced by the onion and seasonings, makes for a restorative and filling meal that will keep you in the game when you think you're out.

Dressing

2 tablespoons olive oil
Zest and juice of 1 lemon
2 tablespoons apple cider vinegar
1 teaspoon maple syrup
1 teaspoon dried oregano
½ teaspoon kosher salt
½ teaspoon ground black pepper

Salad

15 ounces kidney beans
15 ounces black beans
1 shallot, diced
2 scallions, light green and white parts only, chopped
½ bunch cilantro, chopped

1. In a small bowl, whisk together all the ingredients for the dressing.

2. In a medium bowl, combine the beans, shallot, scallions, and cilantro. Lightly toss to mix. Add the dressing and toss until combined. Allow to rest for at least 30 minutes in the refrigerator before serving.

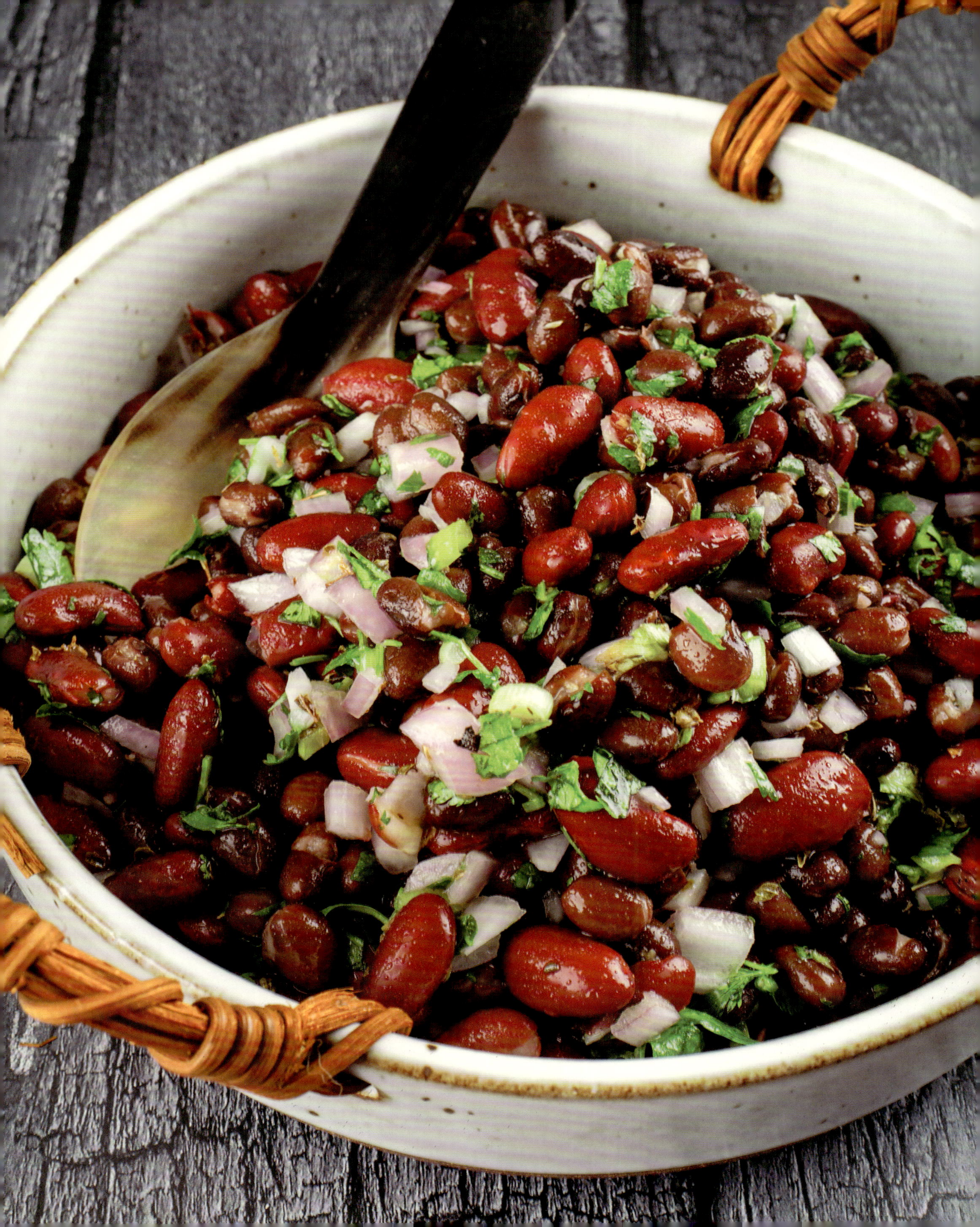

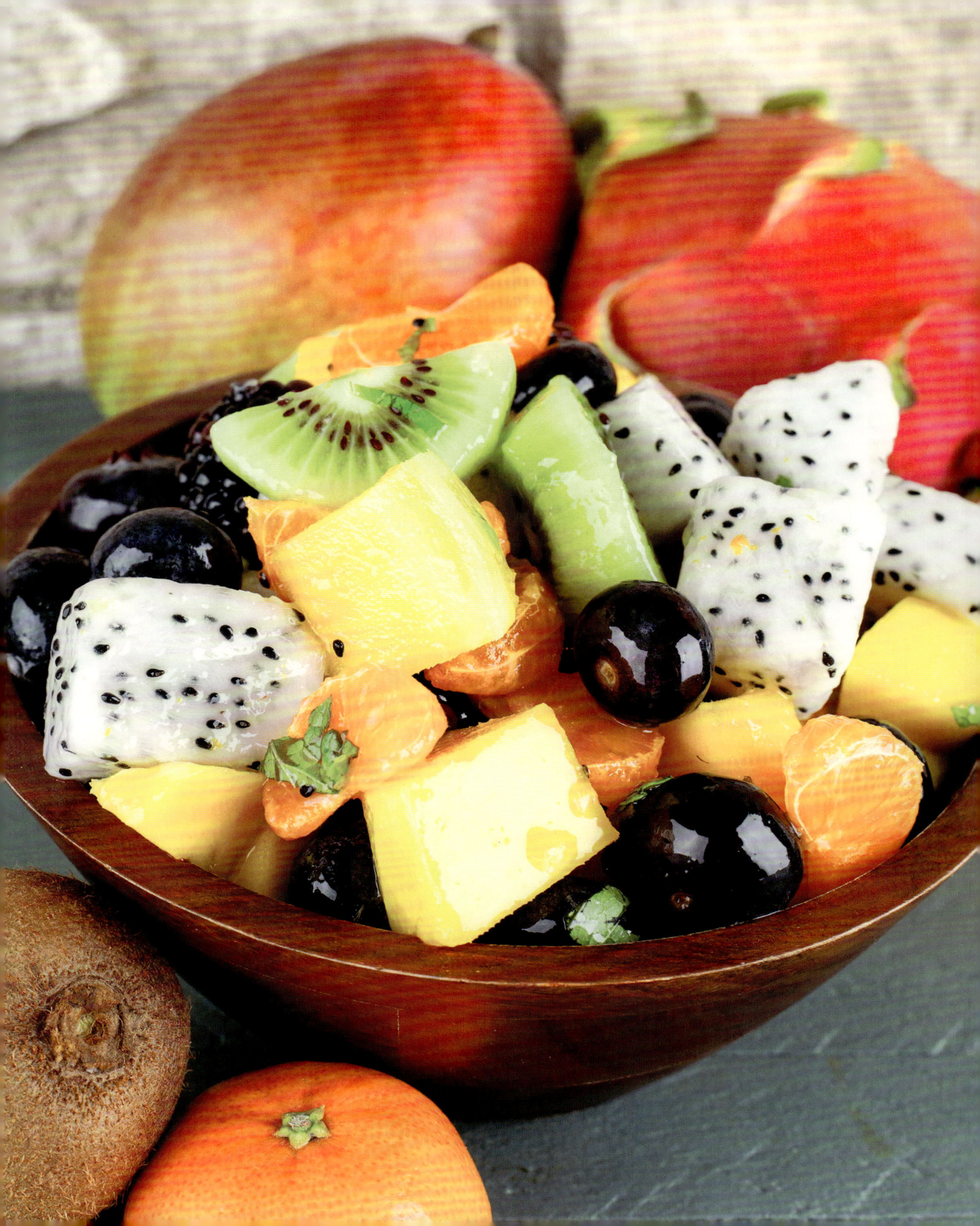

FRUIT SALAD WITH MINT GARNISH

DIFFICULTY
Initiate

PREP TIME
30 minutes

INACTIVE TIME
12 hours

COOK TIME
30 minutes

SERVINGS
6 servings

DIETARY NOTES
Vegan, Gluten free

Researchers always argue back and forth over what exactly makes the fruit of Southsun Cove so distinct. Some propose that it's the island's warm climate. Others say it's the way the currents bring specific nutrients from the Maguuma mainland. I've even heard one culinary scientist theorize that the huge colony of Karka on the island helps fruit grow in some symbiotic relationship! Whatever the reason, it led to Southsun Cove inspiring this tropical salad recipe. With options of juicy mango, tart passion fruit, tangy orange, and more, you can choose whatever fruit suits you—as long as you garnish it with fresh mint.

1. To make the syrup: In a small saucepan, whisk together sugar and water and place over medium-high heat. Once the sugar dissolves, add the mint and bring to a simmer for 1 minute. Remove from the heat and let steep for 30 minutes.
2. Strain into an airtight container. Allow to cool to room temperature. Mix in the lemon and orange zest. Store in the refrigerator for at least 12 hours and up to 2 weeks.
3. To make the salad: In a large bowl, toss all the fruit until well combined. Pour in the simple syrup and toss until the fruit is coated.

Zesty Mint Simple Syrup

¼ cup sugar

¼ cup water

2 mint sprigs

1 tablespoon lemon zest

½ tablespoon orange zest

Fruit Salad

6 mandarin oranges, peeled and divided

1 white dragon fruit, peeled and cut into bite-size pieces

2 mangoes, peeled, seeded, and cut into bite-size pieces

3 kiwis, peeled and cut into bite-size pieces

6 ounces blackberries

6 ounces blueberries

Zesty Mint Simple Syrup

SOUPS AND STEWS

Relations between Cantha and Tyria were nonexistent when I was a young kid, so I never got to see the Jade Sea myself. But during my time on the road, I met another traveling trainee: Hina, a chef's apprentice from Cantha. We traded recipes—she taught me how to make Imperial Chef Jiong's Kimchi Tofu Stew. *Hoo*, the burst of flavor when it hit my tongue! It kicked off a burning passion in my spirit for soups, stews—anything liquid you ate from a bowl. I spent days and nights simmering ingredients in pots, hoping they'd turn into soupy ingenuity.

My favorite stews were made from ingredients that came from different regions, that somehow came together and balanced one another out. When Hina taught me Kimchi Tofu Stew, I taught her the recipe for Spiced Mashed Yams—a norn staple. I can still remember her eyes glittering with delight when she tasted it. I trust that that happiness balanced out the greatness she shared with me! I've picked up many more soup and stew recipes from around the world since meeting Hina, so if we ever meet again, I'll be armed to trade. In the meantime, I'll share those recipes with you.

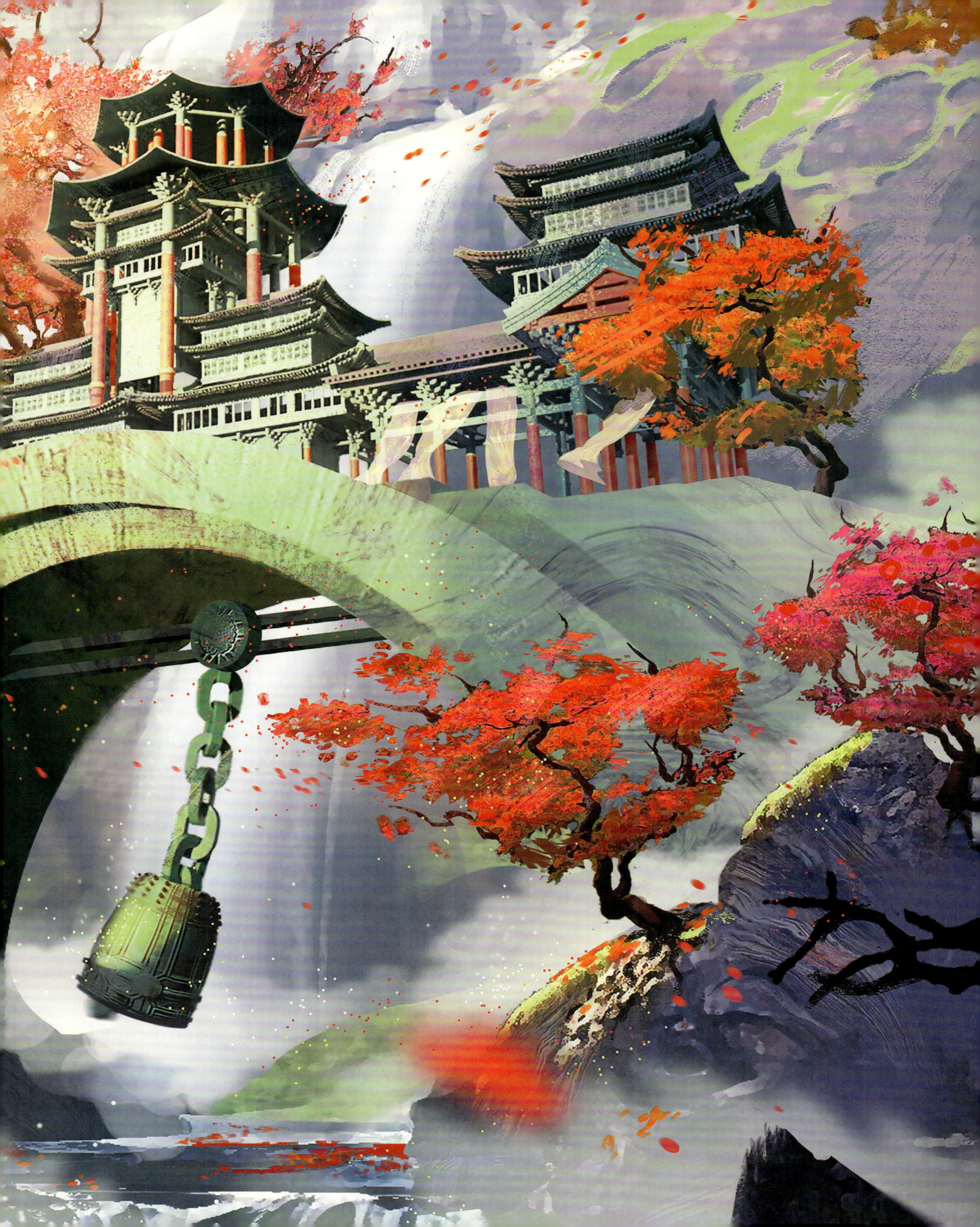

DIFFICULTY
Novice

PREP TIME
30 minutes

COOK TIME
6 hours

SERVINGS
3½ quarts

DIETARY NOTES
Dairy free, Gluten free

POULTRY STOCK

You can't go wrong with a classic poultry stock—a beloved favorite of my friend and mentor Robertus. He always used to beat me over the head with his declarations of love for the stuff. "Poultry stock is the birthplace of contemporary Tyrian cooking, Seimur" and "Anyone who underestimates a good broth of poultry deserves to be eaten by a pack of pocket raptors, Seimur." I roll my eyes, but he's not wrong. I still haven't found the best way to mix bloodstone dust into a poultry stock, but I'm close.

---

2 carrots, cut into chunks
2 onions, quartered
2 celery stalks, cut into chunks
1 whole garlic, halved
1 whole duck, cut into portions
8 chicken wings
2 tablespoons black peppercorns
1 tablespoon coriander seeds
½ tablespoon fennel seeds
3 bay leaves
1 bunch parsley
2 thyme sprigs
1 rosemary sprig
1 gallon water

1. Preheat the oven to 425°F. Place the carrots, onion, celery, and garlic on a large baking sheet. Top with a wire rack. Place all the duck pieces and chicken wings on the wire rack. Roast for 1 hour or until it reaches an internal temperature of 165°F. Remove from the oven and transfer everything into a large pot.

2. Add the remaining ingredients to the pot.

3. Bring the pot to a boil over medium-high heat, then reduce the heat to low. Keep at a slight simmer for 5 hours.
Note: There is no need to add more water as this is cooking. You'll lose about ½ quart of water from the evaporation that is done during the cook time.

4. After the stock has finished simmering, carefully strain through a fine-mesh strainer into another container to separate the stock from all the ingredients, discarding those. Once cooled, the stock can be stored in an airtight container in the refrigerator for up to 7 days or in the freezer for up to 4 months.

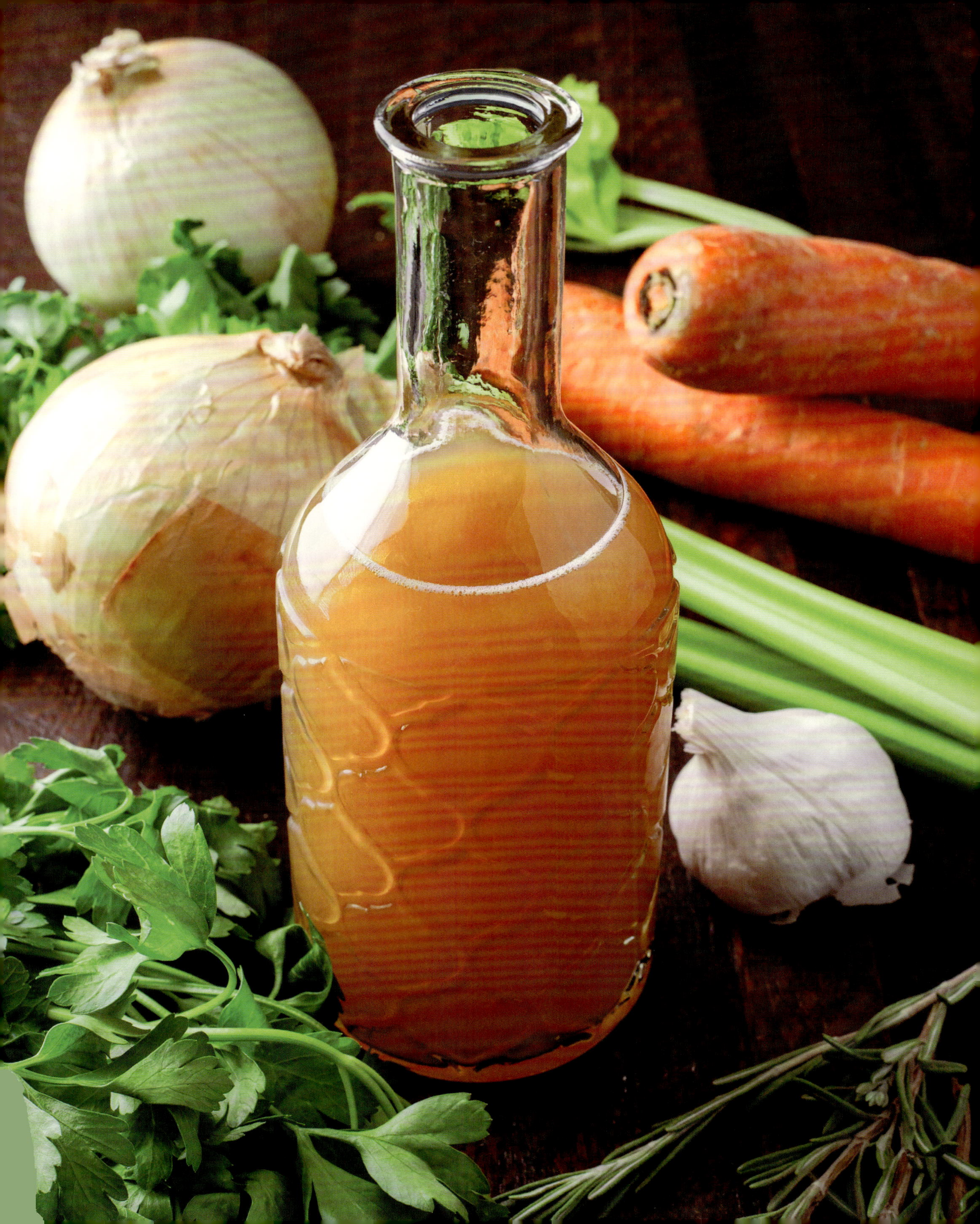

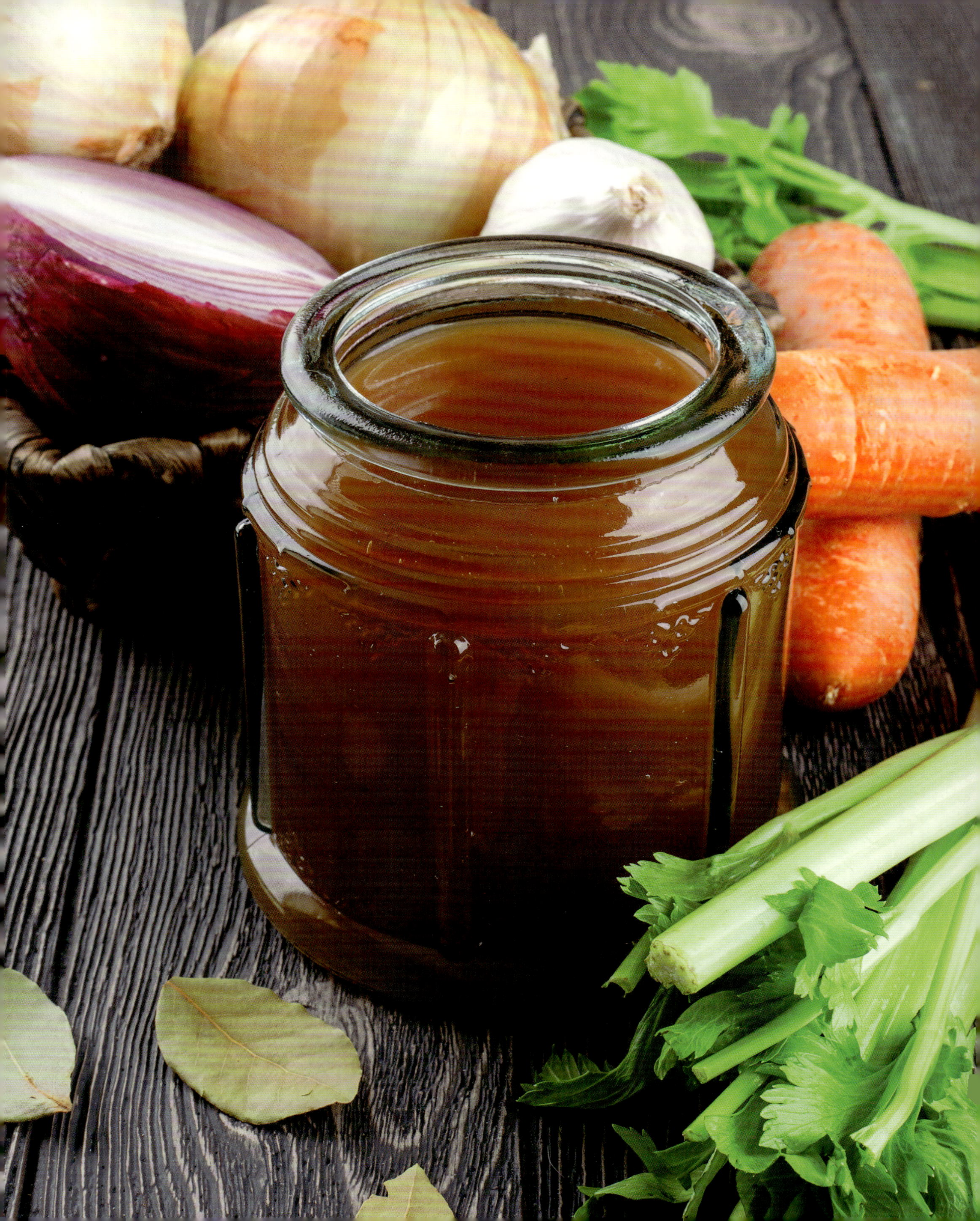

RED MEAT STOCK

DIFFICULTY
Novice

PREP TIME
30 minutes

COOK TIME
7½ hours

SERVINGS
3½ quarts

DIETARY NOTES
Gluten free, Dairy free

A red meat stock will always be hearty and warm, though its taste differs from land to land. In Kryta, they tend to use beef. I'm told they use venison on the Plains of Ashford. At home in the Shiverpeaks, we use moose, bear, or even minotaur! I have fond memories of my mother setting a steaming bowl of minotaur stock down in front of me, with chunks of meat inside. Even thinking of it makes me start to drool . . . but if you're not a fan of minotaur, I recommend trying the lot and seeing what suits you.

1. Preheat the oven to 425°F. Place the beef knuckles and necks on a large baking sheet. Place in the oven and roast for 40 minutes. Add the celery, carrots, and onions. Roast for another 30 minutes.

2. Transfer everything from the baking sheet to a large pot. Add the garlic, bay leaves, peppercorns, and fennel. Top with enough water to just cover everything. Cook over medium-low heat for 6 hours. Check on the stock a few times and use a fine-mesh spoon to skim any scum that forms at the top.

3. Carefully strain through a cheesecloth-lined fine-mesh strainer into another container to separate the stock from all the ingredients, discarding those. Once cooled, the stock can be stored in an airtight container in the refrigerator for up to 7 days or in the freezer for up to 4 months.

3 pounds beef knuckles
2 pounds beef necks
1 whole celery, halved
4 carrots, halved
2 onions, halved
1 red onion, halved
1 whole garlic, halved
3 bay leaves
1 tablespoon black peppercorns
2 teaspoons fennel seeds

DIFFICULTY
Novice

PREP TIME
10 minutes

COOK TIME
30 minutes

SERVINGS
1½ gallons

DIETARY NOTES
Vegan, Gluten free

VEGETABLE STOCK

If you're any kind of chef, you'd be wise to invest some time and energy into a personal garden. And once you do, you'll never be out of the stock to make *this* stock! Carrots, onions, celery, potatoes, corn—the great thing about veggie stock is it's adaptable to whatever's on hand and will always come out light and tasty. My personal taste is to throw in some fennel and parsnip, too. Of course, if you're too busy gallivanting around the world to take proper care of your garden plots, you can always hire someone to take care of them for you—my friend Styrsson might be available for work!

2 onions, quartered
3 carrots, chopped
4 celery stalks, chopped
1 whole garlic, halved
2 leeks, dark green parts only
3 bay leaves
6 thyme sprigs
½ bunch parsley
1 tablespoon black peppercorns
½ teaspoon coriander seeds
¼ teaspoon fennel seeds
1½ gallons water

1. Place all the ingredients in a large stockpot. Heat over medium-high heat and bring to a boil. Reduce the heat to medium-low and simmer for 30 minutes.

2. After the stock has finished simmering, carefully strain through a fine-mesh strainer into another container to separate the stock from all the ingredients, discarding those. Once cooled, the stock can be stored in an airtight container in the refrigerator for up to 7 days or in the freezer for up to 4 months.

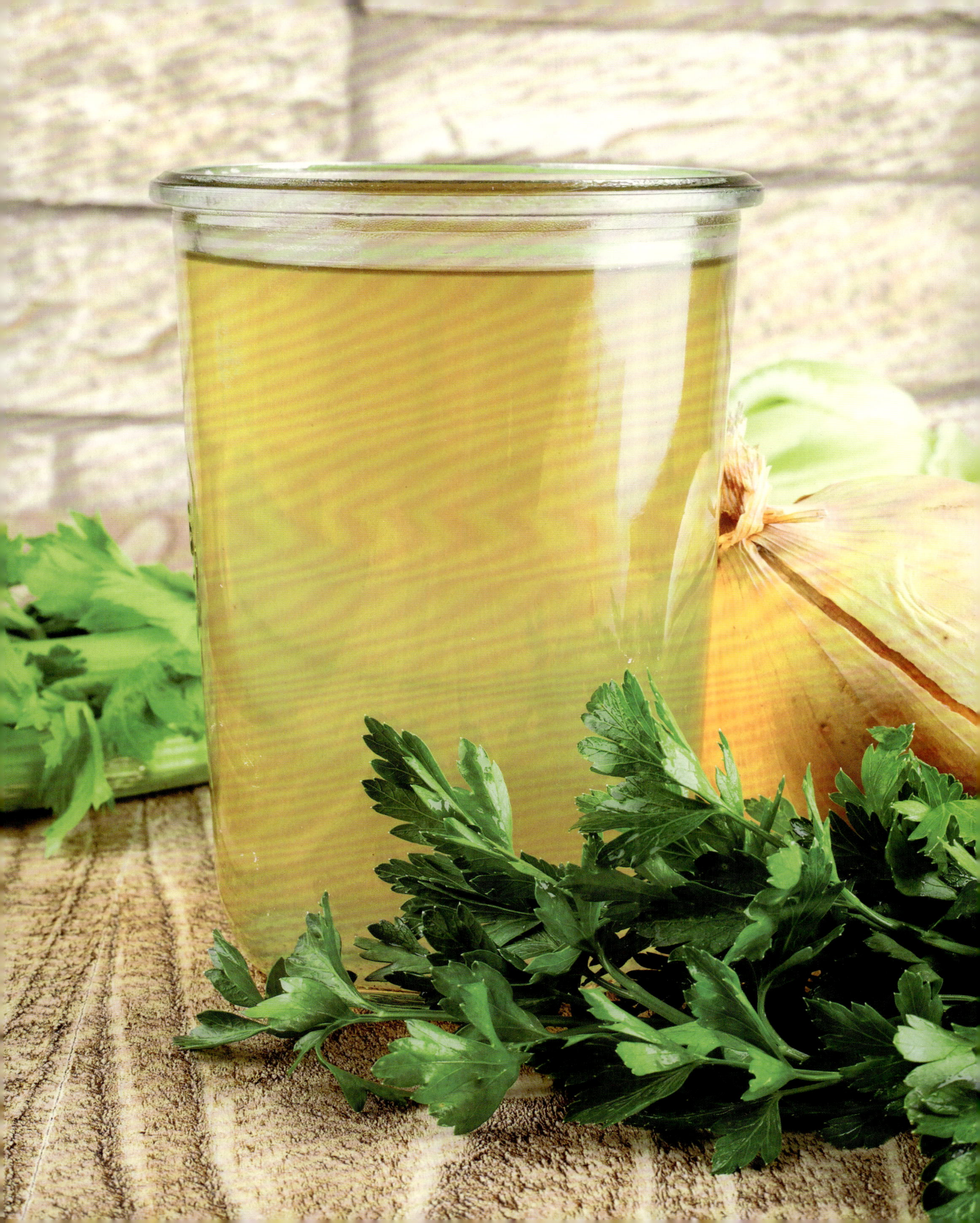

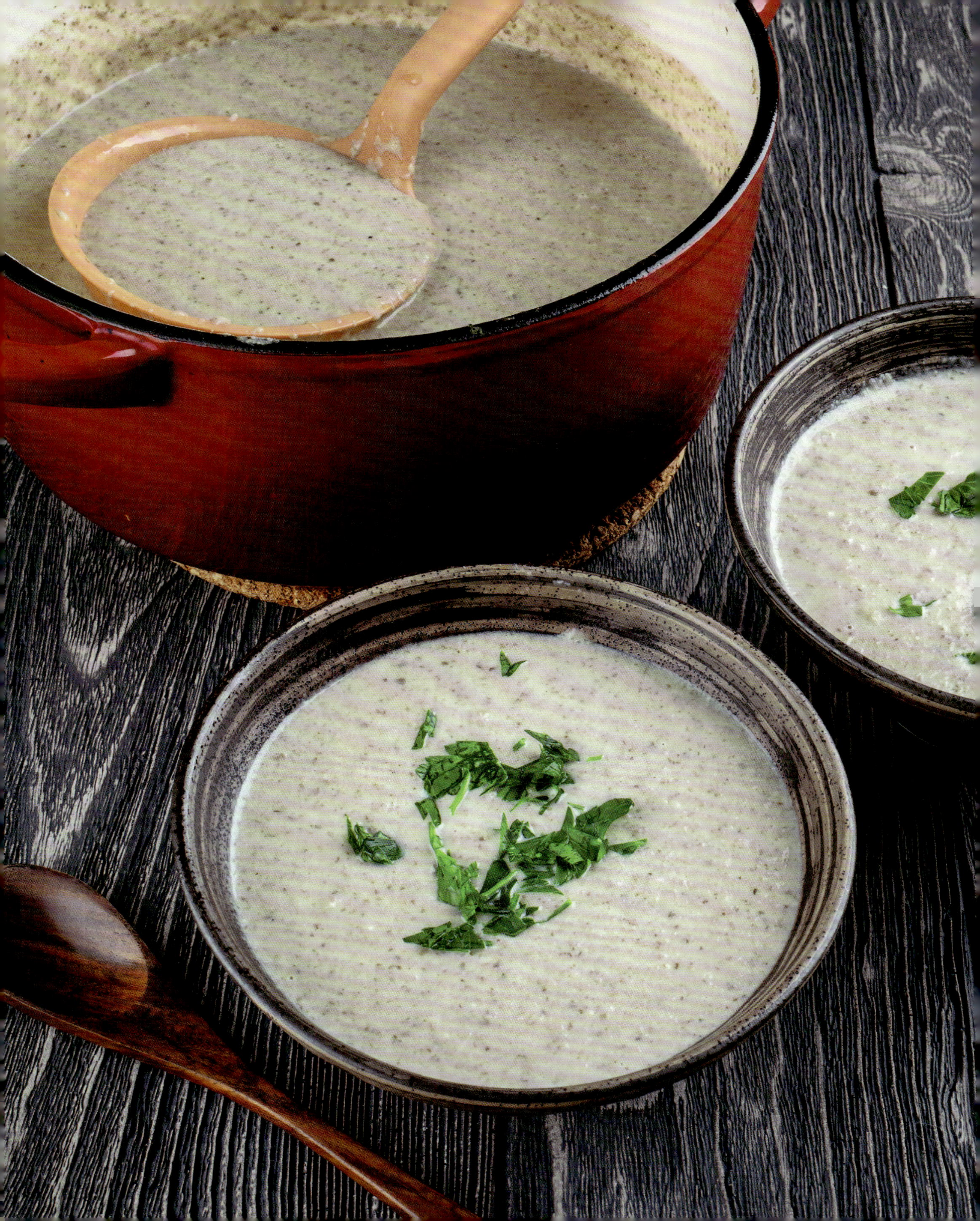

FANCY CREAMY MUSHROOM SOUP

DIFFICULTY
Journeyman

PREP TIME
20 minutes

COOK TIME
40 minutes

SERVINGS
4 servings

DIETARY NOTES
Gluten free

I love the rich savor of a cream of mushroom broth. This recipe is often used with portobellos, but I like to mix in a medley of different fungi. I once met a plucky sylvari who swore by adding redcaps to her creamy mushroom soup. She had to shout the recommendation up at me because she'd been shrunk to the size of a mushroom herself! Elain, if you're reading this, I admire your undefeatable spirit, but you should learn some self-preservation.

---

1. In a medium pot, heat the olive oil over medium-high heat. Add the shallots and onion and cook until softened, 5 to 8 minutes.

2. Add the garlic and mushrooms and cook until the mushrooms have released most of their liquid, 8 to 10 minutes. Add the thyme, salt, and pepper and mix until combined.

3. Add the Dijon mustard and wine and bring to a simmer. Cook until the wine has reduced by half, about 3 to 5 minutes. Add the poultry stock and bring to a simmer for 20 minutes.

4. Remove from the heat and carefully transfer everything to a blender. Blend until smooth. Return to the pot and add the heavy cream. Heat over medium heat and cook until it has warmed through. Serve with freshly chopped parsley.

3 tablespoons olive oil
2 shallots, diced
1 onion, diced
6 garlic cloves, minced
½ pound cremini mushrooms, sliced
¾ pound shiitake mushrooms, sliced
¾ pound oyster mushrooms, chopped
1 tablespoon fresh thyme leaves, chopped
1 teaspoon kosher salt
2 teaspoons ground black pepper
1 teaspoon Dijon mustard
½ cup white wine
3 cups Poultry Stock (page 60)
1 cup heavy cream
Parsley, chopped, for garnish

DIFFICULTY
Initiate

PREP TIME
20 minutes

COOK TIME
40 minutes

SERVINGS
4 servings

DIETARY NOTES
Vegetarian, Gluten free

POTATO AND LEEK SOUP

The night before I left the Shiverpeak Mountains to travel to Tyria, I trekked deep into the frostbitten wilderness and made an offering to the Spirits of the Wild. I've never been the most pious norn, but I prayed that my journey would bring me purpose—something to dedicate my life to. The next day, I made my way down the mountain. I was just at its foot when I had to stop and stare. There, in the middle of the road, stood a giant wolf. It looked at me for a long while. I don't know how long we stood there, just staring at each other, until it finally padded off into the woods. At that moment, I knew I would find my calling. Now that I think about it, it may just have been my friend Hamund in were-form, playing a prank on me! But it lifted my spirits all the same.

---

3 tablespoons unsalted butter

3 leeks, white and light green parts only, roughly chopped

4 cups Vegetable Stock (page 64)

1½ pounds Yukon Gold potatoes, peeled and cut into 1-inch pieces

2 bay leaves

2 thyme sprigs

¾ cup heavy cream

1 teaspoon kosher salt

½ teaspoon ground black pepper

1. In a medium pot, heat the butter over medium-high heat. Once the butter has melted, add the leeks and cook until softened, 8 to 10 minutes.

2. Add the vegetable stock, potatoes, bay leaves, and thyme. Bring to a boil. Reduce the heat to medium and simmer until the potatoes have softened, about 25 minutes.

3. Remove and discard the bay leaves and thyme. Carefully transfer everything else into a blender and blend until smooth. Return to the pot and back over medium heat.

4. Add the heavy cream, salt, and pepper. Heat up before serving.

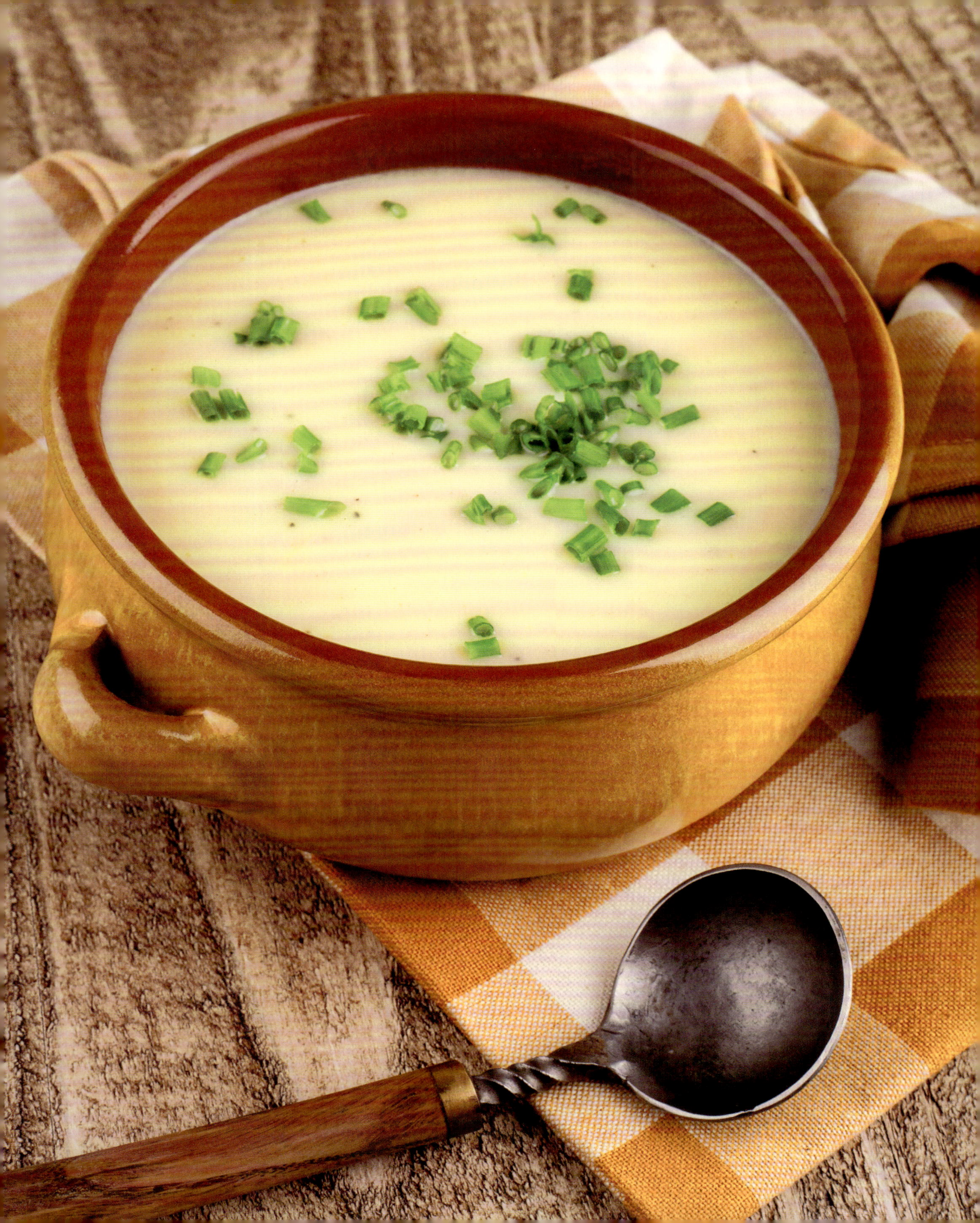

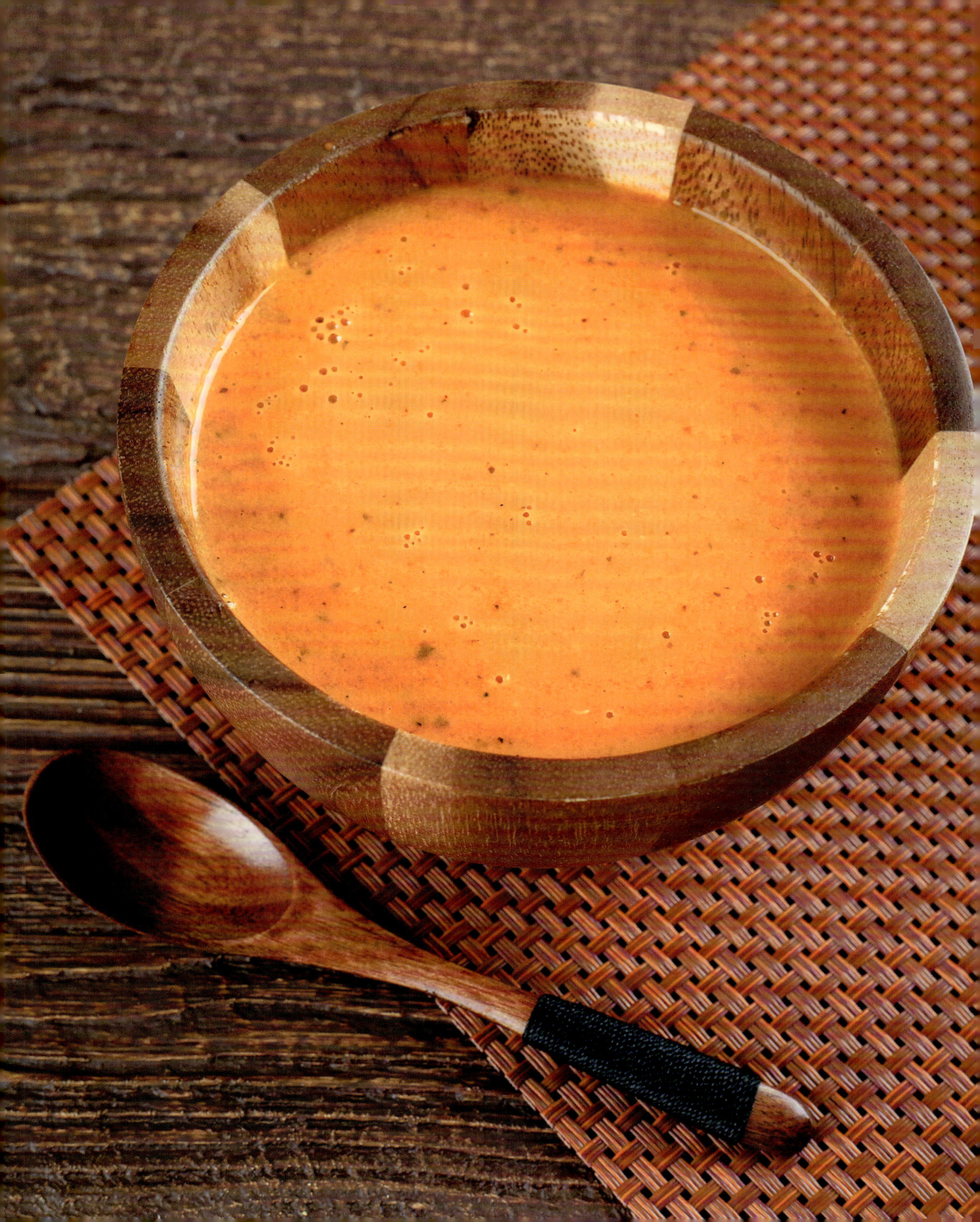

TOMATO SOUP

DIFFICULTY
Initiate

PREP TIME
20 minutes

COOK TIME
1 hour 10 minutes

SERVINGS
4 servings

DIETARY NOTES
Vegetarian

Once the Priory's historians did their initial explorations into the Desolation's Sulfur Quarry, I took a trip there looking for some unique desert herbs I'd heard about. Unfortunately, I hadn't been warned enough about the gross, overpowering smell. Even after I left, the stink stuck to my skin and clothes! I had a fellow member, Sieran, blast me with some magically enhanced water, but nothing. She recommended I try bathing in tomato soup. Well, I made a big batch of it . . . but it smelled SO delectable, so sharp and sweet at the same time, that I ended up eating the whole pot. It was well worth it, even though the rest of the Priory avoided my sulfur stink for weeks.

1. Preheat the oven to 400°F. In a medium bowl, whisk together the olive oil, salt, and pepper. Add the tomatoes and toss to coat. Place the tomatoes on a parchment paper–lined baking sheet and roast in the oven for 45 minutes.

2. In a medium pot, heat the olive oil over medium-high heat. Add the onion and cook until softened, about 8 minutes. Add the garlic and cook for another 2 minutes.

3. Add the roasted tomatoes, oregano, basil, and vegetable stock to the medium pot. Bring to a boil. Reduce the heat to medium and simmer for 10 minutes.

4. Carefully transfer to a blender and blend until smooth. Return the mixture to the medium pot, add the heavy cream, and heat back up before serving.

3 tablespoons olive oil
2 teaspoons kosher salt
1 teaspoon ground black pepper
3 pounds tomatoes, quartered
½ onion, chopped
6 garlic cloves, chopped
1 teaspoon dried oregano
1 teaspoon dried basil
3 cups Vegetable Stock (page 64)
½ cup heavy cream

DIFFICULTY
Journeyman

PREP TIME
20 minutes

COOK TIME
1 hour 15 minutes

SERVINGS
6 servings

DIETARY NOTES
Vegan, Gluten free

BUTTERNUT SQUASH SOUP

This colorful, comforting soup is rumored to have been created by a chef with the Order of Whispers. (I couldn't find out their name—secrecy and all.) Apparently, they were hoping to make a dish that boosted the stealth abilities of the Order members. After various testing, they found that the smooth texture of their soup did seem to help agents move with more precision . . . but its hearty warmth also encouraged their hunger for open battle. Well, our anonymous chef may have no use for this recipe, but it's perfect for us!

- 1 butternut squash (about 3 pounds), peeled and cubed
- 3 tablespoons olive oil, divided
- 1 teaspoon cayenne pepper
- 1 teaspoon ground cumin
- 1 teaspoon kosher salt
- ½ teaspoon ground black pepper
- 3 shallots, diced
- 2 carrots, peeled and chopped
- 3 garlic cloves, minced
- 3 cups Vegetable Stock (page 64)
- 1 sage sprig
- 1 bay leaf
- 13 ounces coconut milk

Additionals
Scallions, chopped
Roasted pumpkin seeds

1. Preheat the oven to 400°F. In a large bowl, combine the butternut squash, 2 tablespoons of olive oil, the cayenne pepper, cumin, salt, and black pepper. Transfer to a parchment paper–lined larger baking sheet and bake in the oven for 20 minutes. Toss and bake for another 15 minutes, or until slightly golden brown. Remove from the oven and set aside.

2. In a medium pot, heat the remaining 1 tablespoon of olive oil over medium-high heat. Add the shallots and carrots and cook until softened, 8 to 10 minutes.

3. Add the garlic and cook for another 3 minutes.

4. Add the vegetable stock, butternut squash, sage, and bay leaf. Bring to a boil. Reduce the heat to medium and simmer for 30 minutes, or until the carrots are softened.

5. Remove and discard the sage and bay leaf. Carefully transfer everything else into a blender and blend until smooth. Return to the pot and place back over medium heat.

6. Add the coconut milk and season with salt and pepper.

7. Heat up and top with scallions and roasted pumpkin seeds before serving.

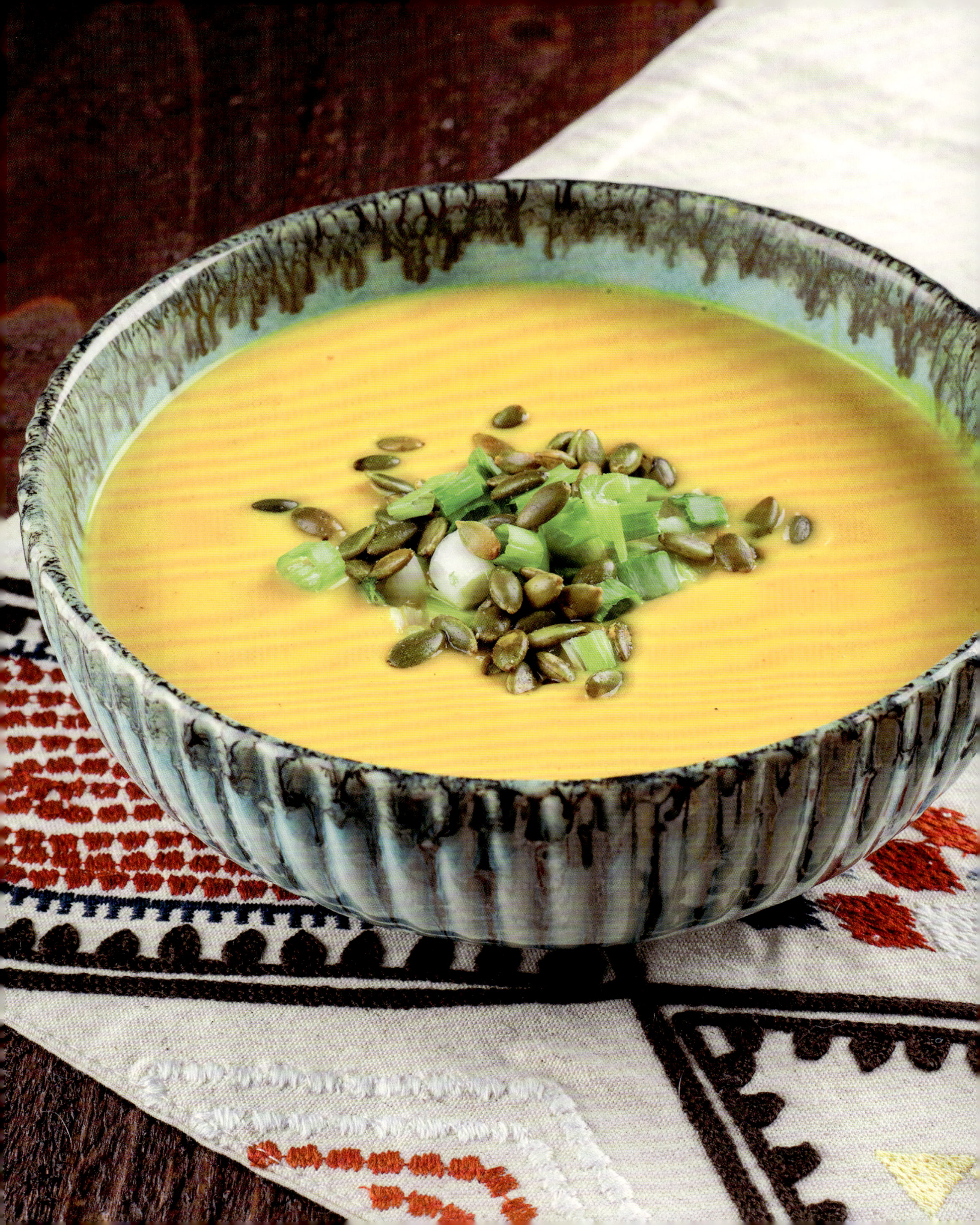

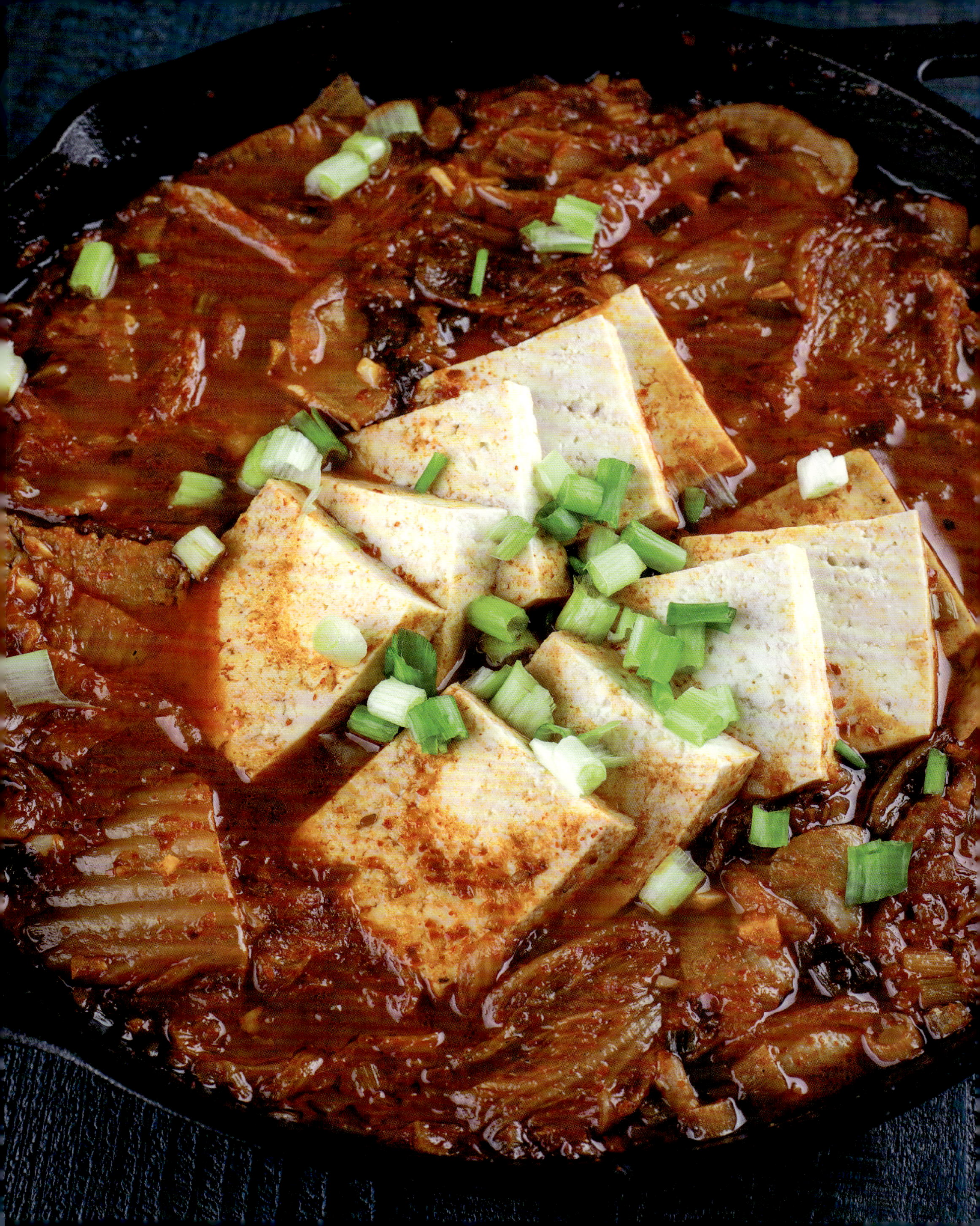

KIMCHI TOFU STEW

Imperial Chef Jiong was renowned among culinary artists for his high-quality soups and stews. Though he's been gone for centuries, his legend lives on in his influential dishes and groundbreaking techniques! He famously declared that his kappa shell soup was his prizewinning dish, but all the Priory chefs agree that his take on this stew is superior. The pleasant sourness and spicy fire of the kimchi! The umami savor of the seafood! And the ingredient that ties them all together: tofu, the most adaptable ingredient known to all the races of Tyria! Of all the glorious foods to come out of Shing Jea Island, I had to include this one—even if I've never been there myself.

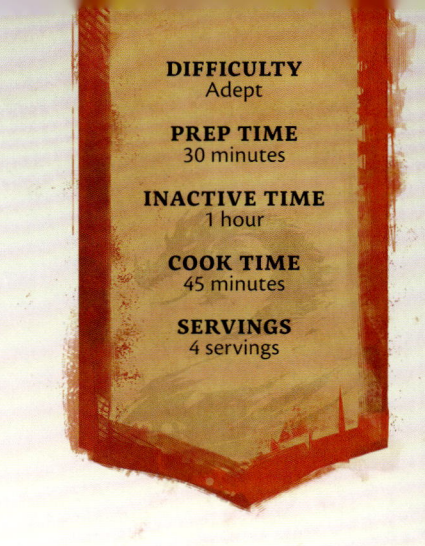

DIFFICULTY
Adept

PREP TIME
30 minutes

INACTIVE TIME
1 hour

COOK TIME
45 minutes

SERVINGS
4 servings

---

1. To make the broth: Place everything in a pot and cover. Allow to soak for 1 hour.
2. Place the pot over medium-high heat and bring to a boil. Once boiling, remove and discard the kombu. Reduce the heat and simmer for 15 minutes.
3. Strain and discard the anchovies and set aside the broth.
4. To make the stew: In a medium, deep nonstick pan, heat the canola and sesame oil over medium-high heat. Add the pork belly and cook until no longer pink.
   Note: Make sure not to overcrowd the pan, cooking the pork belly in batches if needed. Transfer the cooked pieces to a plate.
5. Return all the cooked pork belly to the pan. Add the kimchi, onion, and scallions. Cook until softened, 3 to 5 minutes. Add the garlic and cook for another minute.
6. Add the anchovy broth, kimchi juice, gochujang, gochugaru, brown sugar, salt, and pepper. Mix everything together until well combined. Bring to a boil and reduce the heat to medium. Cover and simmer for 10 minutes.
7. Add the tofu, cover, and cook for another 10 minutes. Serve with rice and garnish with chopped scallions.

Anchovy Broth

2 cups Poultry Stock (page 60)
3-inch piece of kombu
½ cup dried anchovies, head and guts removed

Kimchi Tofu Stew

2 teaspoons sesame oil
1 teaspoon canola oil
½ pound pork belly, thinly sliced
1 pound kimchi, cut into bite-size pieces
1 onion, sliced
6 scallions, chopped
3 garlic cloves, minced
Anchovy Broth
¼ cup kimchi juice
1 tablespoon gochujang
2 teaspoons gochugaru
2 teaspoons dark brown sugar
1 teaspoon kosher salt
½ teaspoon ground black pepper
7 ounces medium-firm tofu, cut into thick slices

Additionals

2 cups cooked rice
2 scallions, chopped

VALRAVN STEW

DIFFICULTY
Apprentice

PREP TIME
30 minutes

COOK TIME
4 hours

SERVINGS
6 to 8 servings

DIETARY NOTES
Dairy free

This recipe originates in Lowland Shore with the kodan. Anyone who's been to Janthir knows that the Lowland kodan and the valravns are eternally at war. The valravns attack and eat the hearts of kodan cubs. Through a mystical process, that gruesome meal causes the birds to become terrifying valravn knights. In return, the kodan slay valravns to protect and avenge their offspring. They use the valravn meat in various foods, including this wild but decadent stew. That said, I'm well aware that valravn meat is hard to come by. It's hard to find hunters who will risk having their hearts torn out. So, in this recipe, venison makes a great lean meat substitute. Normally I'd also recommend bear meat, but . . . well. Seems gauche.

- ⅓ cup all-purpose flour
- 1 tablespoon kosher salt
- 1 tablespoon ground black pepper
- 3 pounds venison stew meat, cut into 1-inch cubes
- 2 tablespoons canola oil, plus more as needed
- 3 onions, thinly sliced
- 1 red onion, thinly sliced
- ¼ cup dark brown sugar
- 6 tablespoons tomato paste
- 2 carrots, peeled and cut into bite-size pieces
- 2 cups Red Meat Stock (page 63)
- 4 cups stout
- 2 bay leaves
- 2 rosemary sprigs
- 1½ pounds Yukon Gold potatoes, cut into bite-size pieces
- 1 pound pumpkin, peeled and cut into bite-size pieces
- 2 tablespoons cornstarch
- 3 tablespoons water
- 12 ounces egg noodles, cooked (optional)

1. In a medium bowl, combine the flour, salt, and pepper. Add the venison and toss until well coated. In a large Dutch oven, heat 1 tablespoon of canola oil over medium heat. Add a single layer of the venison, but do not overcrowd the Dutch oven. Brown all sides of the meat. Remove and transfer to a plate. Add more canola oil if needed and continue this process until all the venison has been browned.

2. Add another tablespoon of canola oil to the Dutch oven. Add the onions and cook until softened, 10 to 12 minutes. Mix in the brown sugar and tomato paste until well combined with the onions.

3. Toss in the carrots and cook for another 2 minutes. Add the venison back to the Dutch oven and stir together. Mix in the red meat stock and stout.

4. Add the bay leaves and rosemary and bring to a boil. Reduce the heat, cover with a lid, and simmer for 3 hours.

5. Add the pumpkin and potatoes, cover, and cook for another 30 minutes until the potatoes are tender. In a small bowl, combine cornstarch and water. Remove the bay leaves and rosemary sprigs from the Dutch oven.

6. Add the cornstarch slurry. Mix until the sauce begins to thicken. Can be served as is or on top of a portion of cooked egg noodles.

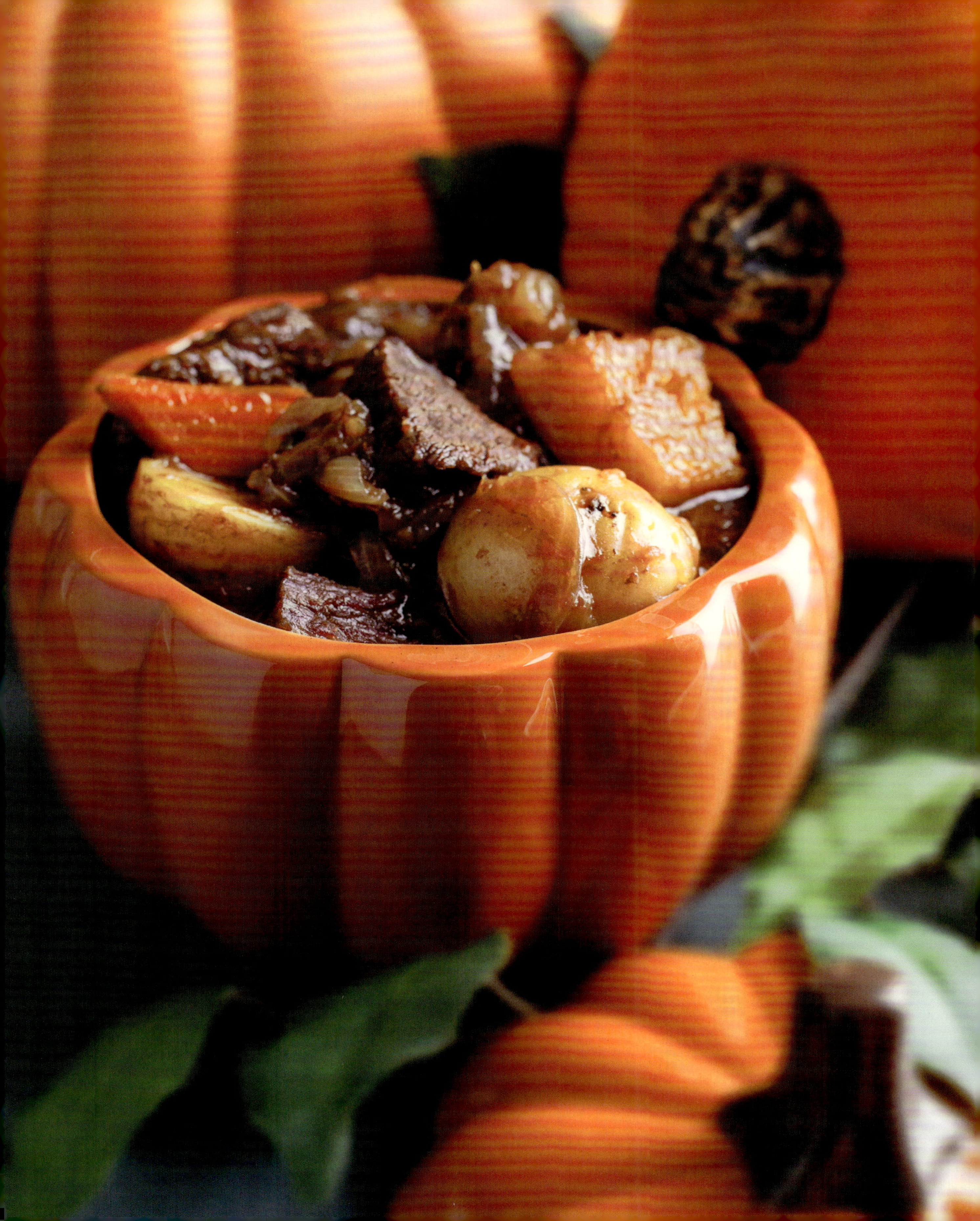

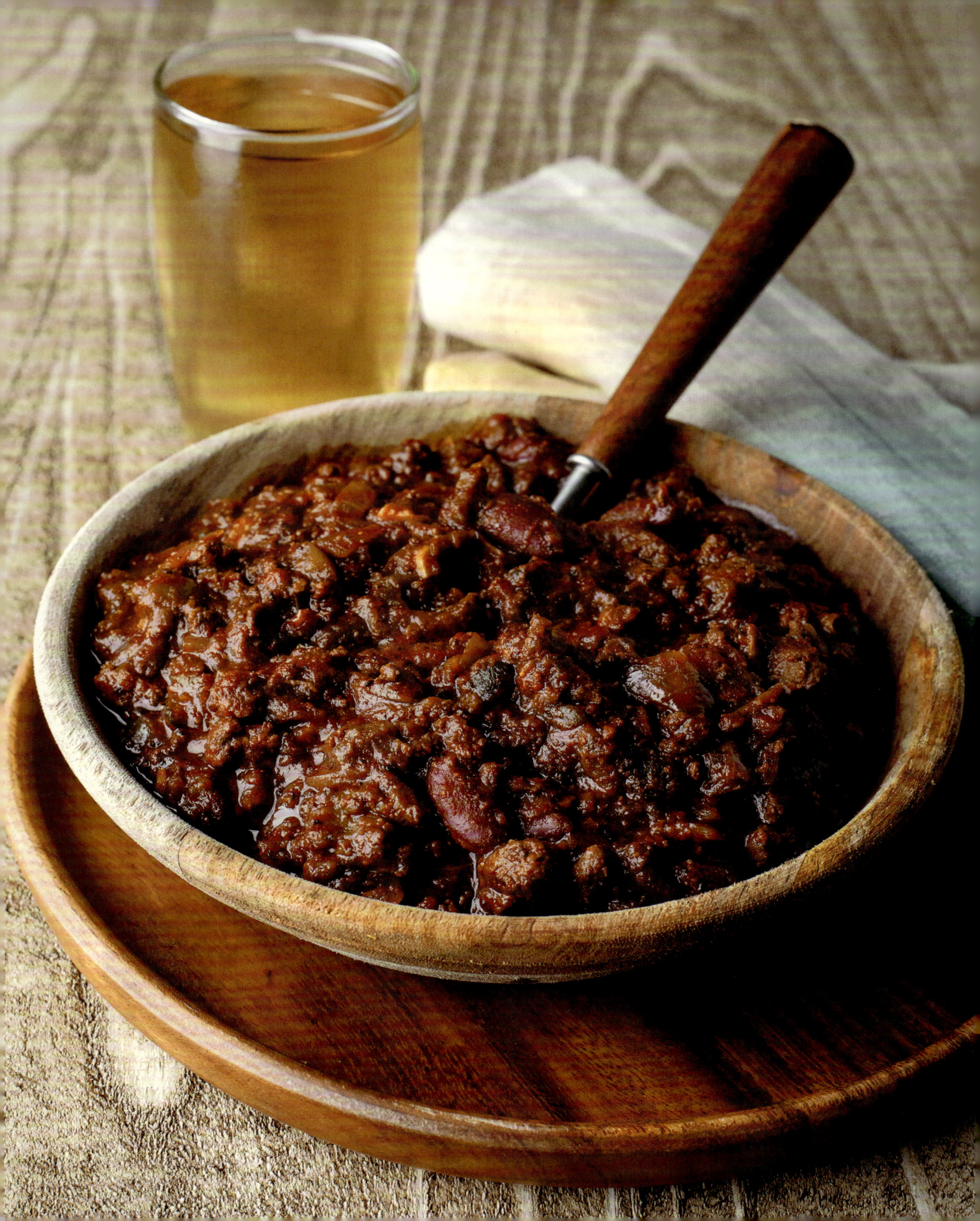

CARNE KHAN CHILI

DIFFICULTY
Adept

PREP TIME
45 minutes

COOK TIME
5 hours

SERVINGS
6 servings

DIETARY NOTES
Dairy free

Though the imperators of the High Legions endlessly squabble over the title Khan-Ur, my friend Arae Lorehunter insists that there has only ever been one true Khan-Ur. Their name has been lost to history, but they've been the namesake of something even greater: this chili! It's a bold recipe: the beans provide groundedness, the charred meat keeps you coming back for more, and the unique blend of spices kick up an amazing heat. Arae found records that document the original Khan-Ur enjoying two bowls before every war meeting. I'd like to think that all the charisma and command he's remembered for were due to this chili.

1. Preheat the oven to 450°F. Place the red onion, bell peppers, jalapeño, hatch, and serrano on a baking sheet. Brush all the vegetables with olive oil and season with salt and black pepper. Bake for 25 minutes. Flip everything over and add the garlic cloves to the tray. Bake for another 15 minutes or until the peppers have softened and start to blacken.

2. Once cooked, take the baking sheet out of the oven and wrap it in foil. Let it rest for 30 minutes or until it is cool enough to work with. Remove the skin from all the peppers. Remove the stem and seeds from the jalapeño, hatch, and serrano peppers. Dice all the roasted vegetables and set aside.

3. Place the guajillo, ancho, and pasilla peppers in a dry skillet over medium-high heat. Toast until fragrant, 2 to 3 minutes per side.

4. Transfer to a small pot and fill with water until the peppers are covered. Heat over high heat and bring to a simmer. Cover, remove from the heat, and let rest for 10 minutes.

5. Remove the peppers from the water and transfer to a blender. Add the tomato paste and half the diced tomatoes. Blend together until smooth and set aside. **Note:** If the mixture is too thick to blend, add a few spoonfuls of the water you used to heat the peppers in. Do not add too much; it should be a thick paste while still being blendable.

6. In a large pot, heat the ground beef and venison over medium-high heat. Cook until it has all browned. Add the salt, pepper, cumin, Kashmiri chili powder, basil, cinnamon, brown sugar, ground coffee, and Worcestershire sauce. Mix until well combined.

7. Mix in the roasted vegetables. Add the red kidney beans, remaining diced tomatoes, and blended dried peppers. Bring to a simmer. Finally, add the bay leaves, cover, and reduce the heat to low. Simmer for 4 hours, making sure to stir once every hour or so. Once cooked, remove and discard the bay leaves.

- 1 red onion, quartered
- 2 green bell peppers, halved and seeded
- 1 jalapeño pepper
- 2 hatch peppers
- 2 serrano peppers
- 1 whole garlic
- 2 guajillo peppers, stemmed and seeded
- 1 ancho pepper, stemmed and seeded
- 1 pasilla pepper, stemmed and seeded
- Olive oil, for brushing the vegetables
- 6 ounces tomato paste
- 28 ounces diced tomatoes
- 1 pound ground beef
- 1 pound ground venison
- 2 teaspoons kosher salt, plus more for seasoning the vegetables
- 2 teaspoons ground black pepper, plus more for seasoning the vegetables
- 2 tablespoons ground cumin
- 2 tablespoons Kashmiri chili powder
- 1 tablespoon dried basil
- 1½ teaspoons ground cinnamon
- 2 tablespoons dark brown sugar
- 1 tablespoon ground coffee
- 1 tablespoon Worcestershire sauce
- One 15-ounce can dark red kidney beans, rinsed
- 2 bay leaves

DIFFICULTY
Adept

PREP TIME
30 minutes

COOK TIME
30 minutes

SERVINGS
5 servings

SAVORY SPINACH AND POULTRY SOUP

Scholar Boki told me a great story that, strangely enough, involved this recipe. They say there was a kooky inventor at the College of Dynamics who dedicated her research to improving golem performance. She insisted the key was in finding a way for golems to eat food—because if golems could convert food into energy the way organic beings do, they'd have access to an endless supply of organic fuel. The inventor gave a lot of spinach and poultry soup to the golem. Apparently, she believed wholeheartedly that the simple nutrition of the soup would be easiest to transfer to the golem's power. To make a long story short, it caused a massive stir in her college. Not because it worked, but because people thought she'd been making it to share and were up in arms about the inefficiencies of wasting good soup! She ended up making another batch for her colleagues—the clear, light, umami broth definitely powered them up.

Meatballs

1 pound ground chicken
⅔ cup panko breadcrumbs
2 tablespoons parsley, chopped
4 garlic cloves, chopped
¼ cup Parmesan Reggiano, shredded
¼ cup Romano cheese, shredded
1 egg
1 teaspoon kosher salt
½ teaspoon ground black pepper
2 tablespoons olive oil, divided

Soup

1 carrot, chopped
1 onion, chopped
2 tablespoons olive oil
5 garlic cloves, minced
2 teaspoons dried basil
6 cups Poultry Stock (page 60)
⅔ cup ditalini rigati
10 ounces spinach
¼ cup Parmigiano Reggiano, shredded

1. In a medium bowl, combine the ground chicken, panko, parsley, garlic, Parmigiano Reggiano, Romano cheese, egg, salt, and pepper. Mix until it just comes together. Split the mixture into tablespoon-size balls. You should end up with 27 to 30 meatballs.

2. In a large pan, heat 1 tablespoon of olive oil over medium-high heat. Add the meatballs and brown each side, 2 to 3 minutes per side.
   Note: The meatballs will not be fully cooked through yet.

3. Once the meatballs have browned, remove them from the pan and transfer them to a plate.

4. In a large pot, heat 1 tablespoon of olive oil over medium-high heat. Add the carrot and onion and cook until softened, 8 to 10 minutes. Add the garlic and basil and cook for another 3 minutes.

5. Add the poultry stock and bring to a boil. Reduce the heat to medium and add the meatballs. Allow to simmer for 5 minutes.

6. Add the ditalini rigati and cook until al dente, 8 to 10 minutes. Finally, add the spinach and Parmigiano Reggiano and cook until the spinach has wilted, 2 to 3 minutes.

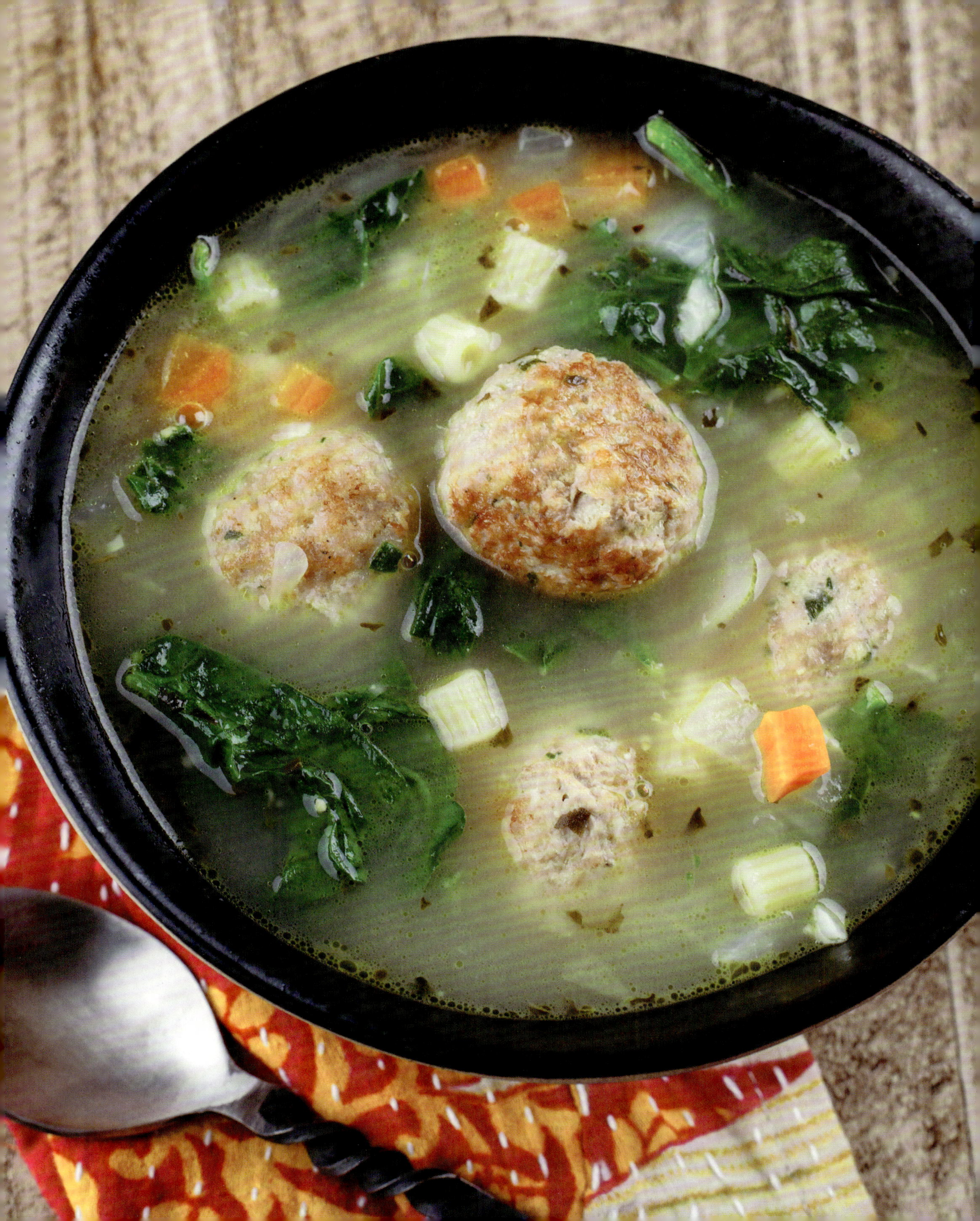

SIDES

The Crystal Desert! That massive expanse of hot sand under a relentless sun is every adventurer's nightmare. You never know what will pop out at you from behind a sand dune! I learned to be well prepared from my mishap in Ascalon, so when I started the trek across the desert, I looked like a snail carrying a giant shell of a pack on my back. I wasn't going to be caught unawares! It wasn't long before I saw a swarthy pair of desert devourers, but they didn't dare attack me. Instead, they attacked a small Elonian caravan going in the same direction.

I jumped to the rescue and made handy work of the devourers, but the people in the caravan were mighty shaken up. I offered to cook them something to settle them—I was eyeing their unique cooking utensils and ingredients! The Elonians were happy to lead me through their recipes. They made a large variety of dishes, but to my utter horror, the plates they prepared were all tiny! And nothing looked to be a main dish. "Impossible that anyone could ever get full from this," I remember thinking. "Let alone a norn who has just finished off two devourers." I figured I shouldn't shake them up further, though, so I dug in. My doubts were shelved by how interesting each little dish was—by the time I'd tried them all, I realized I was stuffed. Turns out, a bunch of sides can be just as filling as one big dish! It also turns out that traveling goes a lot faster when you're with friends—I went the rest of the desert eating those little plates with that caravan.

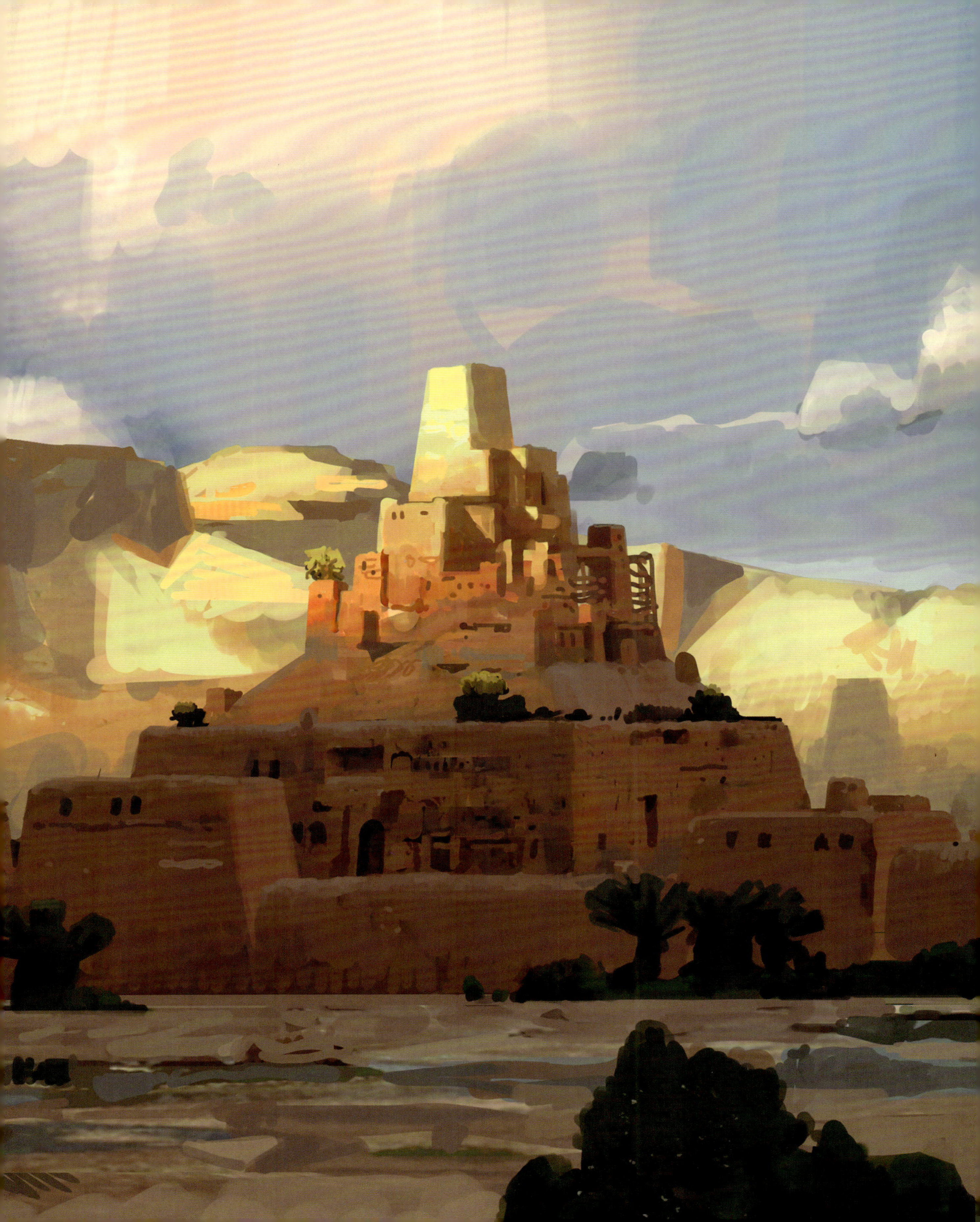

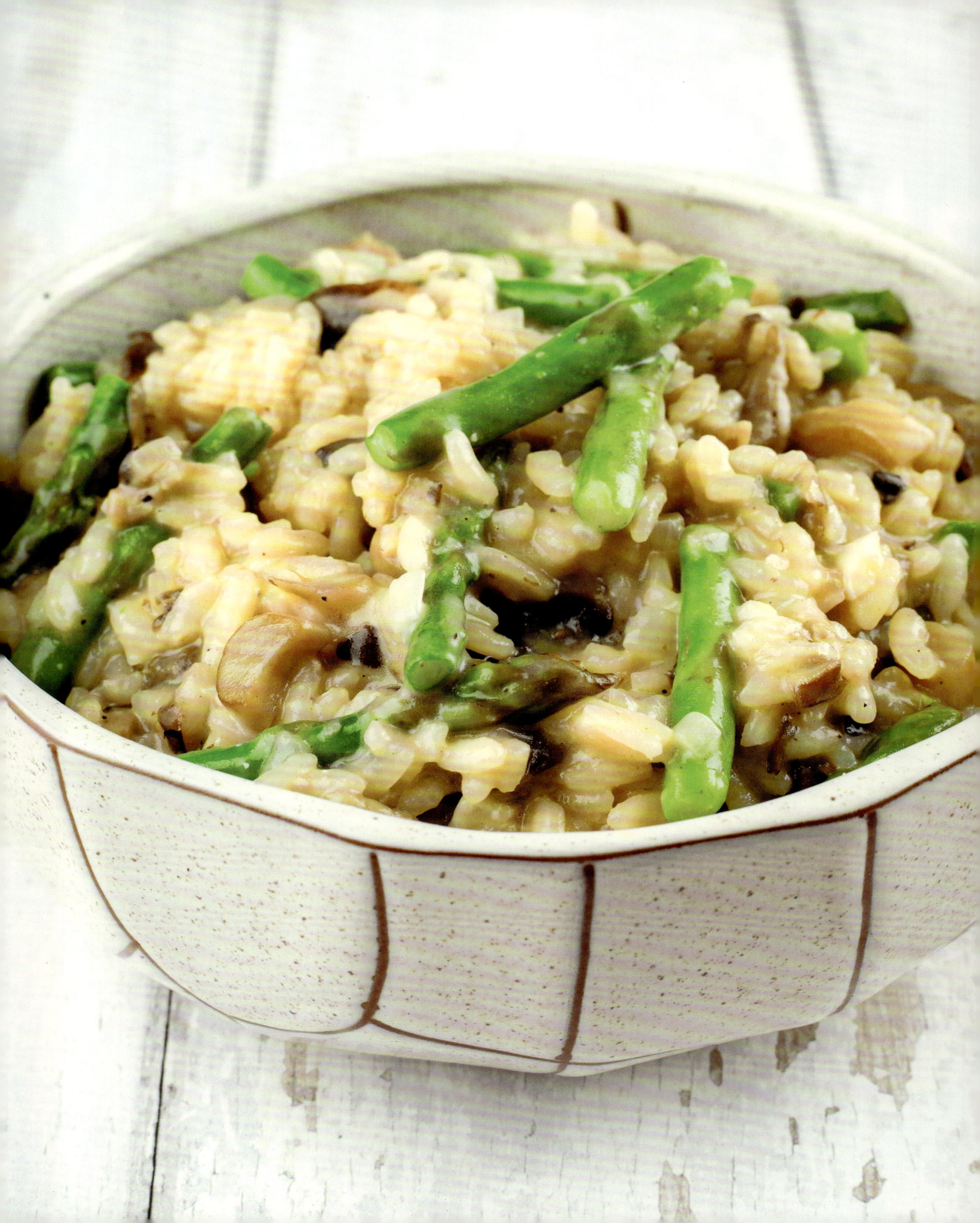

MUSHROOM AND ASPARAGUS RISOTTO

DIFFICULTY
Master

PREP TIME
20 minutes

COOK TIME
45 minutes

SERVINGS
4 servings

DIETARY NOTES
Vegetarian

One summer, the Priory assigned me a mission near the Labyrinthine Cliffs. I just happened to be in the area when the Festival of the Four Winds was in full swing. Walking around and perusing the magnificent banners and lanterns was a delight, but I didn't partake in any activities—that is, until I smelled the lunch of a Zephyrite running the crystal collection stall. It was a creamy, fluffy risotto, with tender bites of mushroom and asparagus throughout the sauce! I almost drooled on the spot. The staff member, named Lumen, told me that if I could win gold in crystal collection, she'd share the recipe with me. Well, here it is.

1. In a medium saucepan, heat the vegetable stock, shiitake mushrooms, and porcini mushroom over medium-high heat. Bring to a boil and then reduce to medium. Simmer for 15 minutes.
2. Remove and discard the mushrooms. Reduce the heat to low and keep the broth warm.
3. In a large nonstick pan, heat ½ tablespoon of olive oil over medium-high heat. Add the asparagus and sauté until softened, 5 to 7 minutes. Transfer to a plate.
4. Add the remaining ½ tablespoon of olive oil and add the mushrooms. Cook until softened, 5 to 8 minutes. Transfer to the plate with the asparagus.
5. Add the butter to the pan. Once the butter has melted, add the shallots and garlic and cook until softened, about 5 minutes. Add the arborio rice and coat the rice with the butter. Sauté for 2 minutes, but do not let the rice brown.
6. Add the white wine and stir in until all the liquid is absorbed. Slowly add the mushroom broth in half-cup increments. Stir until the broth is fully absorbed before adding more liquid. Repeat until all the broth is used and the rice is cooked through.
7. Remove from the heat and stir in the asparagus, mushrooms, and Parmigiano Reggiano cheese. Season with salt and pepper.

Mushroom Broth

5 cups Vegetable Stock (page 64)
3 dried shiitake mushrooms
½ ounce dried porcini mushrooms

Risotto

1 tablespoon olive oil, divided
½ pound asparagus, cut into 2-inch pieces
1 pound mushrooms, sliced*
3 tablespoons unsalted butter
3 shallots, diced
3 garlic cloves, minced
1½ cups arborio rice
1 cup white wine
3 ounces Parmigiano Reggiano, shredded
Kosher salt
Ground black pepper

*****Note:** Any variety of mushroom will work here.

DIFFICULTY
Novice

PREP TIME
30 minutes

COOK TIME
30 minutes

SERVINGS
6 servings

DIETARY NOTES
Vegetarian

MASHED POTATOES

Mashed potatoes are a favorite back home in Hoelbrak. It does a lot to keep the body warm! We made it year-round. Norn don't tend to spend a lot of time in one anothers' company—actually, most of us don't like to spend much time with any company. I'm an exception, of course—but whenever this was on the stovetop, the kitchens were crowded. I've perfected the dish into this recipe, bringing out the moreish flavors and textures. Now, whenever I'm home, people crowd around and wait for me to make it.

- 1½ pounds russet potatoes, peeled and chopped
- 2 teaspoons kosher salt, plus more as needed
- 6 tablespoons unsalted butter
- 1 cup buttermilk
- 2 tablespoons chives, chopped
- 1 teaspoon ground black pepper

1. Place the potatoes in a large pot, add just enough water to cover them, and season with the salt. Bring to a boil over high heat and then reduce the heat to medium and simmer for 15 to 20 minutes, or until the potatoes are tender. Drain and set the potatoes aside.

2. Place the pot back on the stove and heat the butter and buttermilk over medium heat. Cook until the butter has fully melted. Add the potatoes and mash until smooth. Add the chives and season with salt and pepper.

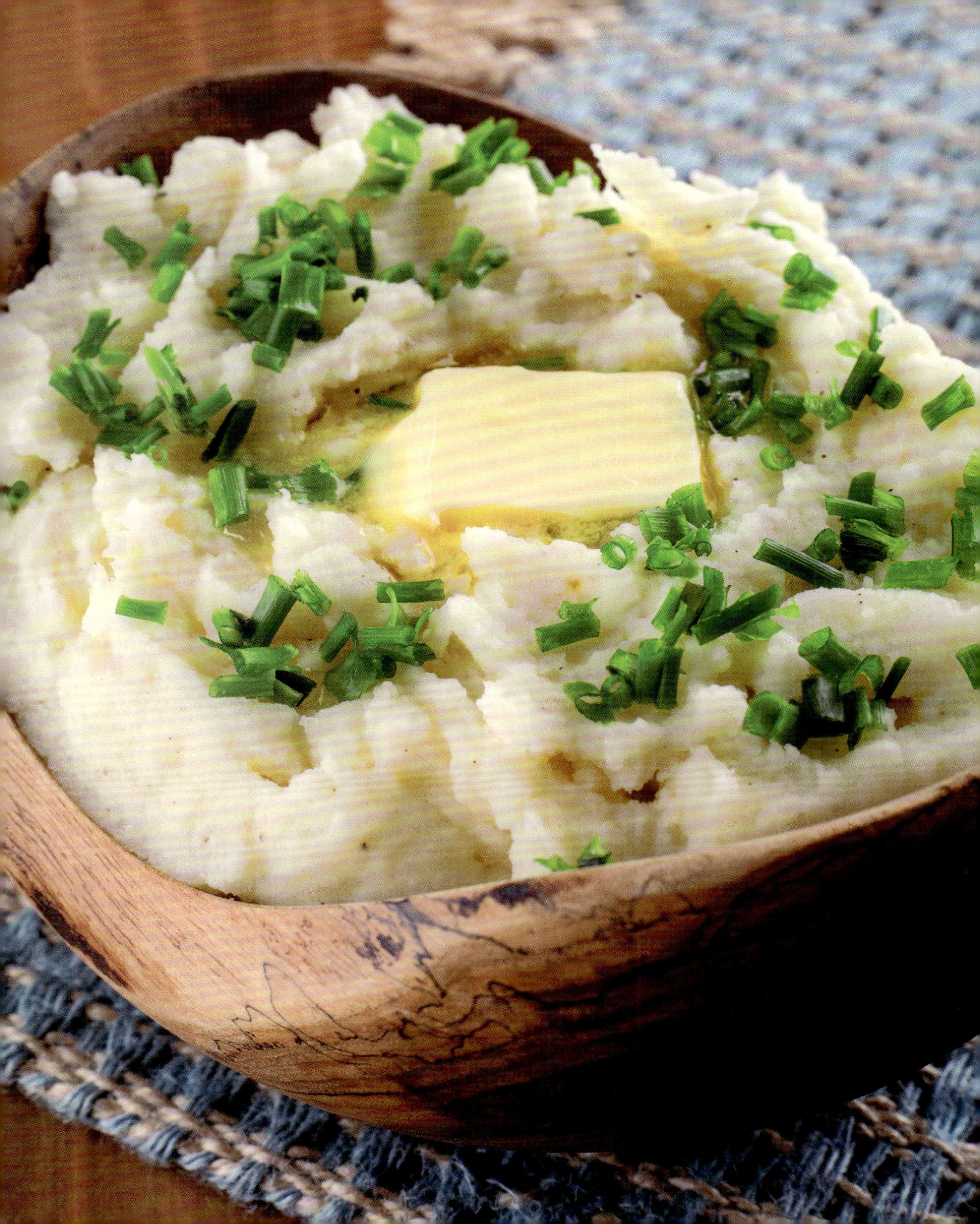

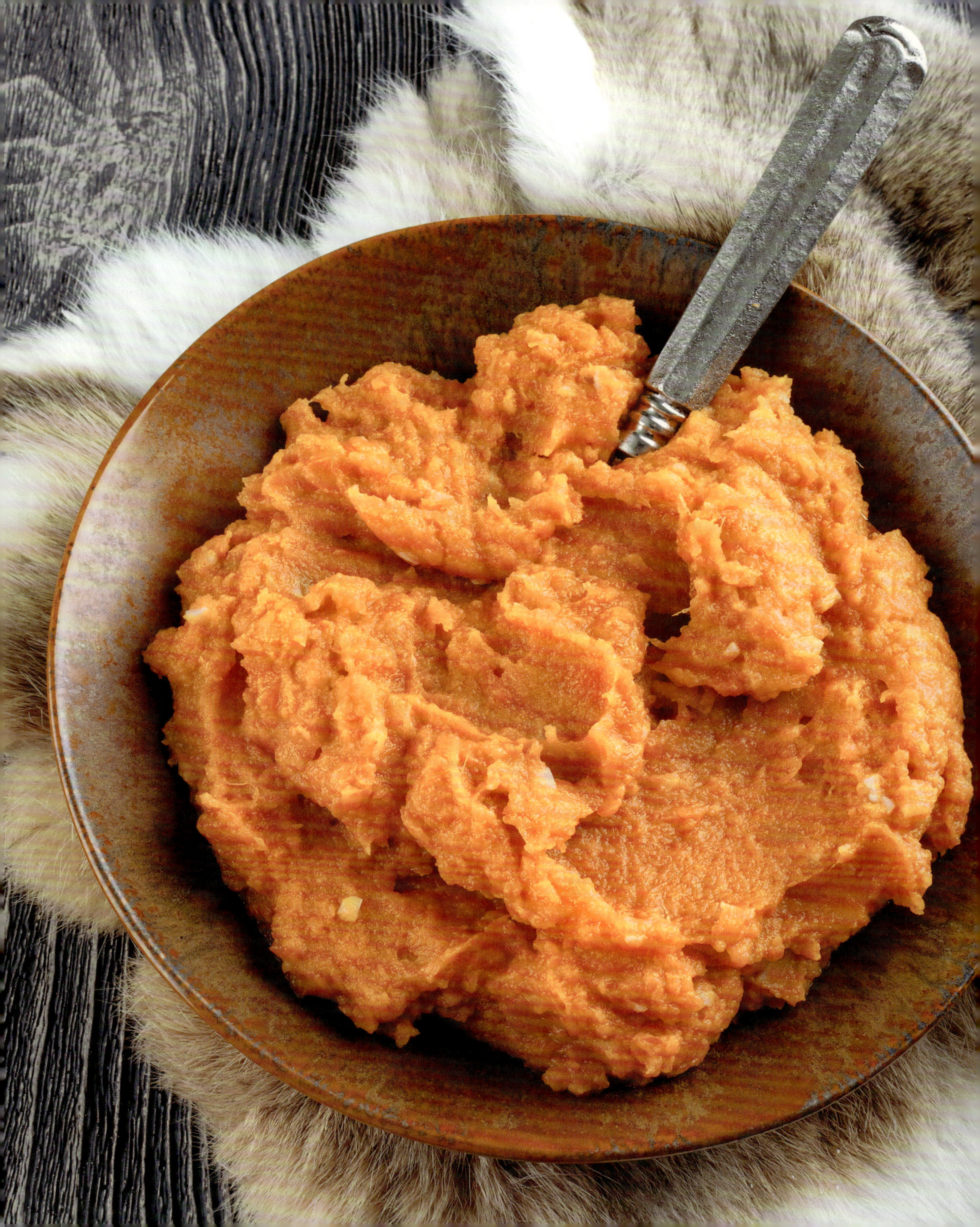

SPICED MASHED YAMS

DIFFICULTY
Apprentice

PREP TIME
20 minutes

COOK TIME
1 hour 45 minutes

SERVINGS
6 servings

DIETARY NOTES
Vegetarian, Gluten free

Whenever I have Spiced Mashed Yams, I think of Forgal Kernsson. I never knew him personally, but he has a reputation as a strange norn who loves discipline and order. After his family fell victim to the Icebrood, he up and joined the Vigil, of all things. But in the Shiverpeaks, the thing people talk about is how every time he came to the taverns, he'd request a plate of mashed yams. He would sit in silence, tasting the sweetness and the velvety texture of the starch. He would close his eyes to savor the warm spices. When a tavern owner finally asked him why, he said it reminded him of Wintersday with his wife and child.

1. Preheat the oven to 400°F. Poke several holes into the sweet potatoes with a fork. Lightly wrap in aluminum, leaving small holes for steam to escape.
2. Bake for 1 to 1½ hours, or until soft and cooked through. Once cooked, set aside until cool enough to work with.
3. In a medium saucepan, melt the butter over medium-high heat. Add the thyme and rosemary and cook until the butter begins to brown slightly, about 2 minutes. Remove and discard the herbs. Add the ginger and garlic and cook until softened, 2 to 3 minutes. Remove from the heat and set aside.
4. Once the sweet potatoes have cooled, remove and discard the skin and place the sweet potatoes in a medium bowl. Mash until smooth. Add the butter mixture, honey, palm sugar, salt, pepper, and buttermilk. Mix until smooth.

2 pounds sweet potatoes
2 tablespoons unsalted butter
2 thyme sprigs
1 rosemary sprig
3 tablespoons ginger, grated
2 garlic cloves, minced
2 tablespoons honey
1 tablespoon palm sugar, chopped
Pinch of kosher salt
Pinch of ground black pepper
2 tablespoons buttermilk

DIFFICULTY
Initiate

PREP TIME
15 minutes

COOK TIME
12 minutes

SERVINGS
4 servings

DIETARY NOTES
Dairy free

MEATY ASPARAGUS SKEWER

Have I got a spooky story for you! My friend Mikna was stationed in the Crystal Desert, researching ancient history for the Priory. One day, another researcher offered her a bit of this skewer. Who would turn down that crunchy, crispy prosciutto or juicy asparagus tossed in soy sauce and rice wine? After snarfing it down, Mikna and her team were ambushed by a group of bandits. But listen—as soon as the bandits raised their swords, sinister black smoke blew up around them. Then mysterious gashes appeared all over their bodies, like they were haunted by ghosts! The bandits ran off in terror. Once the team collected themselves, they realized that none of them knew the researcher that had given them the snack—and he was nowhere to be seen.

---

1 pound asparagus
1 tablespoon perilla oil
2 teaspoons soy sauce
1 teaspoon rice wine
Pinch of kosher salt
Pinch of ground black pepper
½ pound prosciutto, thinly sliced

1. Preheat the oven to 425°F. In a large bowl, toss the asparagus, perilla oil, soy sauce, rice wine, salt, and pepper until the asparagus is fully coated.

2. Take one of the asparagus pieces and wrap with a piece of prosciutto. Make sure to cover about three-quarters of the asparagus, leaving the top and bottom unwrapped. Place on a parchment paper–lined baking sheet. Repeat until all the pieces of asparagus are wrapped.

3. Place in the oven and bake for 10 to 12 minutes, or until the asparagus is softened and the prosciutto is crispy.

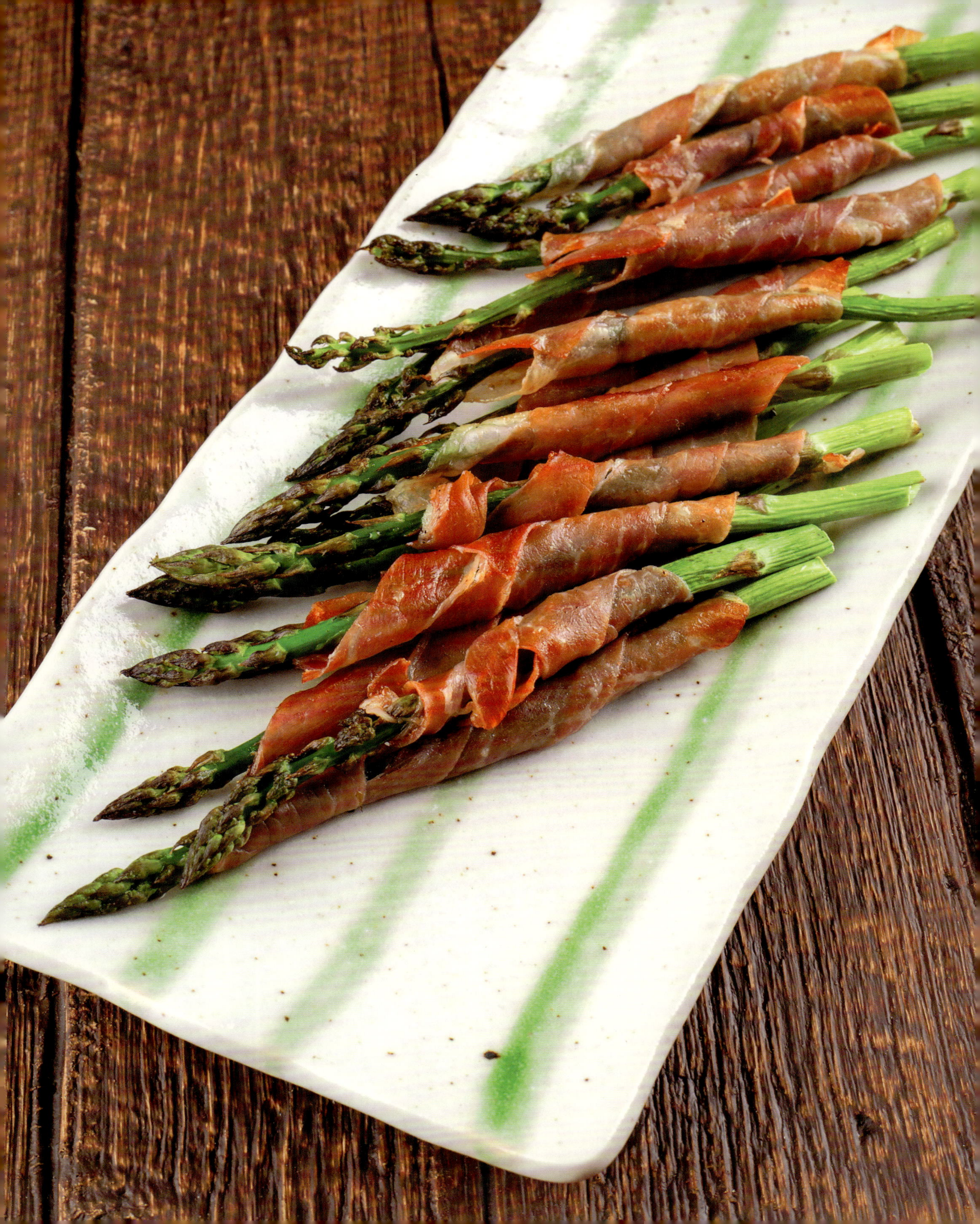

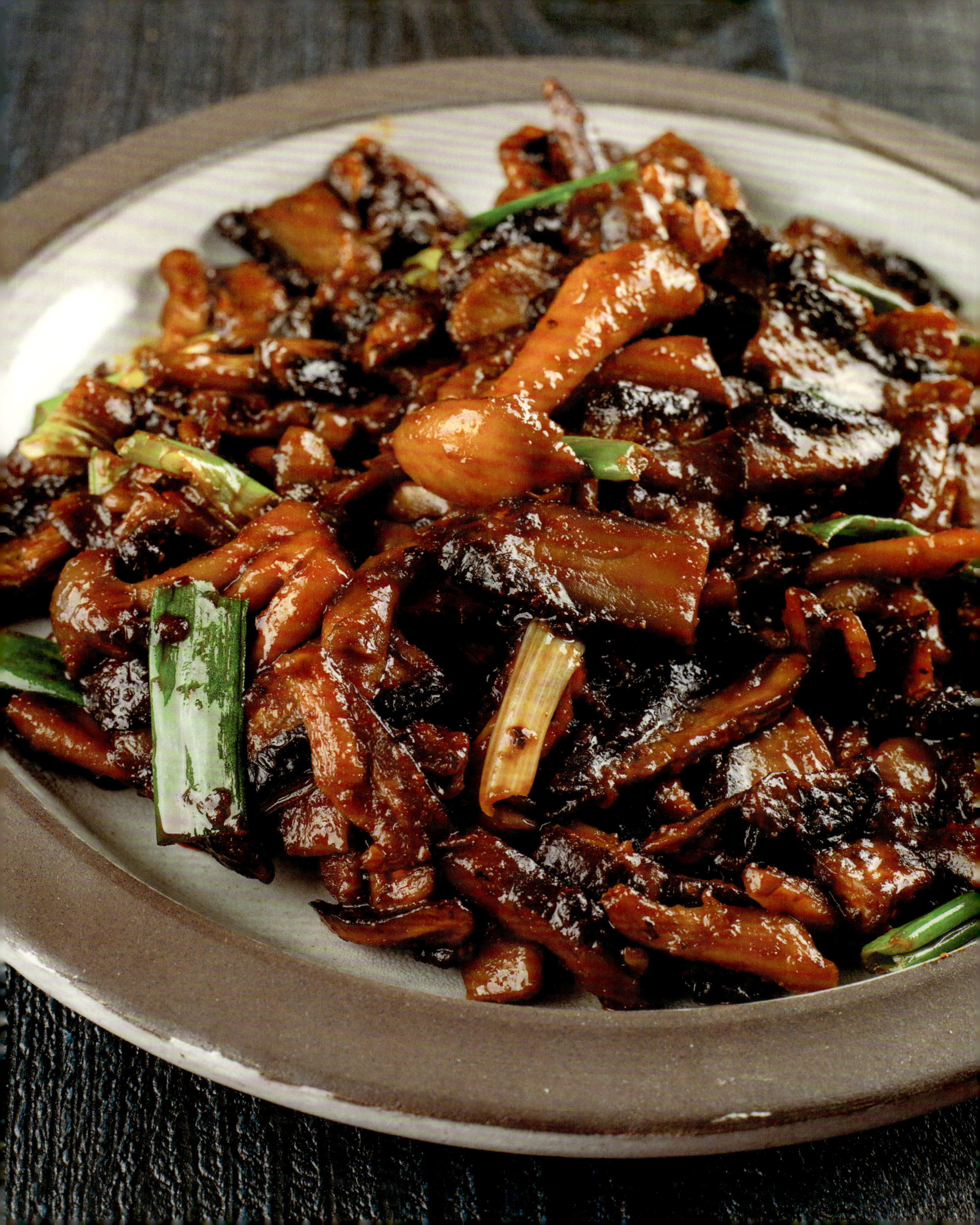

SPICY MARINATED MUSHROOMS

DIFFICULTY
Apprentice

PREP TIME
15 minutes

INACTIVE TIME
2 hours

COOK TIME
10 minutes

SERVINGS
4 servings

DIETARY NOTES
Vegan

I first tried this recipe years ago, at Highjump Ranch over in the Stampede Uplands. My raptor had gotten sick while I passed through that area, and the man who ran the stable was nice enough to help him recover. In exchange, I cooked meals! There was a homemade cookbook that had belonged to the stablemaster's wife gathering dust on a shelf. He hadn't touched it since she'd passed, but he'd never forgotten the spicy burn of this mushroom dish. I can still remember his tiny tyke of a daughter toddling around the kitchen to bring me salt and black peppercorn.

1. In a small bowl, whisk together the gochujang, gochugaru, soy sauce, rice wine, palm sugar, sesame oil, garlic powder, and ginger powder. Add the mushrooms and mix until well combined.
2. Place the mushrooms and sauce in an airtight container. Place in the refrigerator and allow to marinate for 2 hours.
3. In a medium nonstick pan, heat the canola oil over medium-high heat. Add the mushrooms and marinade and cook until softened and slightly browned, about 8 to 10 minutes.

2 tablespoons gochujang
1 tablespoon gochugaru
3 tablespoons soy sauce
3 tablespoons rice wine
1 tablespoon palm sugar
1 teaspoon sesame oil
1 teaspoon garlic powder
1 teaspoon ginger powder
2 portobello mushrooms, sliced
5 shiitake mushrooms, sliced
2 beech mushroom bunches, separated
1 teaspoon canola oil

DIFFICULTY
Apprentice

PREP TIME
1 hour

COOK TIME
2 hours

SERVINGS
8 servings

DIETARY NOTES
Vegetarian

EZTLITL STUFFING

This filling is made with the best ingredient: a storied and violent past! Hylek tribes are historically hostile to outsiders. The Eztlitl hylek tribe of Timberline Falls is an exception, but typically there's no one a hylek tribe hates more than another hylek tribe! For a few years, one common tribe tactic was to inject deadly toxins into an appetizing bowl of rosemary-infused stuffing, sneak it into a rival tribe's camp, and wait until they became fatally sick. The stuffing became so mistrusted after that that no hylek would dare eat it. What a waste of good food! In the last fifty years, the Eztlitl have lately brought the dish back in style and shared it with non-hylek outsiders. Thankfully, they've left out the poison.

---

1 loaf of Rosemary Bread (page 40), cut into 1-inch cubes
¼ cup unsalted butter
1 pound shallots, chopped
½ pound celery, chopped
6 garlic cloves, chopped
3 rosemary sprigs, stemmed
3 thyme sprigs, stemmed
2 eggs
2 cups Vegetable Stock (page 64)
1 teaspoon kosher salt
1 teaspoon ground black pepper
Nonstick spray

1. Preheat the oven to 200°F. Prepare a baking sheet with parchment paper and top with the cubed rosemary bread. Place in the oven and bake for 30 minutes. Toss and bake for another 30 minutes. Toss once more and bake for another 30 minutes or until the bread is crispy and lightly golden brown. Set aside.

2. Increase the oven's temperature to 375°F. While the oven is heating, in a medium nonstick pan, melt the butter over medium-high heat. Once melted, add the shallots, celery, and garlic and cook until softened, about 10 minutes.

3. Add the rosemary and thyme leaves and cook until fragrant, about 2 minutes. Remove from the heat and set aside.

4. In a medium bowl, whisk together the eggs, vegetable stock, salt, and pepper.

5. Transfer the bread into a large bowl. Add the vegetables and toss until combined. Add the egg mixture and mix until well combined.

6. Prepare a deep 13-by-9-inch baking dish by spraying with nonstick spray. Transfer the bread mixture into an even layer into the baking dish. Cover with aluminum foil and bake for 25 minutes.

7. Remove the foil and bake for another 15 minutes, or until golden brown and cooked through. Allow to rest for 10 minutes before serving.

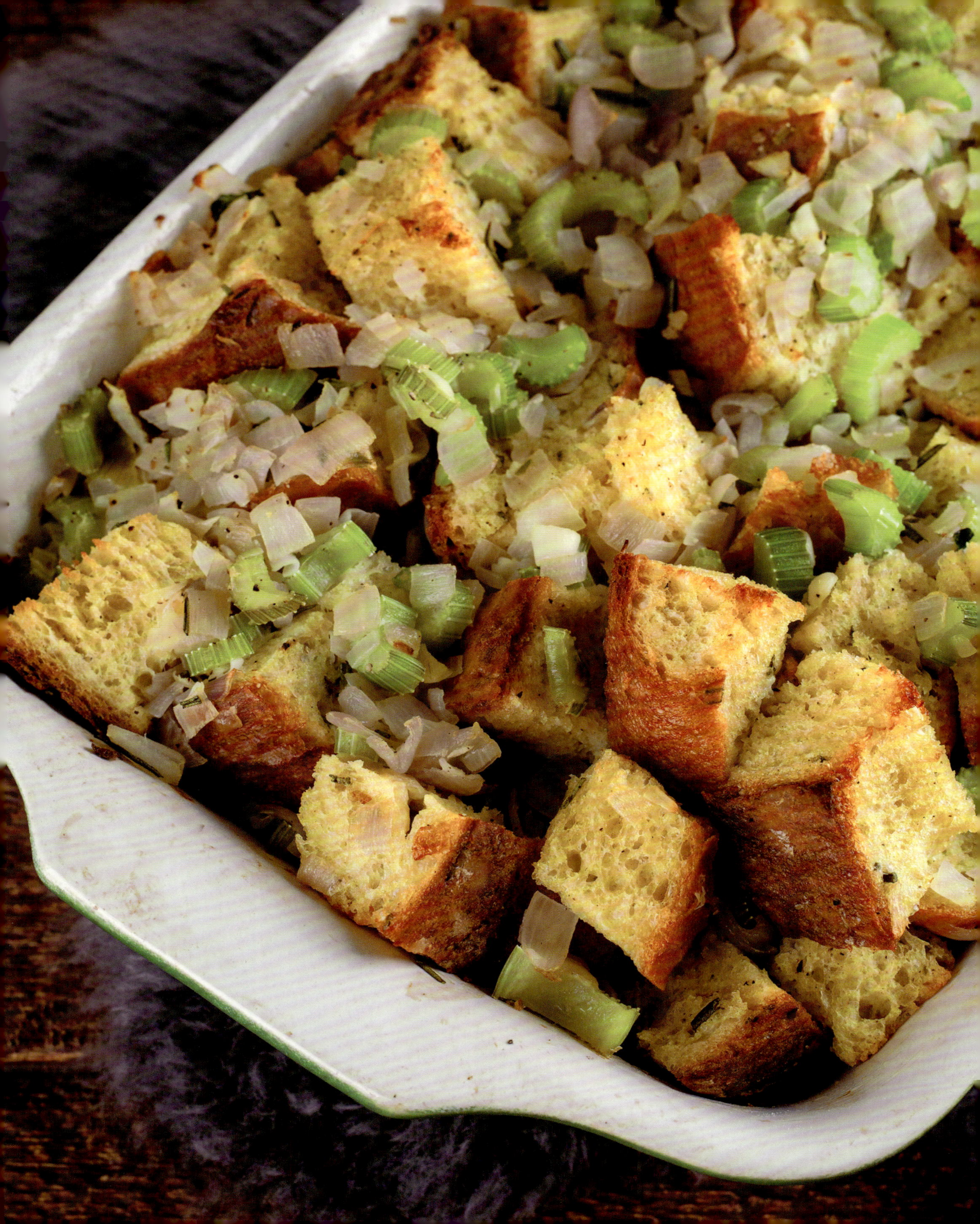

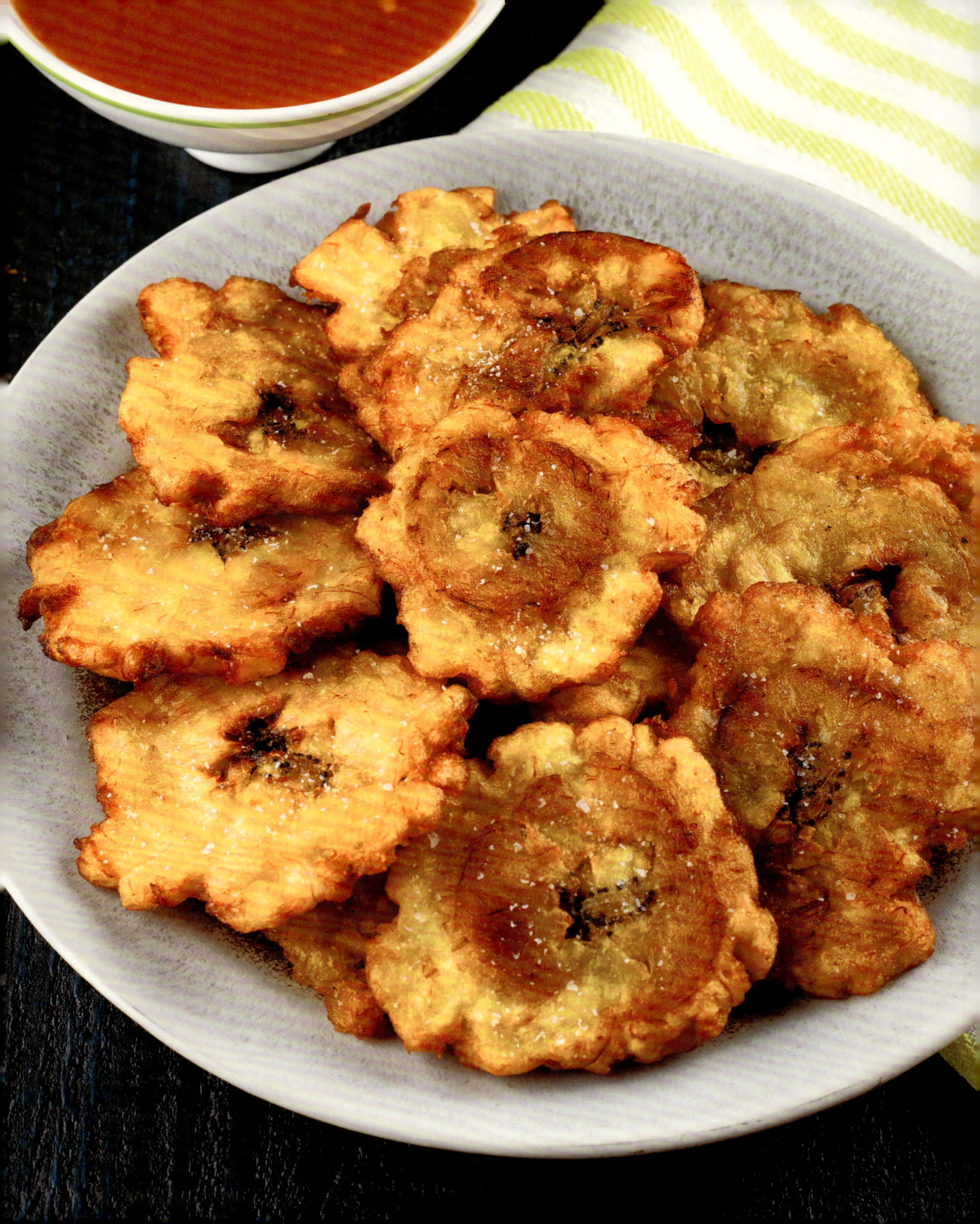

GRILLED PLANTAINS WITH PASSION FRUIT SAUCE

DIFFICULTY
Journeyman

PREP TIME
30 minutes

COOK TIME
30 minutes

SERVINGS
6 servings

DIETARY NOTES
Vegetarian

Behold! This recipe for sweetened plantains is one of the oldest I've found recorded and originates on the shores of Ember Bay. The marooned inhabitants of the Ring of Fire have held outdoor feasts whenever they had anything to celebrate. You have to make the best of what you can get when you're in a rough location like that! These small community jamborees were cooked and served family-style, and on Ember Bay, the tropical blend of plantain and passion fruit was often in demand. There's one recorded instance where they cooked and ate five hundred plantains! Of course, multicourse banquets at Ember Bay fell out of fashion when Primordus's destroyers began running rampant . . . but we can all be a part of bringing this dish back.

1. In a blender, pulse the passion fruit purée, red Thai chiles, ginger, garlic, lime juice, brown sugar, honey, apple cider vinegar, and salt until smooth.

2. Transfer through a fine-mesh strainer into a small saucepan, discarding any large bits. Place the saucepan over medium-high heat and bring to a simmer. Cook for 10 minutes until the sauce has heated through.

3. In a small bowl, whisk together the water and cornstarch and then add to the saucepan. Mix in until the sauce has thickened. Transfer to a small bowl to serve.

4. Cut the plantains into 1-inch-thick slices.

5. Fill a frying pan with ½ inch of oil and heat over medium heat. Once heated, carefully add the plantains and cook each side until golden, 2 to 3 minutes per side.

6. Transfer to a paper towel on a plate to drain off the excess oil. Once cool enough to handle, take the fried plantains and lightly smash them under a plate into a ½-inch-thick disk.

7. Place the smashed plantains back into the oil and fry to golden, about 1 minute per side. Transfer to a paper towel on a plate to drain excess oil off. Season with additional salt and serve with passion fruit sauce.

Passion Fruit Sauce
1 cup passion fruit purée
2 red Thai chiles
2 teaspoons ginger, grated
1 garlic clove
½ tablespoon lime juice
1 tablespoon dark brown sugar
2 tablespoons honey
2 tablespoons apple cider vinegar
½ teaspoon kosher salt
1 tablespoon water
1½ teaspoons cornstarch

Platanos
3 very ripe plantains
Neutral oil, for frying
Kosher salt

ENTRÉES

At one point in the middle of my first year, I received an unexpected summons from Steward Gixx. One of the Priory's excavation teams had been ambushed by a horde of jungle trolls along the Tarnished Coast—including a champion troll. I rushed to their aid armed with all my weapons, ready to fight. The battlefield was a grisly sight: my exhausted comrades littered the ground as the trolls rampaged through the lavender fog of the swamp. Fighters that I considered in my league were retreating because they were so drained. They didn't need me to fight, I realized. They needed me to *cook*.

I immediately started whipping up feasts upon feasts. Meatball dinners! Lemongrass Mussel Pasta! Fishy Rice Bowls! Entrées were the only thing that would power my crew through—big, filling portions that granted strength. As fast as I churned them out, the excavation team ate. Finally, they could stand tall and outlast the horde of enemies—meanwhile, I was exhausted! I'd never undergone a culinary gauntlet like that before. But I'd proven my skill. Word got back to Gixx, and the next message I got from him assigned me as an assistant to Chef Robertus!

Is there a moral to that story? Hmm . . . I'd say this: Cooking main dishes is a challenge, but if you can beat it, the reward will be well worth it! That, and don't poke your nose where jungle trolls are sleeping.

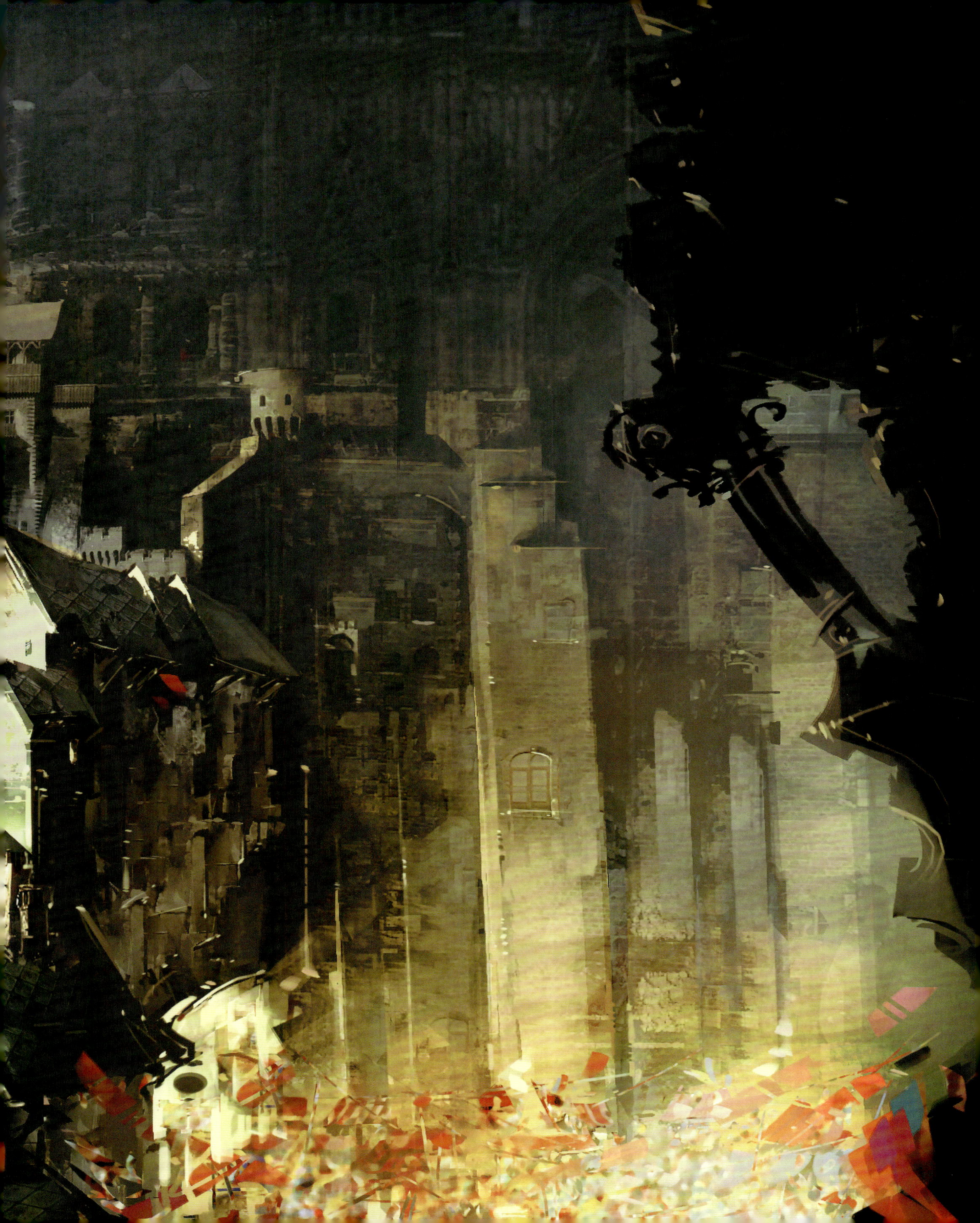

DIFFICULTY
Journeyman

PREP TIME
30 minutes

INACTIVE TIME
2 hours

COOK TIME
45 minutes

SERVINGS
4 servings

DIETARY NOTES
Dairy free

FISHY RICE BOWL

"Simple yet delicious." That was the motto of the legendary Imperial Chef Tian—before he got famous for his over-the-top ingredients like spiderwebs and blobs! Back around 250 years ago, when Tian had just become a grandmaster, his standard menu was much more focused on a balanced diet, and this Fishy Rice Bowl was one of his best. With a mix of sliced veggies, fresh salmon, and a nice, short-grain rice, this nutritious meal will keep you as long-lived as a phoenix. The historian in me liked his recipes way more before the fame, though I'd never turn down a strange ingredient. Maybe the Fishy Rice Bowl could use some bloodstone dust . . .

Soy Salmon
½ cup soy sauce
½ cup rice wine
1 tablespoon granulated sugar
1 tablespoon light brown sugar
2 tablespoons grated ginger
½ teaspoon fish sauce
1 pound salmon, cut into 1½-inch portions

Canthan Vegetable Mix
¼ cup soy sauce
2 tablespoons light brown sugar
¼ cup Vegetable Stock (page 64)
1 teaspoon sesame oil
1 teaspoon fish sauce
2 teaspoons cornstarch
1 teaspoon canola oil
1 onion, sliced
½ carrot, peeled and julienned
1 zucchini, cut into ½-inch pieces
4 shiitake mushrooms, sliced
1 bunch beech mushrooms, roughly chopped
1 king oyster mushroom, sliced
3 scallions, cut into 2-inch-long pieces
¼ napa cabbage, cut into 1-inch pieces

Additionals
2 cups cooked rice
4 pan-fried eggs
White sesame seeds

1. To make the salmon: In a large plastic sealable bag, combine the soy sauce, rice wine, sugars, ginger, and fish sauce. Add the salmon and marinate for at least 2 hours.

2. Preheat the oven to 400°F. Place the marinated salmon on a baking sheet and bake for 16 to 18 minutes.

3. To make the vegetables: In a small bowl, whisk together the soy sauce, brown sugar, vegetable stock, sesame oil, fish sauce, and cornstarch. Set aside.

4. In a large nonstick pan, heat the canola oil over medium-high heat. Add the onion and carrot and cook until softened, 5 to 8 minutes.

5. Add the zucchini and mushrooms. Cook until softened, about 5 minutes. Add the scallions and napa cabbage and cook until wilted, about 5 more minutes. Mix in the sauce and cook until it thickens and all the vegetables are cooked through, about 3 to 5 minutes.

6. To serve: Split the rice among four bowls. Top each with the Canthan vegetable mix. Place one of the salmon portions and fried egg on top. Sprinkle with sesame seeds and serve.

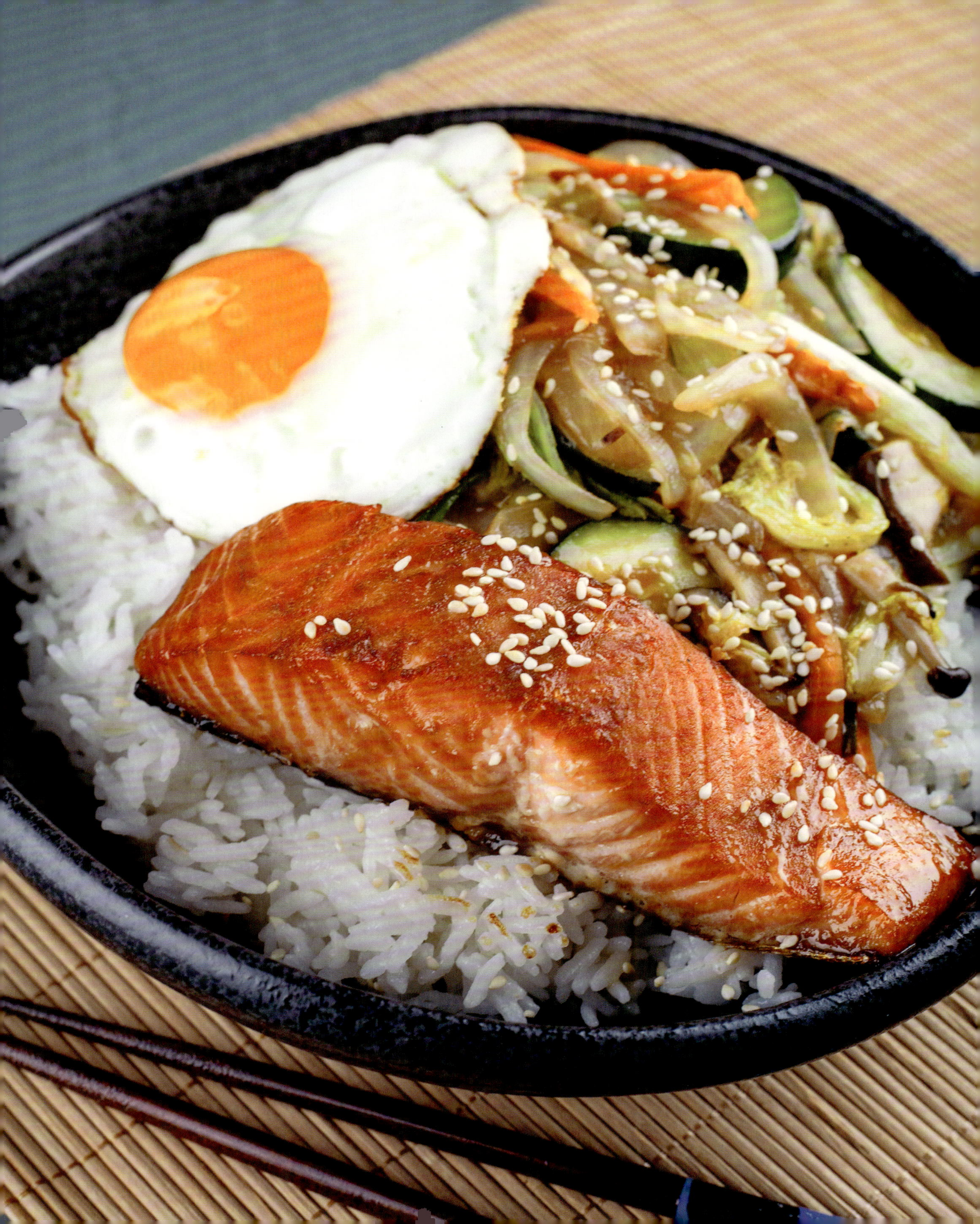

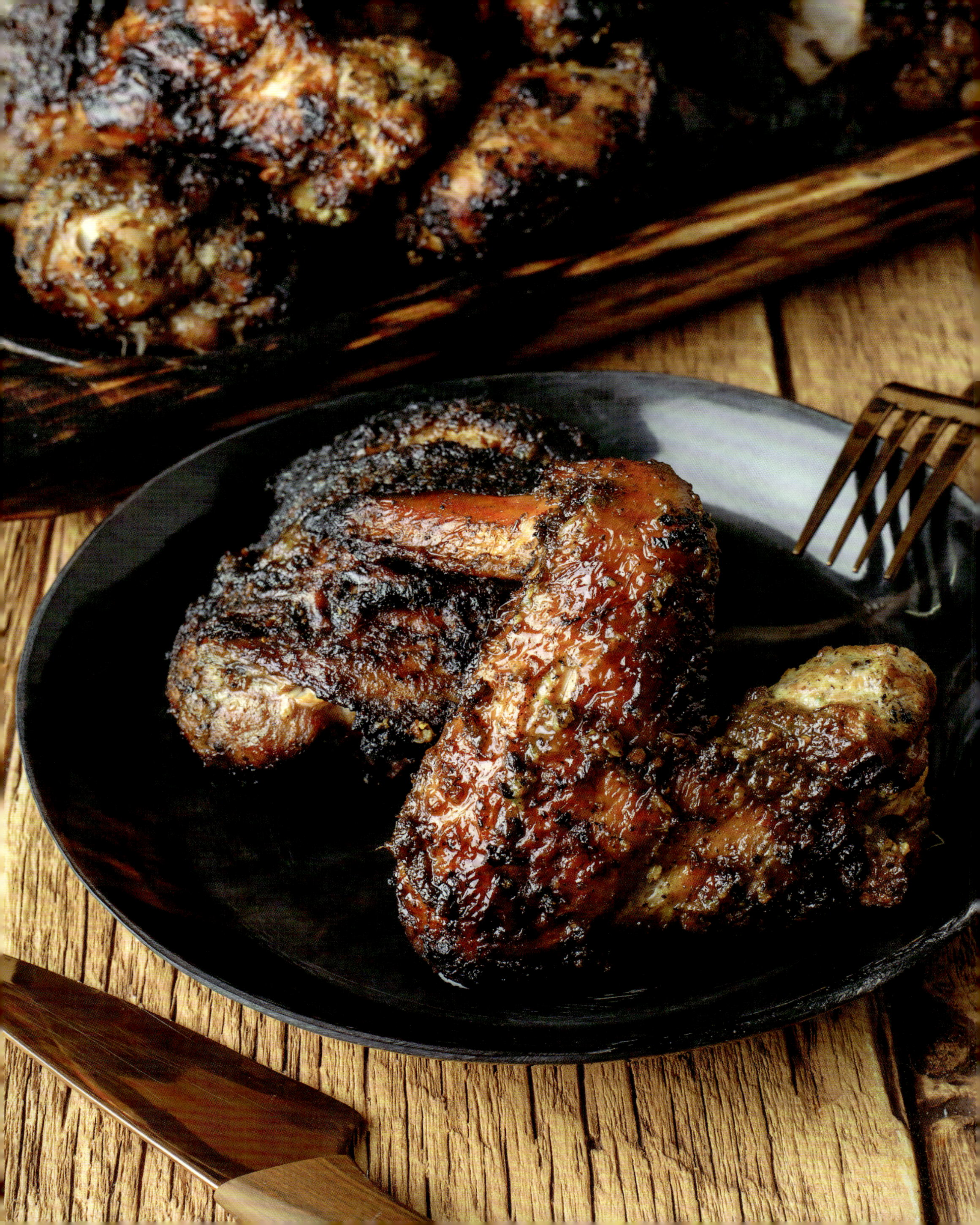

JERK POULTRY

The art of jerk seasoning originated in Elona and was popularized in Tyria around 1135, when Palawa Joko's reemergence in the nation caused a wave of Elonian refugees to flee their home. Since then, the practice of marinating poultry and other meat with allspice, peppercorn, and more has become common in certain corners of Tyria. And for good reason! Jerk chicken is some of the most flavorful, tender poultry I've ever had. The first time I had a bite, I couldn't believe how much of my childhood I'd spent eating unseasoned meats . . . Never again!

DIFFICULTY
Apprentice

PREP TIME
30 minutes

INACTIVE TIME
12 hours

COOK TIME
30 minutes

SERVINGS
6 servings

DIETARY NOTES
Dairy free

1. Place the allspice berries and black peppercorns in a spice grinder or mortar and pestle. Grind until the spices are fully ground.
2. Transfer to a food processor with the garlic, ginger, thyme, scallions, bay leaf, Scotch bonnets, soy sauce, brown sugar, and canola oil. Pulse until smooth. Transfer one-quarter of the mixture into an airtight container, seal, and refrigerate until needed.
3. Split the remaining mixture between two 1-gallon resealable bags. Add half of the chicken to one bag and the remaining chicken to the other. Seal and shake until the chicken is fully covered. Place in the refrigerator and let marinate overnight.
4. About 30 minutes before you are ready to grill, soak a handful of cherry wood chips in water.
5. Preheat the grill. Make sure to have your heat source over only one side of the grill. The side that has no coals is called the indirect-heat section. Right before you are going to add the chicken, strain the wood chips from the water and place the soaked wood chips directly on the fully heated charcoal.
6. Place the chicken legs and thighs over the direct-heat section of the grill. Cover the grill. Cook for 10 minutes.
7. Remove the cover and flip all the pieces of chicken. Brush the reserved marinade over the chicken. Cover and cook for another 10 minutes. Transfer to the indirect-heat side of the grill and cook until it reaches an internal temperature of 165°F. Transfer to a plate and wrap in aluminum foil until served.
8. Place the chicken wings over the direct-heat section of the grill. Cover the grill. Cook for 6 minutes.
9. Remove the cover and flip all the pieces of chicken. Brush the reserved marinade over the chicken. Cover and cook for another 6 minutes. Transfer to the indirect-heat side of the grill and cook until it reaches an internal temperature of 165°F. Transfer to a plate and wrap in aluminum foil until served.

1 tablespoon allspice berries
2 teaspoons black peppercorns
5 garlic cloves, smashed
1-inch piece of ginger, sliced
2 tablespoons fresh thyme leaves
6 scallions, chopped
1 bay leaf
2 Scotch bonnets
3 tablespoons dark soy sauce
2 tablespoons dark brown sugar
3 tablespoons canola oil
4 chicken thighs
5 chicken legs
2 pounds chicken wings

Equipment
Charcoal grill
Cherry wood chips

DIFFICULTY
Journeyman

PREP TIME
15 minutes

COOK TIME
25 minutes

SERVINGS
4 servings

LEMONGRASS MUSSEL PASTA

While traveling near Sandycove Beach, I was attacked by a band of sylvari. I put up my fists, but they almost had me. The next thing that happened was a blur: a glowing purple ghost slammed into the earth! Everything shook! The rogues scattered, and were replaced by a tall, commanding druid. I was pretty stunned—in hindsight, probably more from his storm spirit than from the Nightmare Court—which inspired this dish. The light tenderness of the mussels over a bed of lemony linguine was exactly what I needed to get back on my feet.

---

1 bay leaf
2 cups white wine
2 lemongrass stalks
2 pounds fresh mussels*
2 tablespoons olive oil
4 garlic cloves, thinly sliced
1 shallot, chopped
1 pound linguine, cooked and 1 cup of water reserved
¼ cup unsalted butter
2 tablespoons lemon juice
2 teaspoons lemon zest
Kosher salt
Ground black pepper
3 tablespoons parsley, chopped

1. In a large nonstick saucepan, heat the wine, bay leaf, and lemongrass over medium-high heat. Bring to a boil.

2. If your mussels are sitting in a bowl of water, drain them and then transfer to the pan. Cover and cook until all the mussels have opened, about 3 minutes. Discard any mussels that don't open.

3. Transfer everything into a large bowl and return the pan to the heat. Remove and discard the lemongrass and bay leaf. Add the olive oil and heat up for 2 minutes. Add the garlic and shallot and cook until softened, 5 to 8 minutes.

4. Strain the mussels from the liquid and transfer the liquid back into the pan. Bring to a simmer and allow to cook until it reduces by half, 5 to 8 minutes.

5. Add the butter, lemon juice, and lemon zest and cook until the butter has melted completely. Season with salt and pepper. Add the linguine and toss until it is coated in the sauce. Add the mussels and parsley and toss until all combined. Serve immediately.

---

*Note:** It is vital to clean and check that your mussels are alive before cooking them. If any of them are open, give them a tap with a spoon and discard them if they don't close. To clean them, place them in a large bowl of heavily salted, cold water and let them rest for 15 minutes. Carefully scrub them. Remove any beards on them by pulling them off and discarding them.

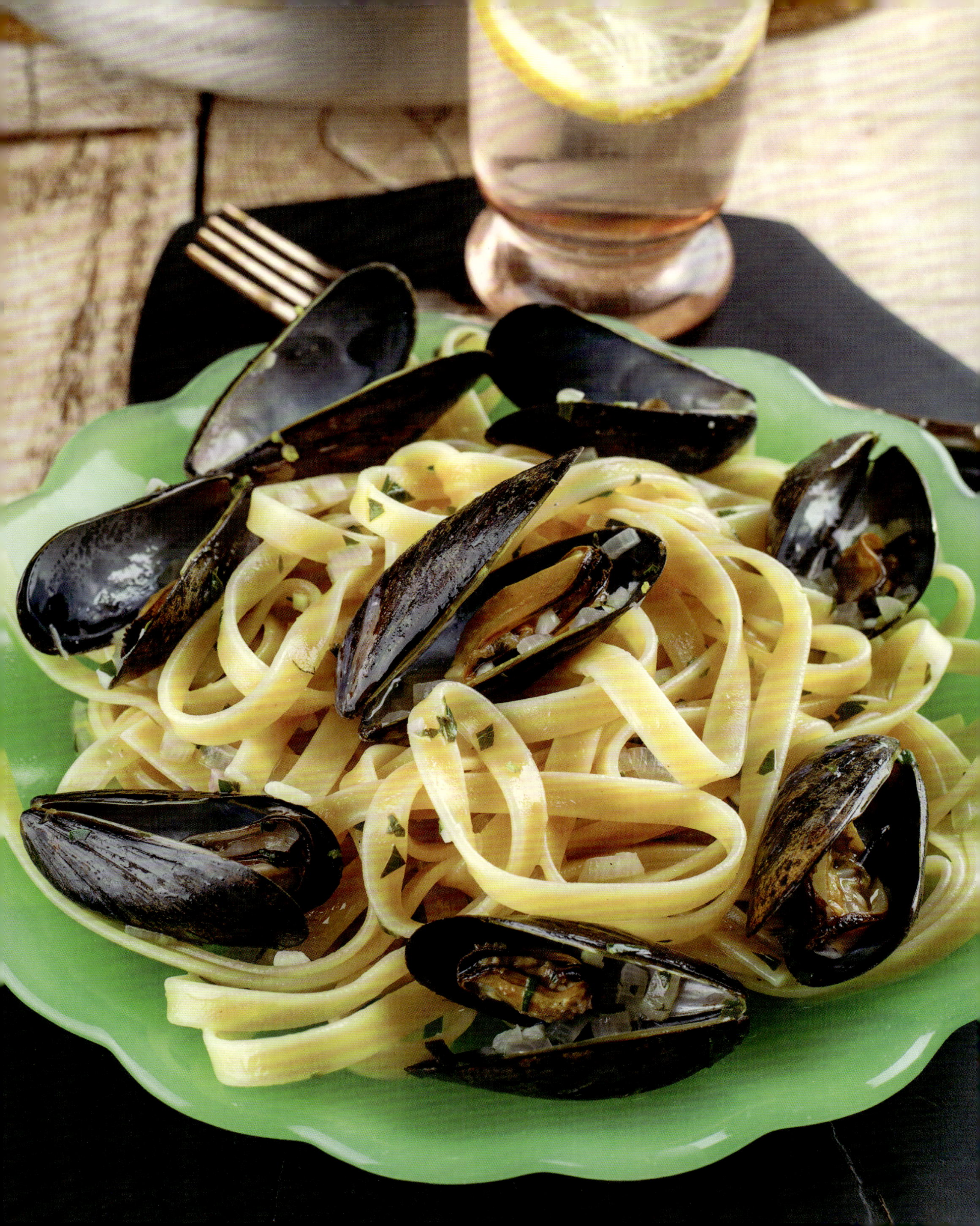

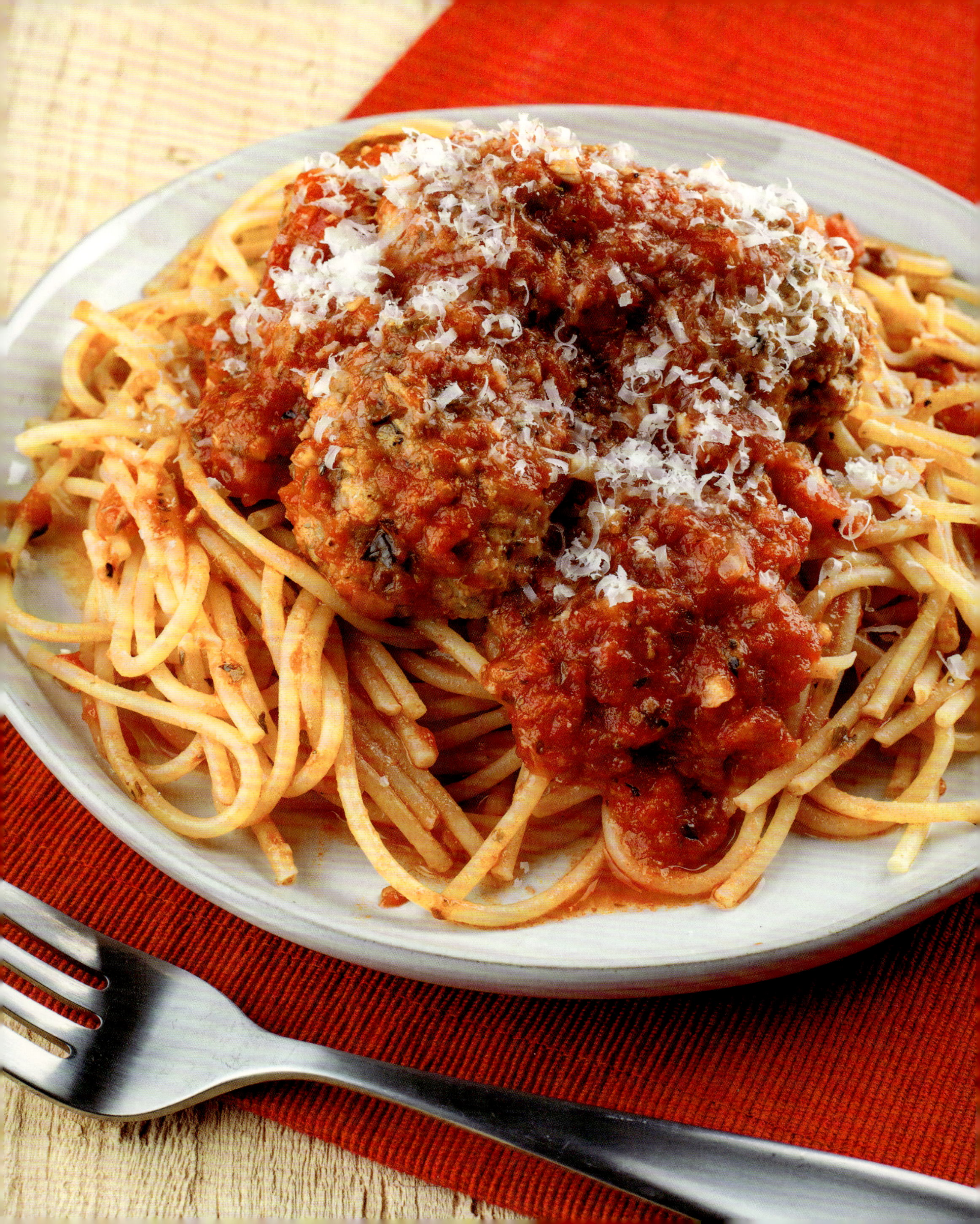

FEAST OF MEATBALL DINNER

DIFFICULTY
Adept

PREP TIME
30 minutes

COOK TIME
1½ hours

SERVINGS
4 servings

One of the Priory's magisters picked up this recipe in Lion's Arch and sent it my way with curious instructions. "Must include a coin and a crystal." He must have been making half-hearted notes, because that makes no blasted sense! Luckily, these herbaceous meatballs are still fantastic without the addition of gold and rocks. Hand-crushing the tomatoes makes sure the pasta soaks them up, giving each bite of spaghetti a steaming burst of flavor. The magister also sent me a bottle of fine Elonian wine with a note: "When complete, say a prayer to Zommoros." No idea what that means, but it makes a great pairing for your feast!

1. In a medium saucepan, heat the olive oil over medium-high heat. Add the sardine and lightly mash into small pieces. Add the garlic and onion. Cook until softened and slightly golden brown, 5 to 8 minutes. Add the tomatoes, crushing each in your hand as you add them, and stir together well.

2. Mix in the oregano, basil, red pepper flakes, and sugar. Add the basil stem. Reduce the heat to low or medium-low and allow the sauce to simmer for about 30 minutes. Make sure to stir often and mash the tomatoes fully by the time it is done cooking.

3. Taste and season with salt and pepper to your liking. If the sauce has thickened too much, add a bit of reserved pasta water to loosen it up. Keep the sauce warm as you prepare the meatballs.

4. In a medium bowl, combine the ground lamb, egg, olive oil, garlic, panko, Parmigiano Reggiano, oregano, basil, salt, and pepper. Mix until it just comes together. Split the mixture into 16 equal balls.

5. In a large pan, heat the olive oil over medium-high heat. Add the meatballs and brown each side, 2 to 3 minutes per side.

6. Once the meatballs have browned, remove them from the pan and transfer them to the saucepan with the marinara. Cover and cook over medium-low heat for 25 minutes, or until the meatballs are cooked through.

7. Take a portion of sauce and toss it with the cooked pasta. Plate some pasta and top with the meatballs and additional sauce. Serve with freshly grated Parmigiano Reggiano.

Marinara

1 tablespoon olive oil
1 sardine
10 garlic cloves, minced
¼ onion, minced
28 ounces whole tomatoes
28 ounces San Marzano tomatoes
2 teaspoons dried oregano
1 teaspoon dried basil
Pinch of red pepper flakes
2 teaspoons sugar
1 fresh basil stem
Kosher salt
Ground black pepper

Meatballs

1 pound ground lamb
1 egg
1 tablespoon olive oil, plus more as needed
5 garlic cloves, minced
¾ cup panko breadcrumbs
¼ cup Parmigiano Reggiano, shredded, plus more for serving
1 tablespoon dried oregano
2 teaspoons dried basil
1 teaspoon kosher salt
1 teaspoon ground black pepper

Additionals

1 pound spaghetti, cooked and some water reserved

DIFFICULTY
Apprentice

PREP TIME
30 minutes

COOK TIME
20 minutes

SERVINGS
4 servings

POULTRY PICCATA

I don't have much time for his stuffy traditional preferences, but I admit that my friend Chef Robertus is a master of classic recipes. His version of Poultry Piccata, passed down through his family, is superior to any other I've had. The key, he says, is to be "exceedingly generous" with salt and pepper to boost the flavor of the chicken. And adding the capers, lemon, parsley, and basil for three minutes—just three!—gives a tang that simply can't be beat. This is the entrée that made me proud to be Robertus's disciple, and though we argue often, I've never regretted my choice. I've tried to poke and prod at this recipe over the years, but nothing of mine has won over Robertus's version.

- 2 chicken breasts, halved crosswise and pounded thinly
- Kosher salt
- Ground black pepper
- ⅓ cup flour
- ½ cup lemon juice
- 1 cup white wine
- ¾ cup Poultry Stock (page 60)
- 2 tablespoons olive oil
- ¼ cup capers, rinsed
- 2 teaspoons lemon zest
- 3 tablespoons parsley, chopped, plus more for garnish
- 3 tablespoons basil, chopped, plus more for garnish
- 4 lemon slices
- 1 pound spaghetti, cooked
- 5 tablespoons unsalted butter

1. Generously season the chicken portions with salt and pepper. Coat with flour and set aside.
2. In a small bowl, combine the lemon juice, white wine, and poultry stock. Set aside.
3. In a medium nonstick pan, heat the olive oil over medium-high heat. Add two portions of chicken and cook for 4 to 5 minutes on each side, or until lightly browned and cooked through to 165°F. Transfer to a plate. Repeat with the remaining two portions of chicken.
4. Add the stock mixture to the pan and bring to a boil. Cook until the sauce reduces by half, 5 to 8 minutes.
5. Add the capers, lemon zest, parsley, and basil and cook for 3 minutes.
6. Place the chicken and cook for 2 to 3 minutes to heat the chicken through. Transfer each portion of chicken to a plate and top each with a lemon slice.
7. Toss in the cooked spaghetti and butter to the pan. Mix until the sauce has thickened. Split among the four plates with the chicken.

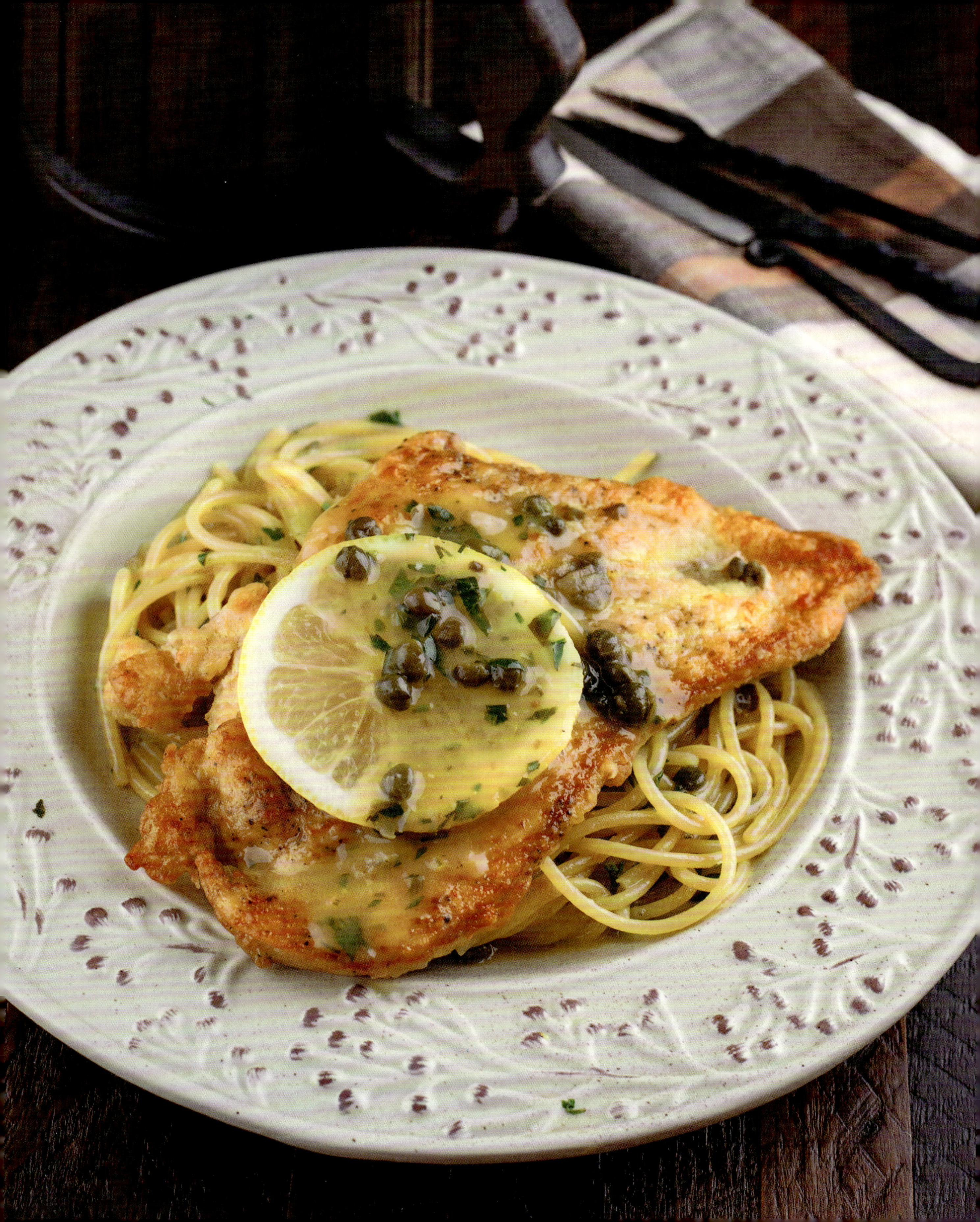

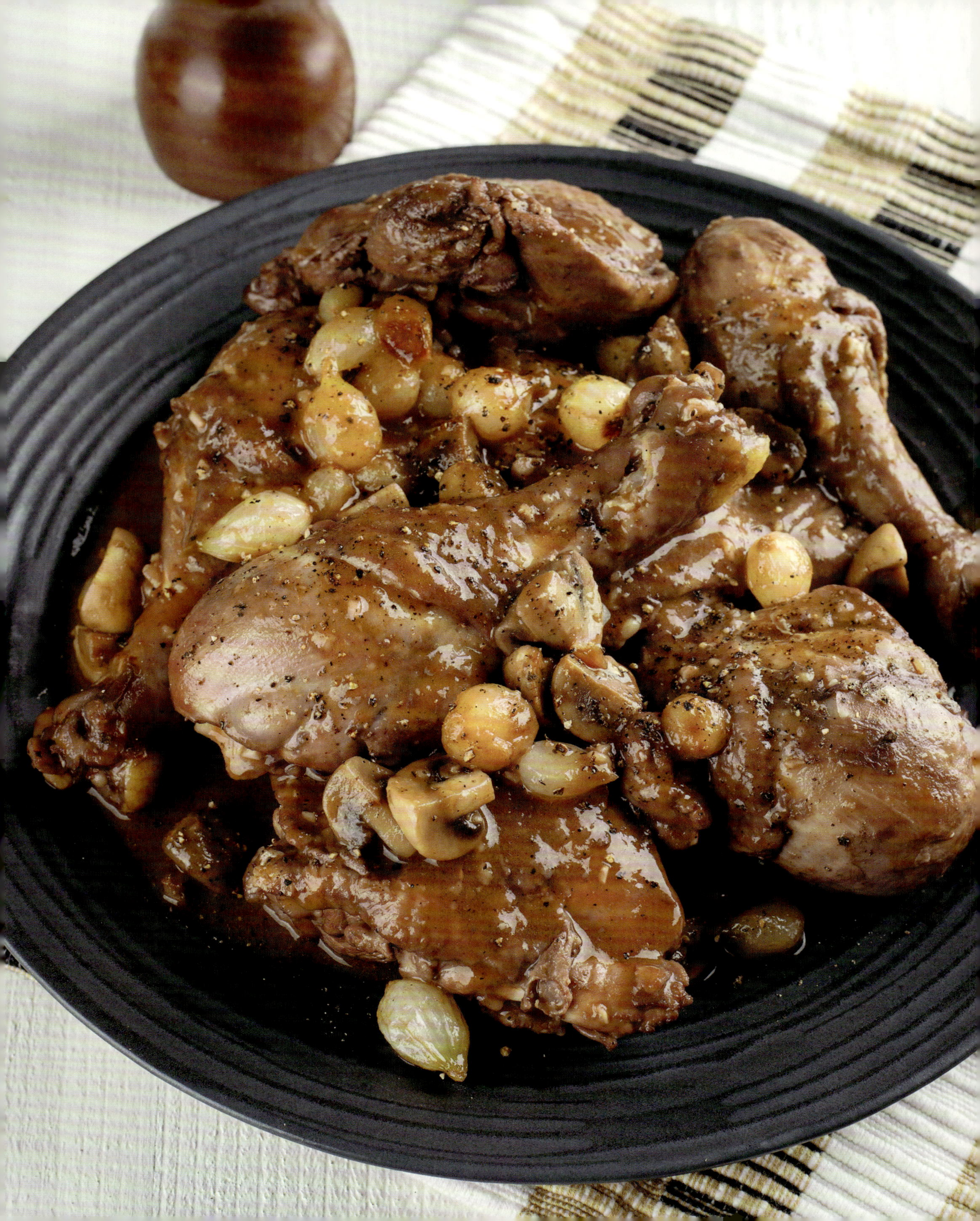

PEPPERCORN-SPICED COQ AU VIN

DIFFICULTY
Adept

PREP TIME
20 minutes

INACTIVE TIME
20 minutes

COOK TIME
1 hour

SERVINGS
5 to 6 servings

"Food to nourish the heart and mind." There was a time you couldn't walk down the street in Divinity's Reach without seeing that motto on some newspaper or poster! It's the slogan of a renowned master chef named Jacqueline, who for a while was one of the world's leading voices in the culinary arts. It was hard to get a table at one of her many establishments. And once the bill came, you'd regret ever sitting down! Jacqueline always insisted that a sophisticated coq au vin required only the finest, most perfectly aged, most *expensive* ingredients. I couldn't disagree more—my version of this traditional chicken stew is easier on the wallet! The way the spiced meat of the chicken melts in your mouth will still do plenty for your heart and mind. Thinking about it, Jacqueline mysteriously disappeared from the public eye at the height of her fame. I hope she's reconsidered her philosophies on expense.

1. In a large bowl, combine the chicken, salt, pepper, wine, bay leaves, and thyme. Cover and let marinate in the refrigerator for at least 1 hour, up to 2 hours.

2. Remove the chicken from the marinade. Set the marinade aside. Pat the chicken pieces dry. In a large Dutch oven over medium-high heat, heat 1 tablespoon of duck fat. Add a single layer of chicken. Cook until each side has browned, 3 to 4 minutes per side. Transfer to a plate.
   Note: This will have to be done in batches. Make sure to add extra duck fat between each batch if the pot becomes too dry.

3. Once all the chicken has browned, add a small amount of duck fat and the garlic and cook for 2 minutes.

4. Return the chicken to the pot. Carefully add the brandy to the pot and cook until it reduces by half. Cover the pot and cook the chicken for 2 minutes. Flip the chicken, cover, and cook for another 2 minutes.

5. Add the reserved marinade, poultry broth, and tomato paste to the pot. Mix everything until well combined. Bring to a simmer and reduce the heat to medium. Cover and simmer for 30 minutes, or until the chicken is cooked through.

8 chicken thighs, bone-in and skin on

5 chicken legs, bone-in and skin on

2 teaspoons kosher salt

2 teaspoons ground black pepper, plus more as needed

3 cups burgundy wine

2 bay leaves

5 thyme sprigs

2 tablespoons duck fat

3 garlic cloves, minced

2 tablespoons brandy

2 cups Poultry Stock (page 60)

1 tablespoon tomato paste

1 pound white mushrooms, quartered

Nonstick spray

1 pound pearl onions, peeled

¼ cup water

2 tablespoons unsalted butter

2 tablespoons all-purpose flour

Recipe continued on next page

6. While the chicken is cooking, place a pan over medium-high heat. Spray with nonstick spray and cook the pearl onions until they start to brown. Add the ¼ cup of water and cover. Reduce the heat to medium and allow the onions to soften (do not allow them to become mushy and lose their shape), about 15 minutes. Remove any remaining liquid and set aside until the stew is ready.

7. In another pan, over medium-high heat, cook the mushrooms until just browned, 8 to 10 minutes. Set aside until the chicken is ready.

8. Remove the chicken from the pot and place on a plate and cover in aluminum foil. Increase the heat to medium-high and bring the stock to a boil. Cook until it has reduced by half.

9. Add the butter and flour and mix until the sauce has thickened. Generously season with ground black pepper. Add the chicken, onion, and mushrooms back to the pot and mix until well combined.

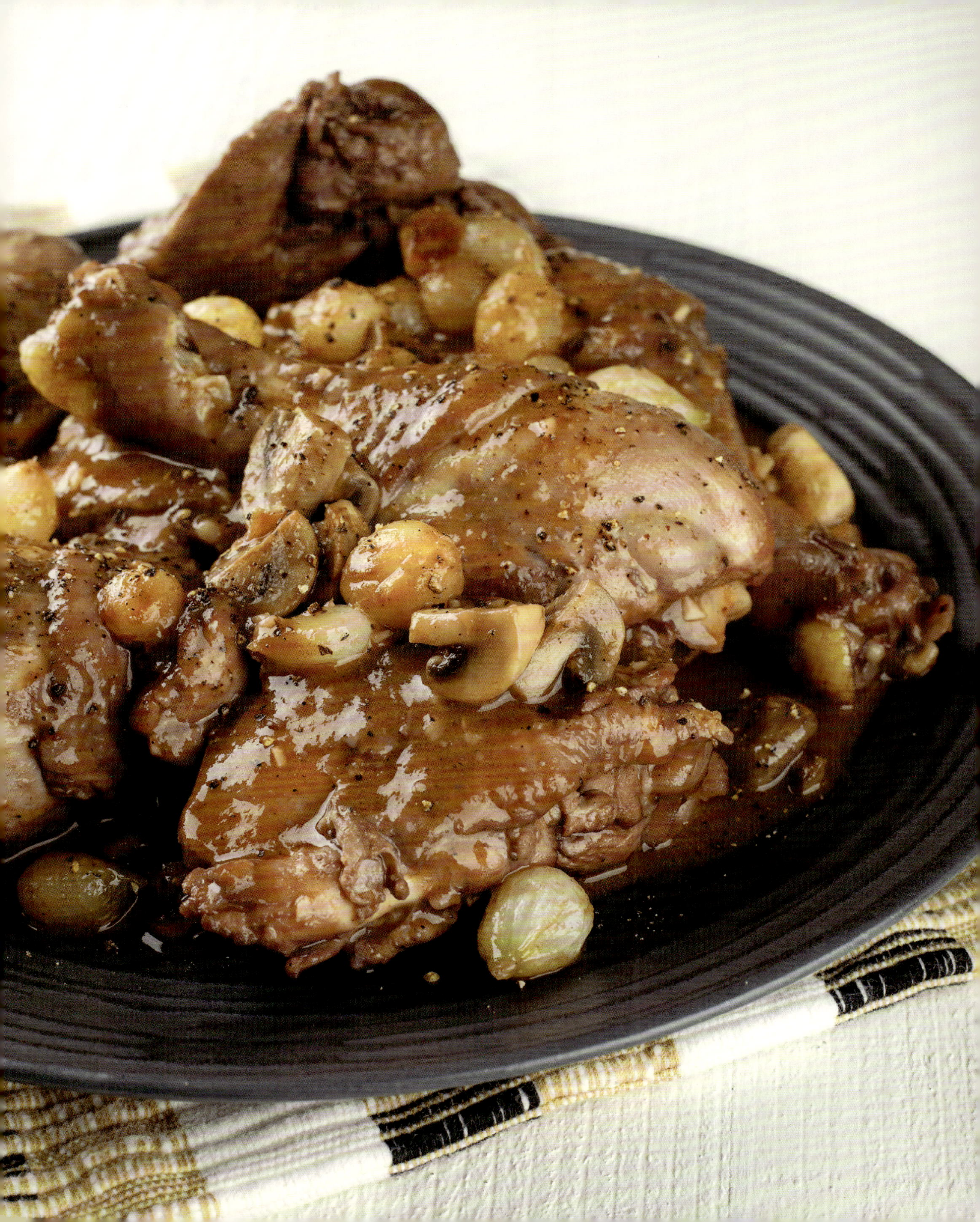

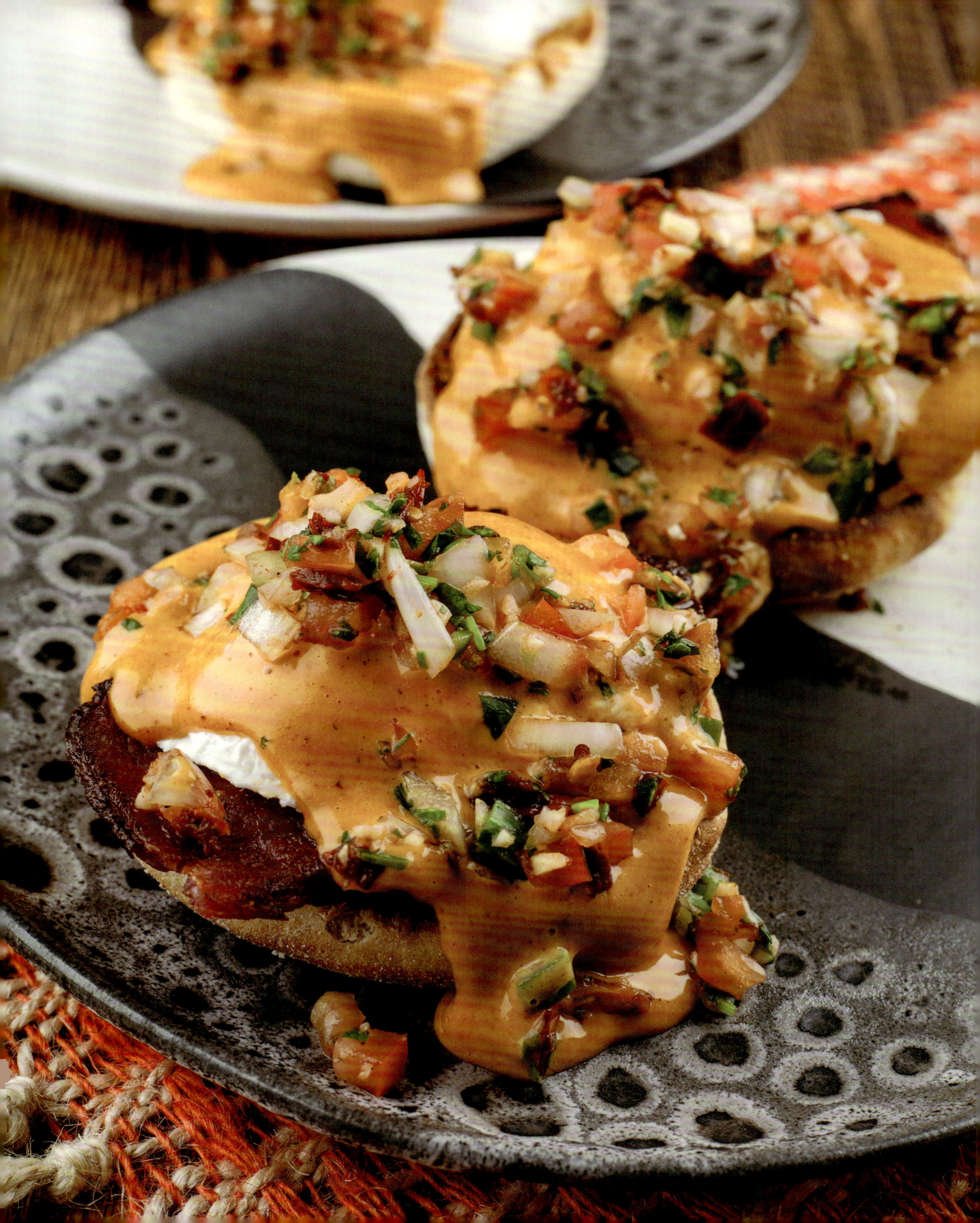

SALSA EGGS BENEDICT

DIFFICULTY
Grandmaster

PREP TIME
25 minutes

COOK TIME
20 minutes

SERVINGS
4 servings

This zesty twist on a Krytan classic makes good for breakfast, lunch, or dinner! I say this because I've heard that the legendary Eir Stegalkin was so fond of salsa on her eggs benedict that she'd sometimes have it for all three meals a day. I'm not usually one for repeating dishes—too much good stuff out there—but I understand her enthusiasm. The salsa adds a real nice heat to the rich, buttery mix of hollandaise and poached egg.

1. To make the salsa: In a small bowl, combine all the ingredients. Taste and season with salt and pepper. Store in an airtight container in the refrigerator until ready to use.

2. To make the hollandaise: Fill a pot with an inch and a half of water and place over medium-high heat. Make sure the bowl you will be making the hollandaise sauce in fits above the pot and does not touch the water. In that bowl, combine the egg yolks, salt, cayenne pepper, and adobo sauce. Whisk together for about 2 minutes.

3. When the pot of water comes to a low boil, place the bowl above it. Begin to whisk and try not to stop. Occasionally remove the bowl from the heat while maintaining your whisking to keep the temperature from rising too quickly. If the yolks cook too quickly, they will scramble.

4. Keep whisking until the mixture becomes ribbony. Slowly add the melted butter, 1 tablespoon at a time. It is very important to add the butter slowly and continue whisking to incorporate the butter.
   Note: If you add the butter too quickly, the sauce will break and you will have to start again. A broken hollandaise means the butter and the yolks are just not combining and begin to separate.

5. Once all the butter has been added, set aside but keep warm. The sauce will thicken as it cools. If you need to, place it back on the steaming water before serving and add water to loosen the sauce up.

6. In a medium nonstick pan, heat the bacon over medium-high heat. Cook until both sides are crispy and cooked through, 3 to 5 minutes per side.

7. Place an inch of water in a medium nonstick pan and bring it to a boil. Add the vinegar and salt. Carefully take the eggs and slowly pour them in the water. Place all the eggs in the water and cook them for 4½ minutes. Remove the eggs and place them on a paper towel to dry.

8. To assemble, place a toasted egg muffin on a plate. Top with a piece of bacon and then the poached egg. Drizzle with hollandaise and top with the salsa. Serve immediately and enjoy.

Salsa
2 Roma tomatoes, chopped
½ jalapeño, chopped
2 chipotles, chopped
¼ onion, chopped
3 tablespoons cilantro, chopped
2 garlic cloves, minced
2 teaspoons lime juice
Salt
Ground black pepper

Chipotle Hollandaise
4 egg yolks
Pinch kosher salt
½ teaspoon cayenne pepper
3 tablespoons adobo sauce
12 tablespoons butter, melted

Assembly
8 eggs, each opened in a separate small bowl
2 teaspoons vinegar
Pinch of salt
4 English muffins
8 pieces shoulder bacon

DIFFICULTY
Master

PREP TIME
30 minutes

INACTIVE TIME
45 minutes

COOK TIME
40 minutes

SERVINGS
4 servings

DIETARY NOTES
Dairy free

SUGAR RIB ROAST

Ah, the Free City of Amnoon! I joined a tour group while visiting to get in as much sightseeing as possible. Amnoon's incredible architecture was on display everywhere, from the Civic Center to the Altar of the Six Gods. We walked through the Grand Sahil Casino and even trekked out to the Tomb of the Primeval Kings. My favorite spot, though, was the Emporium. As soon as I stepped into the plaza, my nose was bombarded with incredible smells. I found myself drawn to a booth where a rack of lamb rib, shining with marinade, cooked over a fire. The vendor offered me a sample. Hoo boy! The smokiness of the mustard! The crisp of the herb crust! The welcome intensity of the coriander and the tenderness of the lamb itself! All of it came together and walloped me in the taste buds. I bought their whole stock on the spot—the merchant was grinning ear to ear, and so was I!

Lamb
2-pound rack of lamb
1 tablespoon olive oil
1 tablespoon kosher salt
2 teaspoons ground coriander
1 teaspoon ground black pepper
2 tablespoons Dijon mustard

Herb Crust
½ cup panko breadcrumbs
½ bunch cilantro
5 garlic cloves
½ bunch parsley
2 mint sprigs
½ jalapeño pepper
1 serrano pepper
2 teaspoons sugar
1 tablespoon olive oil

1. Prepare a baking sheet with aluminum foil and top with a wire rack. Place the lamb on the wire rack. Let rest at room temperature for 45 minutes. Preheat the oven to 400°F.

2. While the oven is preheating, prepare the herb crust. In a food processor, pulse the panko, cilantro, garlic, parsley, mint, jalapeño, serrano, sugar, and olive oil until well crumbled and combined. Set aside.

3. In a medium pan, heat the olive oil over medium-high heat. Season the lamb with salt, coriander, and pepper. Place the lamb, fat-side down, into the pan and sear until browned, 3 to 5 minutes. Sear every side of the lamb and then transfer back to the wire rack, fat-side up.

4. Brush the Dijon mustard on the lamb. Take the herb crust and press onto the lamb until the part facing upward is well covered.

5. Place in the oven and roast until the meat reaches the desired temperature:
   Medium-Rare: 125°F – 15 to 20 minutes
   Medium: 135°F – 25 to 30 minutes
   Medium-Well: 140°F – 35 minutes

6. Remove from the oven and cover in aluminum foil. Let rest for 10 minutes. To serve, use a sharp knife and cut portions between the bones.

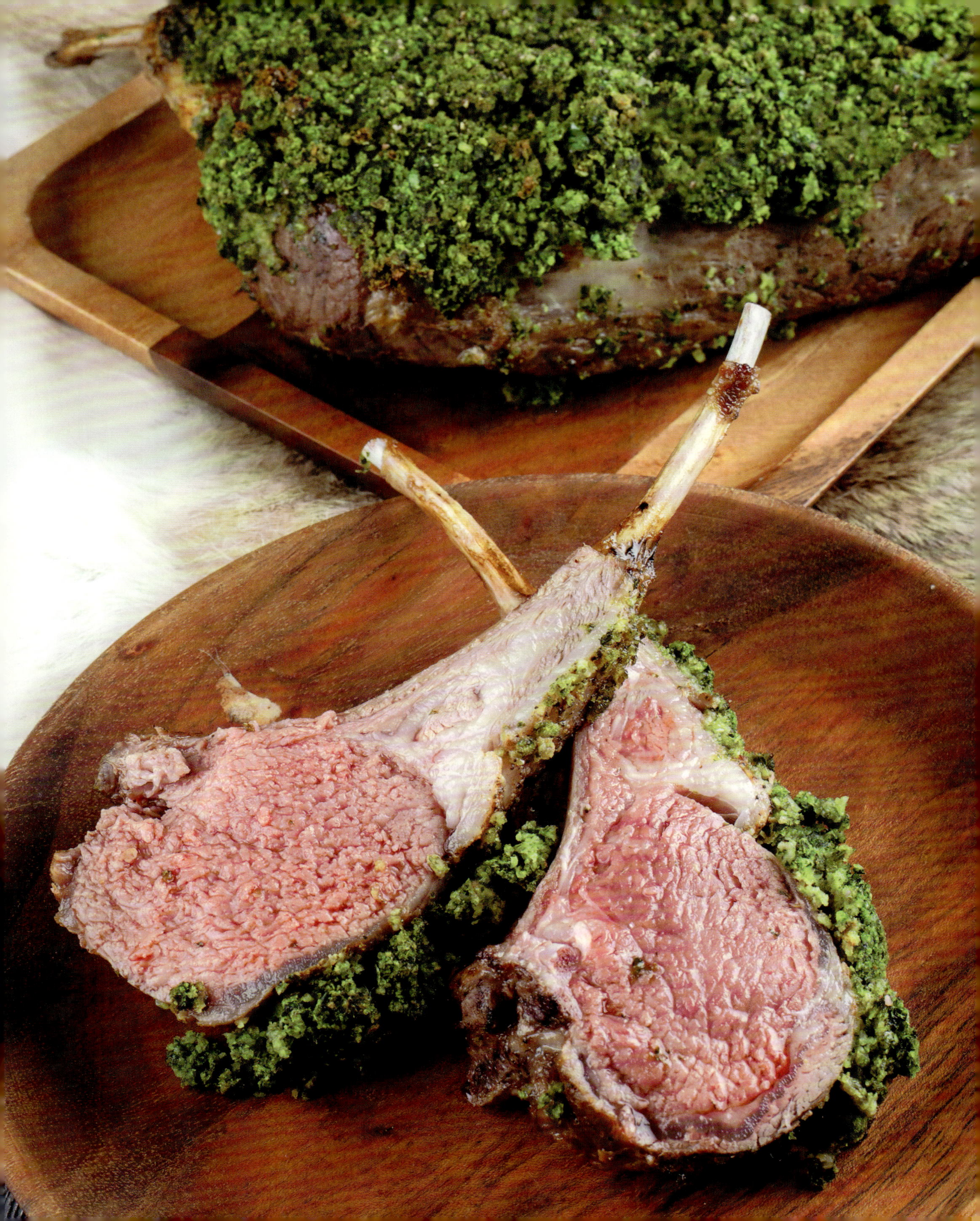

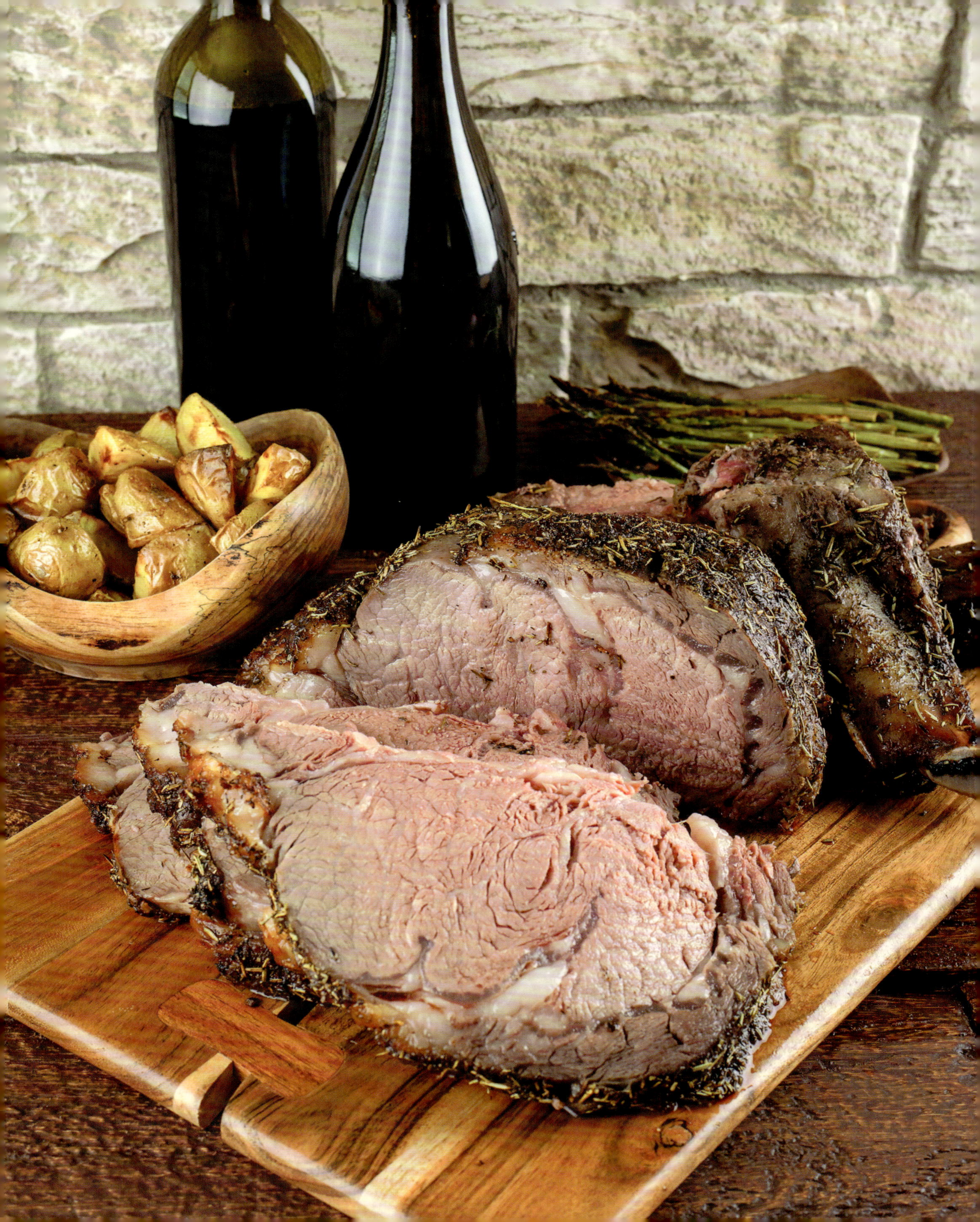

FILET OF ROSEMARY-ROASTED MEAT

DIFFICULTY
Adept

PREP TIME
30 minutes

INACTIVE TIME
48 hours

COOK TIME
5 hours

SERVINGS
8 to 10 servings

DIETARY NOTES
Gluten free, Dairy free

While poring over the Priory's library, I came across a pile of crumbling papers that piqued my curiosity. After some research, I matched it to the writing in the biography of Jalis Ironhammer of Thunderhead Keep, last king of the Deldrimor dwarves! My findings seemed to be a discarded draft of that manuscript—they went into excruciating detail about King Ironhammer's favorite dinner. Whole paragraphs on how exactly to infuse the rosemary into prime rib, so that the seasoning brought out the tenderness of the cut without overpowering it! Pages on how long to cook it for, and how to cut it for best enjoyment, and the best full-bodied red wine to pair it with! No wonder it was cut from the final manuscript.

1. Two days before you plan on serving the roast, in a small bowl, combine the salt, rosemary, and thyme. Rub the mixed seasoning over the entire prime rib. Place on a baking sheet with a wire rack and into the refrigerator uncovered. Allow the prime rib to rest for at least 48 hours and up to 96 hours.

2. Take the prime rib out of the refrigerator 1 hour before it goes into the oven. Adjust the oven racks to the middle-lower position. Preheat the oven to 250°F. In a deep baking dish with a wire rack, fill the bottom with celery, carrots, onion, garlic, rosemary, and thyme. Heavily season the prime rib with pepper. Place the prime rib, fat-side up, on a wire rack. Place in the oven and roast until the meat reaches the desired temperature:
130°F for medium-rare, 3½ to 4 hours
135°F for medium, 4 to 4½ hours

3. Remove the prime rib from the oven, loosely cover with aluminum foil, and let rest for 45 minutes. Increase the oven temperature to 500°F. Move the oven rack up about two levels. Remove the aluminum foil from the prime rib and place it in the oven. Cook until the fat begins to crisp up, 8 to 10 minutes. Remove the roast from the oven and place on a cutting board. Remove the bone and slice the meat into ½- to ¾-inch-thick pieces.

- 3 bone-in prime ribs (about 8 pounds)
- 3 tablespoons kosher salt
- 2 tablespoons dry rosemary
- 1 tablespoon dry thyme
- 3 celery stalks, cut into large chunks
- 2 carrots, cut into large chunks
- 1 onion, cut into large chunks
- 1 whole garlic, halved
- 5 rosemary sprigs
- 5 thyme sprigs
- 2 tablespoons ground black pepper

DIFFICULTY
Master

PREP TIME
45 minutes

COOK TIME
1 hour

SERVINGS
2 medium pizzas

DIETARY NOTES
Vegetarian

FANCY VEGGIE PIZZA

In the last year, this vegetarian pizza has become a fad among the hoity-toity. I served it just last month at a banquet in Divinity's Reach. The lords and ladies were enthralled to learn that the chewy mushrooms and savory shallots they were eating had been picked off ruins in the Brisban Wildlands. They listened with rapt attention as I recounted the ghosts, drakes, and raptors that I'd fought off to obtain the culinary treasures that topped the crust—crunchy on the outside, fluffy in the body! One gentleman offered to fund further exploits into the ruins. He didn't care so much about the different varieties of shrooms but more the possibility of discovering precious gems or artifacts. Of course, I'm not interested in picking apart old civilizations for the fleeting whims of some moneybag. Now, if they wanted to fund my bloodstone experiments, that's another story . . .

Pizza Dough

2⅔ cups bread flour, plus more for dusting

1 teaspoon active dry yeast

2 teaspoons sugar

1 teaspoon kosher salt

2 teaspoons garlic powder

1 teaspoon ground fennel

1¼ cups water

2 tablespoons olive oil

Nonstick spray or olive oil, for greasing

1. To make the dough: The day before you plan to make the pizza, prepare the dough. In the bowl of a stand mixer, combine the flour, yeast, sugar, salt, garlic powder, and ground fennel. In a small bowl, combine the water and olive oil. Pour the liquid into the bowl of the stand mixer.

2. Place the bowl in the stand mixer and mix on low with a dough hook until all the ingredients come together. When it has formed into a ball, increase the speed of the mixer to medium and knead in the machine for 5 minutes.

3. Lightly dust your countertop with flour and place the kneaded dough on it. Smooth the dough into a ball. Spray a large bowl with nonstick spray (or rub with olive oil). Place the dough ball into the bowl and cover the bowl with plastic wrap. Place in the refrigerator for 24 to 48 hours.

4. The next day, remove the dough from the refrigerator at least 30 minutes before you start to prepare your pizza. Punch down the dough and place it onto a lightly floured countertop. Split into two portions and form into balls. Cover with a clean towel and let it rest for 30 minutes.

Recipe continued on page 123

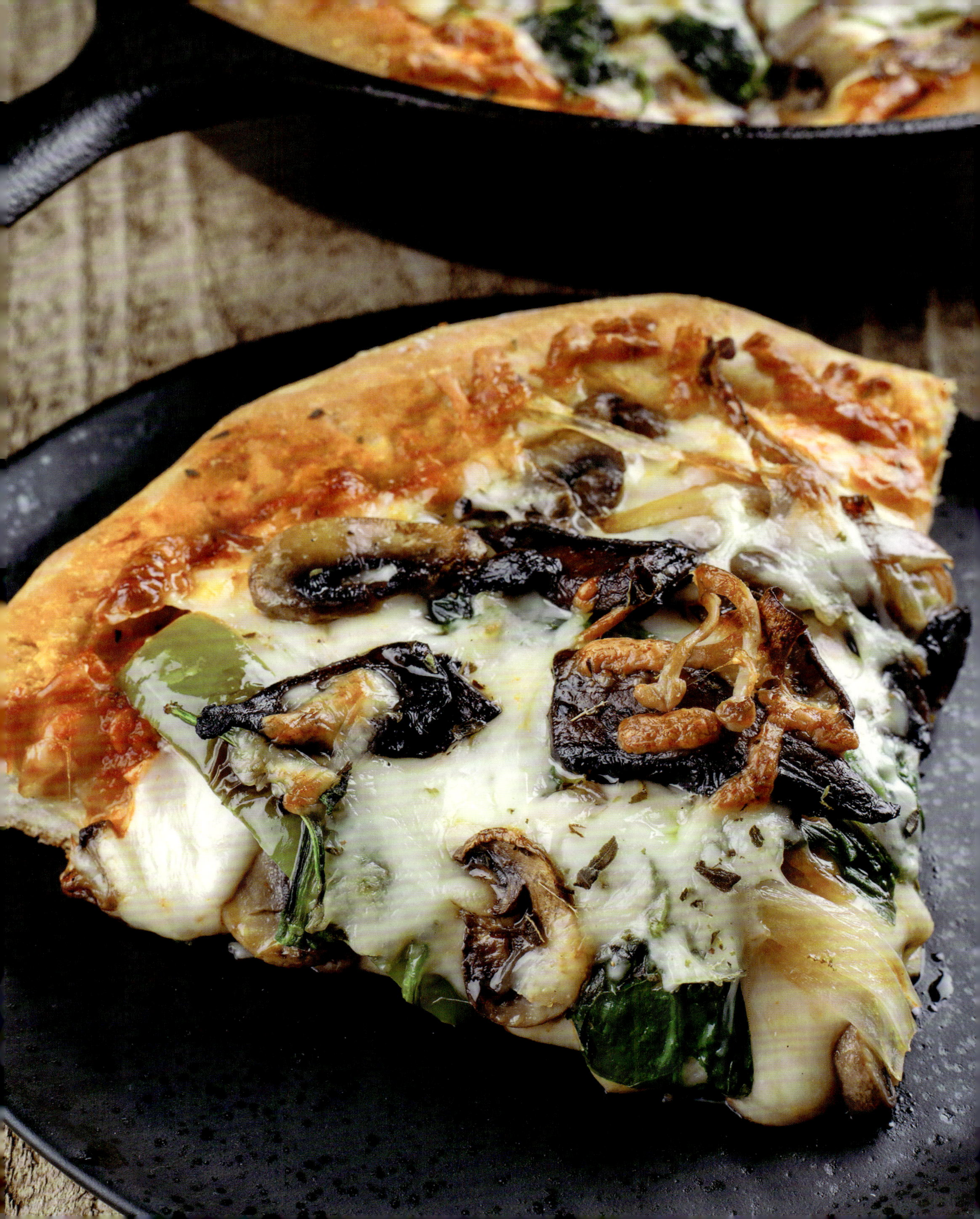

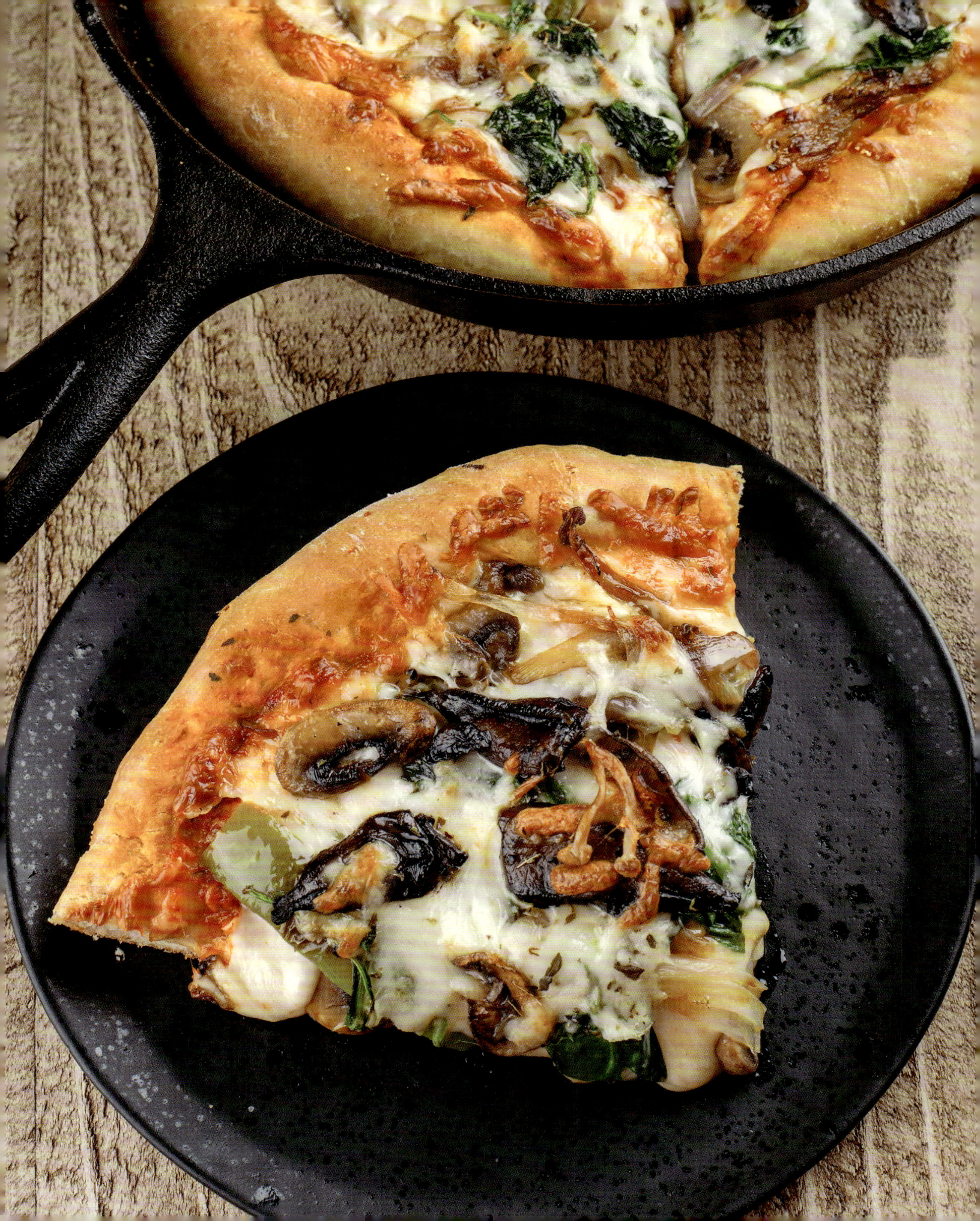

Vegetables

¼ cup olive oil

2 portobello mushrooms, sliced

6 cremini mushrooms, sliced

1 bunch beech mushrooms, separated

2 king oyster mushrooms, sliced

3 shallots, sliced

½ bell pepper, sliced

8 ounces spinach

Additionals

2 tablespoons olive oil

2 tablespoons cornmeal

12 ounces pizza sauce

16 ounces mozzarella cheese, shredded

2 teaspoons dried oregano

2 teaspoons dried basil

5. To make the vegetables: Preheat the oven to 475°F. In a medium nonstick pan, heat the olive oil over medium-high heat. Add the mushrooms and cook until softened and slightly browned, 8 to 10 minutes. Transfer to a plate. Return the pan to the heat and add more olive oil. Add the shallots and sauté until softened and golden brown, 8 to 10 minutes. Transfer to a plate. Set these aside until you are ready to assemble the pizzas.

6. Return the pan once again to the heat and add more olive oil. Add the bell peppers and cook until softened, 6 to 8 minutes. Transfer to a plate. One last time, return the pan to the heat and add a very small amount of olive oil. Add the spinach and cook until wilted, 3 to 5 minutes. Transfer to a plate and set aside.

7. Lightly dust a countertop with flour and take one of the dough portions. Pound the dough into a disk shape. Continue to stretch the dough into a disk shape slightly wider than a 10-inch cast-iron pan. Prepare the cast iron by rubbing all parts with olive oil. Sprinkle a generous amount of cornmeal in the pan. Transfer the dough onto the cast iron. Repeat with the other portion.

8. Top each of the doughs with pizza sauce. Top with mozzarella, mushrooms, shallots, bell pepper, and spinach. Sprinkle oregano and basil on top of the pizza. Brush the crust on the edge with additional olive oil. Place on a stovetop over medium-high heat. Cook until the bottom of the dough begins to turn brown, about 5 minutes.

9. Transfer the cast iron to the oven and cook until the cheese has melted and the crust has lightly browned, 12 to 15 minutes.

DIFFICULTY
Adept

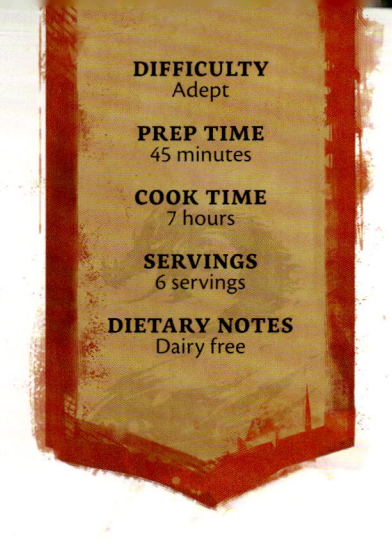

PREP TIME
45 minutes

COOK TIME
7 hours

SERVINGS
6 servings

DIETARY NOTES
Dairy free

BEEF RENDANG

This recipe has been the subject of hot debate by culinary historians in recent years. Most agree that beef rendang has Kurzick roots. For ages, stubborn Krytan scholars—not us at the Priory—insisted the recipe had first been created after Shiro Tagachi died and war broke out between the Kurzicks and the Empire. We have evidence that Beef Rendang, when available, was a part of many wartime diets, as the protein kept Kurzick soldiers strong. However, since the reopening of the border to Cantha in 1325 AE, Canthan experts have corrected the recipe's origin date to around 462 BE, when the Kurzicks fought against the recently assimilated Luxons. It's embarrassing that the records were wrong for so long, but after savoring the rich, aromatic bits of slow-cooked beef myself, I can picture the soldiers wolfing this meal down.

Kerisik
⅓ cup dehydrated shredded coconut

Rendang Paste
4 green cardamom

1 cinnamon stick

2 cloves

2 tablespoons coriander seeds

6 guajillo chiles, stemmed

4 large red chiles

Note: Seeds of the chiles can be removed if you want to reduce the spice level

3 lemongrass stalks, sliced

2 inches galangal, peeled and chopped

2 inches ginger, peeled and chopped

4 shallots, chopped

5 garlic cloves, crushed

1 tablespoon canola oil

1. In a small nonstick pan, toast the coconut over medium-high heat. Cook and constantly toss until lightly browned, 3 to 5 minutes. Transfer to mortar and pestle and mash to release the oils. Set aside.

2. To make the paste: In a small nonstick pan, combine the cardamom, cinnamon stick, clove, and coriander seeds. Cook until toasted, about 3 minutes. Transfer to a spice grinder, grind, and set aside.

3. Place the guajillo chiles in hot water and let soak for 5 minutes. Transfer to a food processor. Add the red chiles, lemongrass, galangal, ginger, shallots, garlic, and canola oil. Pulse until chopped.

4. Add the ground spices and then pulse into a smooth paste.

Recipe continued on page 127

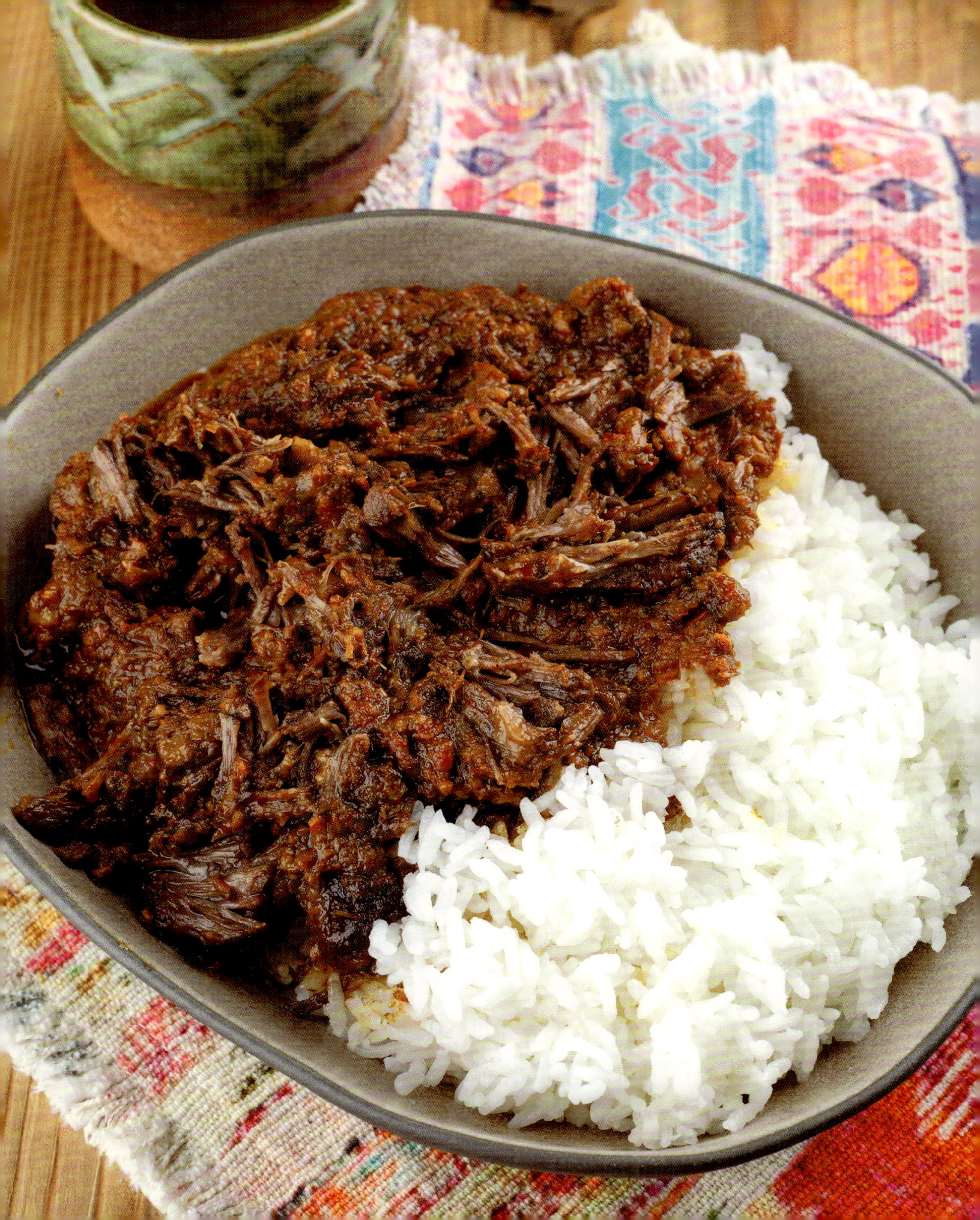

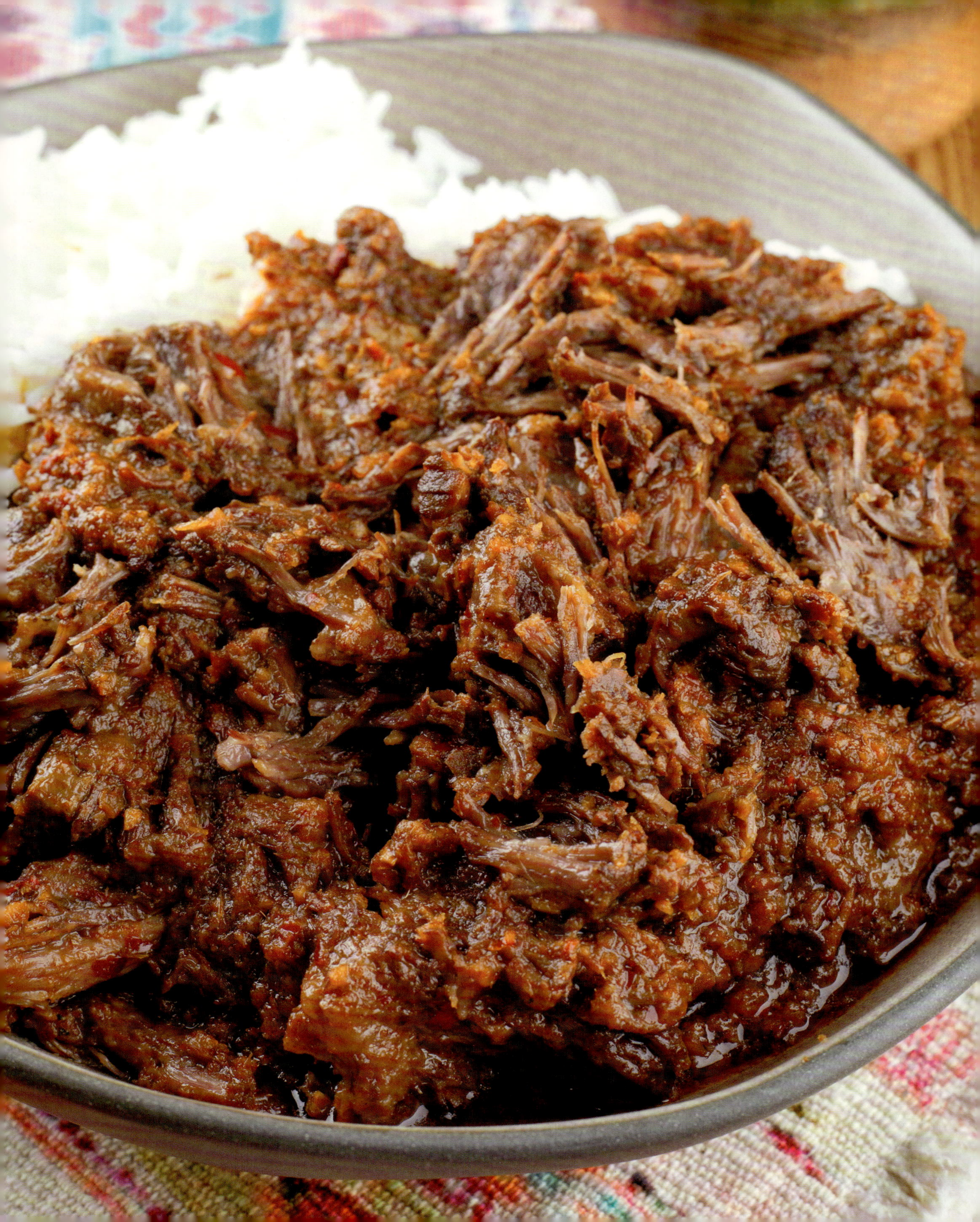

Rendang

3 tablespoons canola oil, divided, plus more as needed

2 pounds boneless beef short ribs, cut into large chunks

6 kefir lime leaves, stemmed and thinly sliced

2 lemongrass stalks

1 cinnamon stick

1 teaspoon salt

½ teaspoon monosodium glutamate

30 ounces coconut milk

1 tablespoon dark soy sauce

2 tablespoons tamarind paste

2 tablespoons palm sugar, chopped

Additionals

3 cups cooked rice

5. To make the rendang: In a Dutch oven, heat 2 tablespoons of canola oil over medium-high heat. Add a single layer of short ribs, but do not overcrowd. Brown all sides of the meat, 2 to 3 minutes per side. Remove and place on a plate. Add more canola oil if needed and continue this process until all the beef has been browned.

6. Add the rendang paste with another tablespoon of canola oil. Cook until the moisture has been removed from the paste, 8 to 10 minutes.

7. Transfer the short ribs back to the pot and toss until well coated in the paste. Add the kerisik, kefir lime leaves, lemongrass, cinnamon stick, salt, and monosodium glutamate and toss until mixed well.

8. Add the coconut milk, dark soy sauce, tamarind paste, and palm sugar. Bring to a simmer and simmer for 20 minutes, stirring often to keep the bottom from sticking.

9. Preheat the oven to 300°F. Place a cover on the pot, transfer to the oven, and cook for 5 hours, stirring every hour.

10. Remove the lid and cook for another hour. Serve over rice.

DIFFICULTY
Master

PREP TIME
1 hour

INACTIVE TIME
12 hours

COOK TIME
30 minutes

SERVINGS
4 servings

MEATY RICE BOWL

The authentic version of this dish has had a recent resurgence in Tyria! When the Meaty Rice Bowl first came from Cantha to Divinity's Reach, people turned their noses up at the "exotic" food. After that, Canthan cooks adjusted their recipe more to Tyrian tastes in order to find mercantile success. Over time, the Meaty Rice Bowl and other adapted Canthan dishes have become staple comfort foods across Kryta and the Shiverpeaks. Enjoy the complexity of flavors that dances over the toppings: mung beans, crispy veggies, egg, and beef. This recipe is a known favorite of Marjory Delaqua, head of Delaqua Investigations!

Mung Beans
½ pound mung bean sprouts
2 garlic cloves, finely minced
1 teaspoon fish sauce
1 teaspoon sesame oil
Pinch of kosher salt

1. Prepare a bowl with 4 cups of water and several ice cubes. Place in the refrigerator until ready to use.
2. In a medium pot, bring 4 cups of water to a boil. Add the mung bean sprouts and cook for 30 seconds. Strain and transfer to the prepared bowl with cold water. Allow to sit for 5 minutes.
3. Strain once again and pat completely dry. Transfer to an airtight container.
4. Add the remaining ingredients and toss until well coated. Can be sealed and stored in the refrigerator for up to 5 days.

Carrots
1 teaspoon canola oil
1 carrot, peeled and julienned
2 tablespoons ginger, grated
1 tablespoon fish sauce

5. In a small nonstick pan, heat the canola oil over medium-high heat. Add the carrot and cook until softened, 5 to 7 minutes. Transfer to an airtight container.
6. Add the ginger and fish sauce and toss until well coated. Can be sealed and stored in the refrigerator for up to 5 days.

Mushrooms
1 teaspoon canola oil
8 shiitake mushrooms, sliced
1 tablespoon soy sauce
1 teaspoon honey

7. In a small nonstick pan, heat the canola oil over medium-high heat. Add the mushrooms and cook until softened, 5 to 7 minutes. Add the soy sauce and honey and toss until coated and the liquid has fully evaporated, about 3 minutes.
8. Transfer to an airtight container. Can be sealed and stored in the refrigerator for up to 5 days.

Spinach
8 ounces spinach
1 teaspoon toasted sesame oil
1 teaspoon toasted sesame seeds, crushed

9. Prepare a bowl with 4 cups of water and several ice cubes. Place in the refrigerator until ready to use.
10. Bring 4 cups of water to a boil. Add the spinach and cook until it wilts, about 30 seconds. Strain and transfer to the prepared bowl with cold water. Allow to sit for 5 minutes.
11. Strain once again and squeeze out the excess liquid. Transfer to an airtight container.
12. Add the sesame oil and seeds and toss until well coated. Can be sealed and stored in the refrigerator for up to 5 days.

Recipe continued on page 131

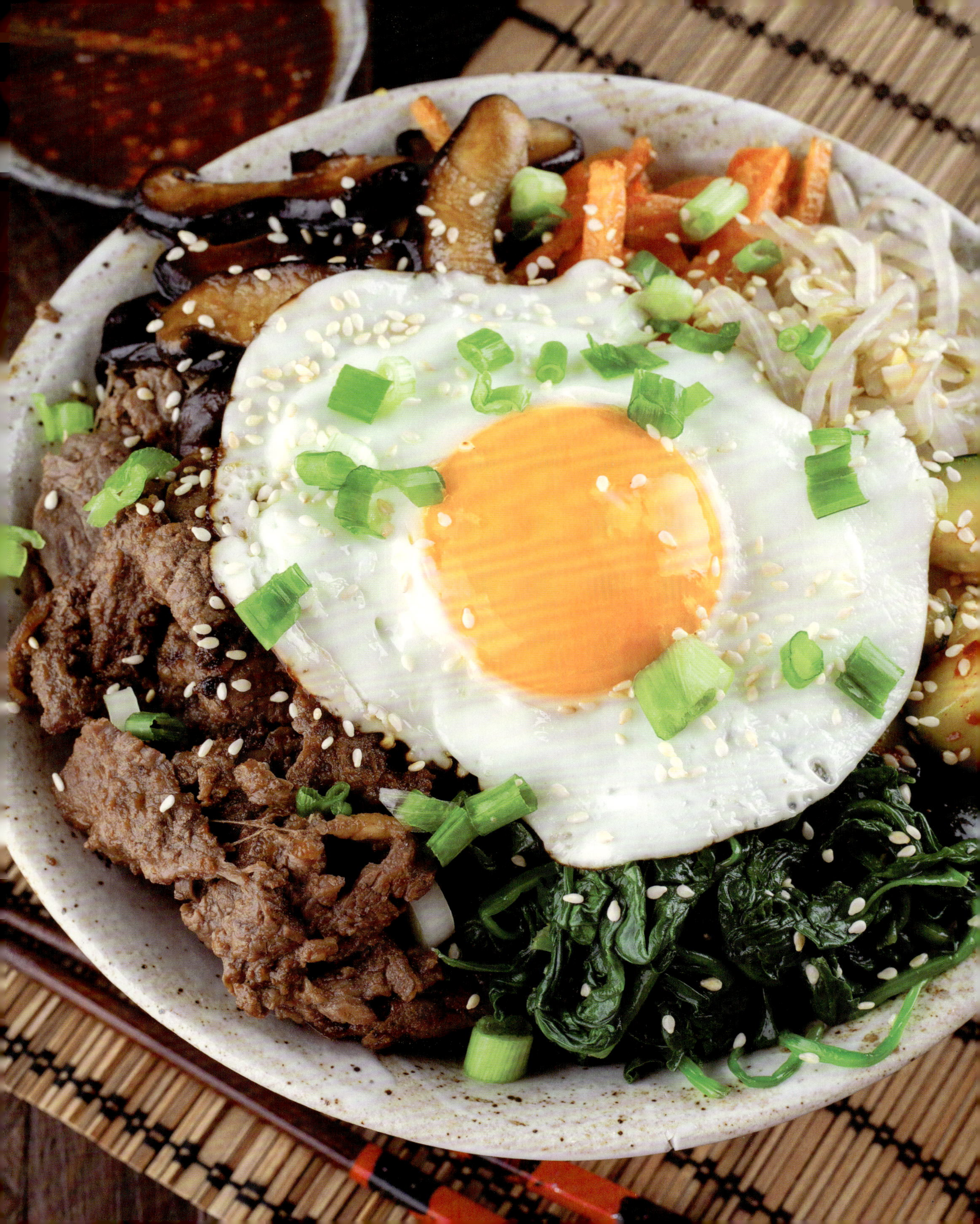

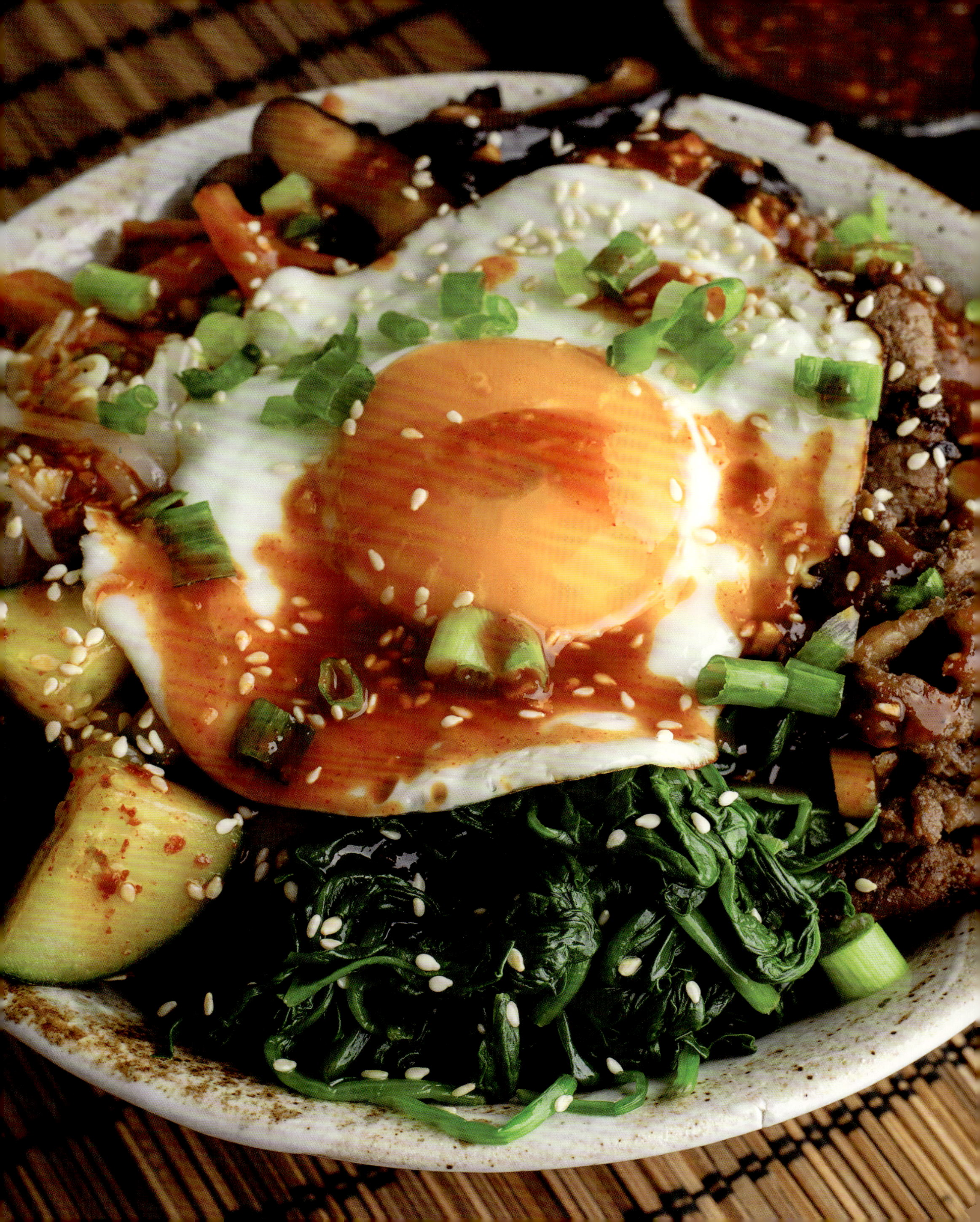

Cucumber

1 cucumber, quartered and sliced
½ teaspoon kosher salt
2 tablespoons rice vinegar
1 tablespoon honey
2 teaspoons sesame oil
2 teaspoons gochugaru
1 teaspoon toasted sesame seeds

13. In a small bowl, combine the cucumber and the salt and let rest at room temperature for 30 minutes.
14. Pat the cucumber dry and transfer to an airtight container.
15. Add the remaining ingredients and toss until well coated. Can be sealed and stored in the refrigerator for up to 1 week.

Sauce

¼ cup gochujang
2 tablespoons rice vinegar
1 tablespoon rice wine
1 tablespoon honey
1 tablespoon light brown sugar
2 teaspoons soy sauce
2 teaspoons toasted sesame oil
2 teaspoons garlic, grated
2 teaspoons ginger, grated

16. To make the sauce: In an airtight container, whisk everything together. Can be sealed and stored in the refrigerator for up to 2 weeks.

Beef

½ Korean pear, peeled and grated
2 tablespoons soy sauce
1 tablespoon rice wine
1 tablespoon honey
½ tablespoon brown sugar
2 teaspoons sesame oil
2 teaspoons garlic powder
½ teaspoon ground ginger
¼ teaspoon onion powder
¼ teaspoon ground black pepper
1 pound boneless beef short ribs, sliced thinly
2 teaspoons canola oil

17. To make the beef: In a gallon-size airtight bag, combine the Korean pear, soy sauce, rice wine, honey, brown sugar, sesame oil, garlic powder, ginger, onion powder, and pepper. Mix everything well together. Add the beef, seal the bag, toss to completely coat the meat, and place the bag in the refrigerator overnight.
18. Remove the beef from the marinade and set aside.
19. In a large cast-iron pan, heat the canola oil over high heat. Add a single layer of beef to the pan and cook until lightly charred, 2 to 3 minutes per side. Transfer to a plate. Repeat this until all the beef has been cooked.

Additionals

2 cups cooked rice
4 sunny-side up eggs
2 teaspoons toasted sesame seeds
3 scallions, minced

20. To assemble a bowl, place ½ cup of cooked rice in a bowl. Top with the cooked beef and any variety of the prepared vegetables. Top with a sunny-side up egg. Sprinkle sesame seeds and scallions on top. Serve with the prepared sauce.

DESSERTS

Toward the end of my journey, I boated out to the Ring of Fire hoping to pick up some tropical recipes. I didn't like to admit it to myself, but I was worn out! I'd been traveling for nearly a year and gone all around the continent. I was ready to kick back and relax a bit. Of course, Abaddon's Mouth isn't the most relaxing place to vacation—legend has it that the inside of the volcano holds a mystical passageway to the underworld. You wouldn't know that the islanders' lives are in constant danger when you're partying with them! If I lived in a place where mangoes, passion fruit, and coconut grew like no tomorrow, I guess I would be celebrating, too. And why not let loose and enjoy the moment—or the ginger-lime ice cream—while it lasts?

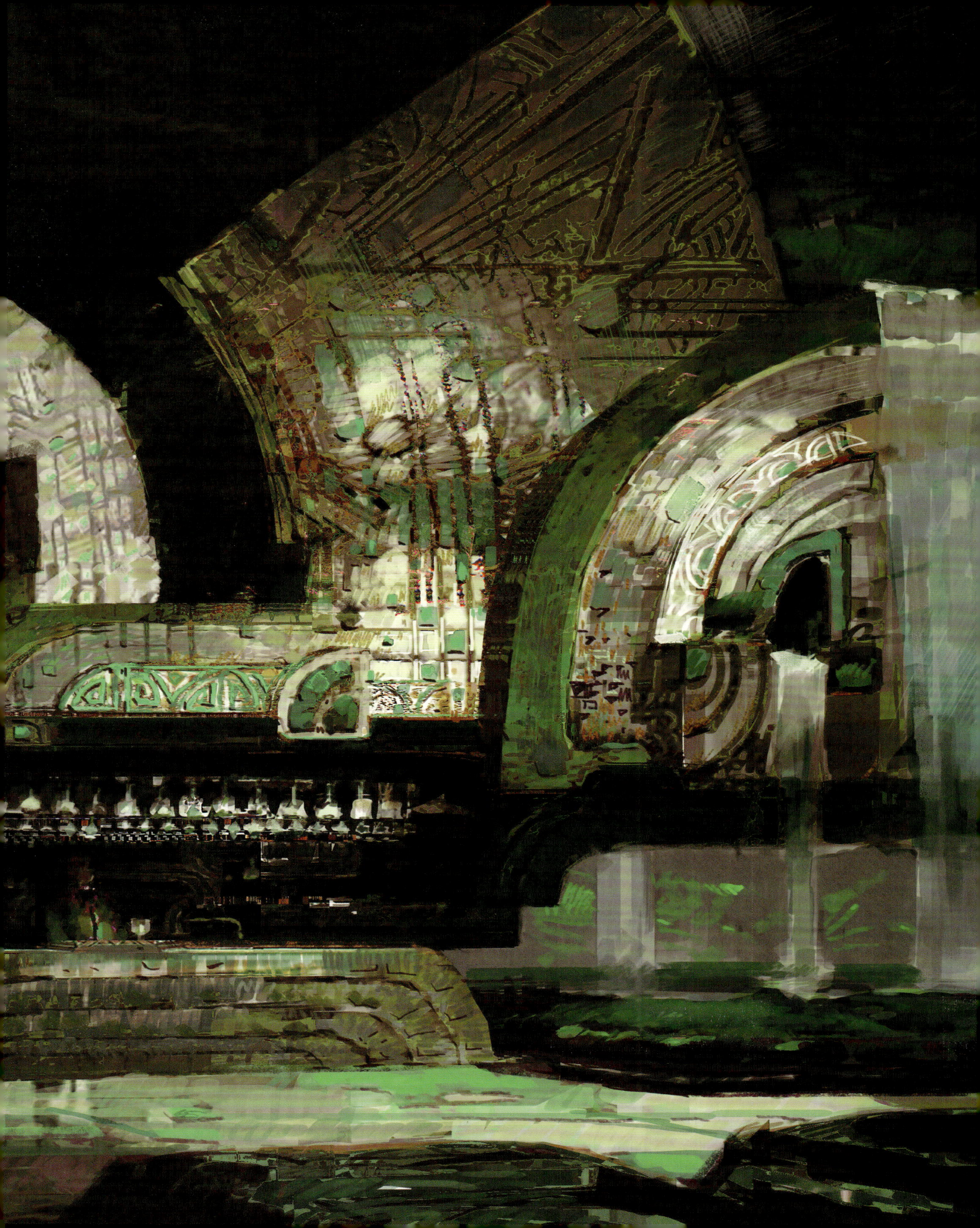

DIFFICULTY
Master

PREP TIME
45 minutes

INACTIVE TIME
2 hours

COOK TIME
1 hour

SERVINGS
1 pie

DIETARY NOTES
Vegetarian

PEACH PIE

I made a trip to Watcher's Hollow to see if the rumors I'd heard were true—an otherworldly peach tree that supposedly grants the strength of a thousand men. I never found the magic fruit. What I did find was a very friendly and very chatty ranger who was overflowing with ideas for this cookbook. She opined for hours on the values of including a "mashed animal fertilizer" dish for treants, which I was strictly against including. It's barely a recipe! In the end, I appeased her by promising to include this recipe. The sweet juices of the peach, heightened by sugar and a beautifully flaky golden crust, could please the taste of a thousand men! You *could* use magic peaches, but it's plenty invigorating with regular ones.

Pie Dough

2½ cups all-purpose flour, plus more for dusting

1½ tablespoons sugar

1½ teaspoons kosher salt

1 cup unsalted butter, cold and cubed

½ cup water, cold, plus more as needed

Peach Filling

3 pounds peaches, cut into large chunks

2 tablespoons lemon juice

¼ cup all-purpose flour

⅓ cup granulated sugar

¼ cup light brown sugar

1 teaspoon ground cinnamon

½ teaspoon ground cardamom

¼ teaspoon grated nutmeg

Pinch of kosher salt

Additionals

1 egg

1 tablespoon coconut milk

2 tablespoons turbinado sugar

1. To make the dough: In a food processor, pulse the flour, sugar, and salt a few times to combine. Add butter and pulse until it resembles a coarse meal.

2. Add the cold water slowly while the food processor runs until it just comes together. If the dough is too dry, add more water 1 teaspoon at a time.

3. Remove the dough from the food processor and transfer onto a lightly floured surface.

4. Split into two equal portions. Flatten each into a disk and wrap in plastic wrap. Refrigerate for at least 2 hours and up to 24 hours.

5. In a large bowl, combine all the ingredients for the filling. Toss until the peaches are completely coated.

6. Transfer to a strainer and place a bowl underneath to drain excess liquid from the filling. Allow this to sit for at least 30 minutes.

7. Preheat the oven to 425°F. When the filling is just about done, take out one of the pie dough portions. Place on a lightly floured work surface and roll out into a ¼-inch-thick circle, about 12 inches in diameter. Transfer to a 9½-inch pie dish. Carefully press the dough into the dish making sure there are no air gaps between the dough and the dish.

8. Place the filling on top of the dough and spread into an even layer. Place in the refrigerator until you've rolled out the other dough portion.

Recipe continued on page 137

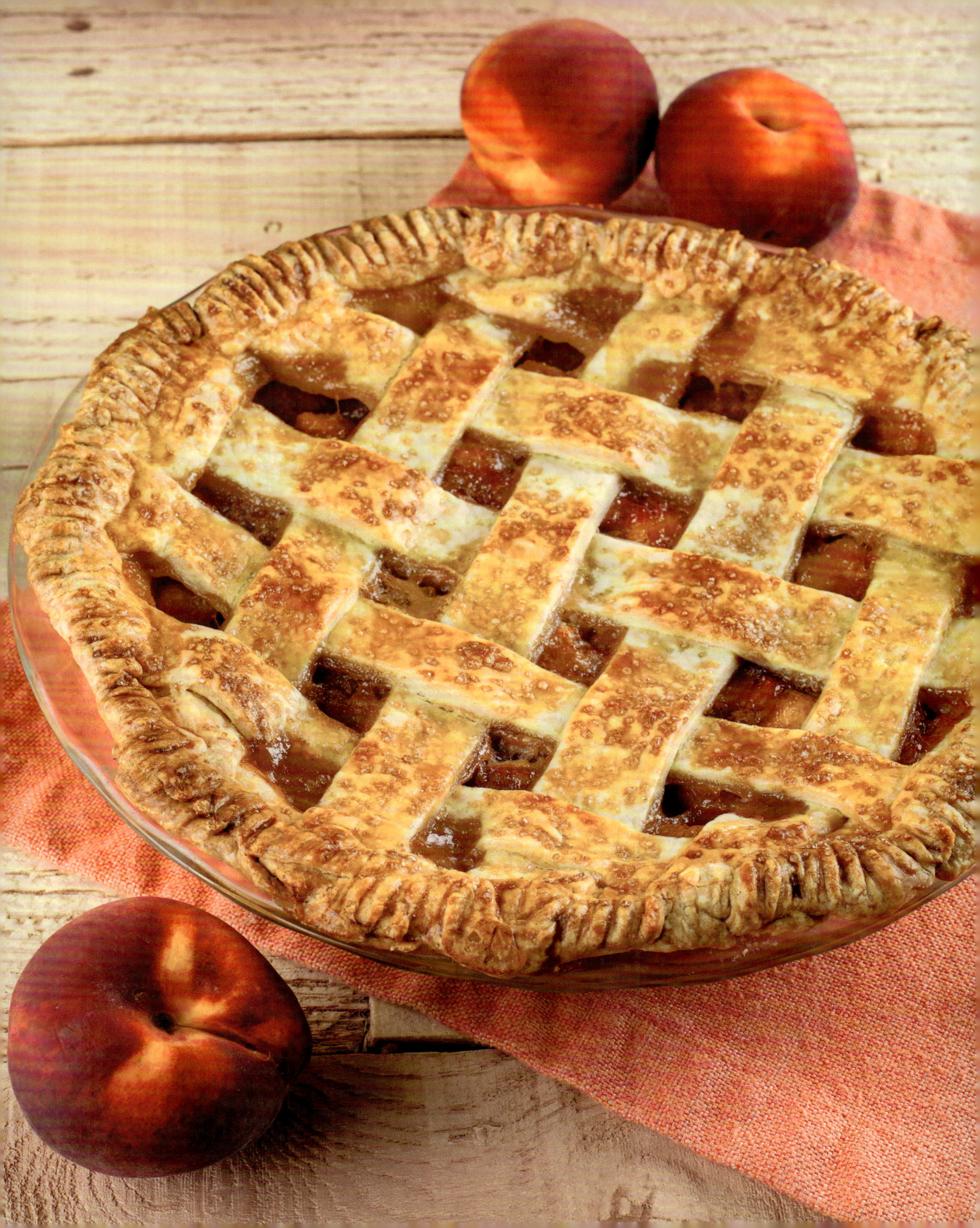

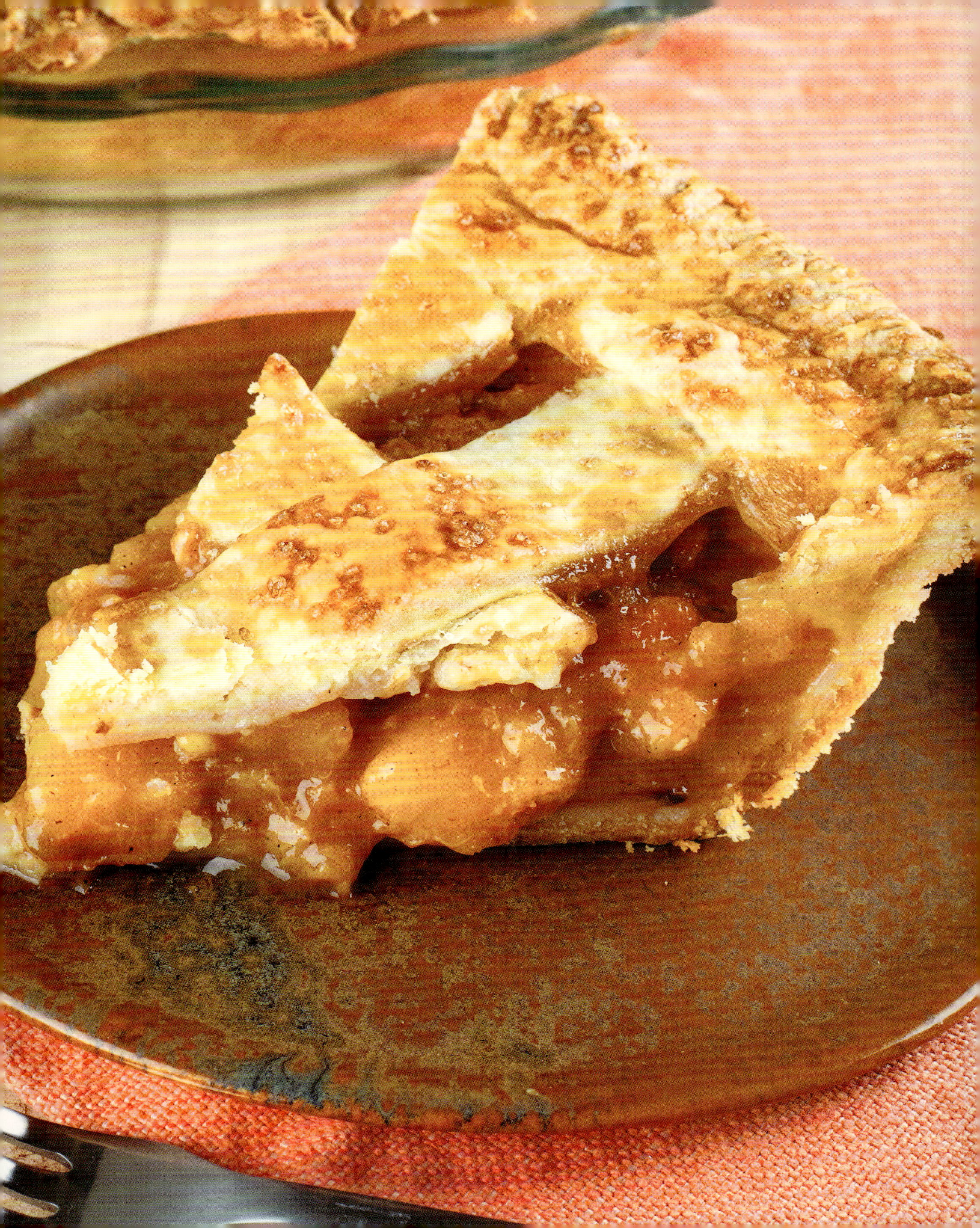

9. Take the other portion of dough out of the refrigerator and roll it out in a circle. Cut 1-inch-wide strips in the rolled-out dough. Remove the pie from the refrigerator.

10. Arrange the strips over the pie into a lattice pattern. Once all the strips have been placed, connect the edge of the pie to the lattices by removing any excess lattice portions and pinching the crust together.

11. In a small bowl, combine the egg and coconut milk. Brush the egg wash on top of the pie and sprinkle with turbinado sugar.

12. Carefully wrap the pie edge with aluminum foil. Place in the oven and cook for 20 minutes.

13. Reduce the heat to 375°F and cook for 40 minutes. Remove the foil and cook for 15 to 20 minutes or until the crust has nicely browned.

14. Allow the pie to completely cool, at least 4 hours, before serving.

DIFFICULTY
Adept

PREP TIME
45 minutes

INACTIVE TIME
12 hours

COOK TIME
35 minutes

SERVINGS
22 to 24 cookies

DIETARY NOTES
Vegetarian

STRAWBERRY COOKIES

While traveling in Ascalon, I heard that one could find fresh strawberries around Diessa Plateau. I explored the rocky ruins overgrown with moss, but it was only after some tricky footwork and tunnel-going that I heard a growly voice humming. The voice belonged to a young charr named Anya tending a small garden of strawberries in an obscure area of the Crimson Plateau. At first, she hesitated to share with me, but I managed to convince her by promising to make her a dessert. The next day, I returned with these cozy cookies. The light crumble and delicate flavor of the cookie allows the sweet, homemade strawberry jam to really dance on the tongue! Anya was delighted. She said she'd happily share strawberries with the next explorer who could find her garden plot, but she was keeping the cookies all to herself.

Strawberry Jam
12 ounces strawberries, hulled and quartered

½ cup sugar

Pinch of kosher salt

1 tablespoon lemon juice

Cookie
2¼ cups all-purpose flour

1 tablespoon cornstarch

½ teaspoon kosher salt

1 cup unsalted butter, room temperature

¾ cup sugar

1½ teaspoons vanilla paste

1 egg

Strawberry Jam

1. To make the jam: In a medium saucepan, combine the ingredients. Place over medium-high heat and bring to a boil. Reduce the heat and simmer for 15 to 20 minutes, until it thickens.

2. Remove from the heat and transfer into an airtight container. Once cooled, cover and refrigerate for at least 12 hours and up to 2 weeks.
Note: This makes enough jam for two batches of these cookies.

3. To make the cookies: Prepare two baking sheets with parchment paper and set aside. In a small bowl, combine the flour, cornstarch, and salt.

4. In a large bowl, cream the butter. Add the sugar until combined and slightly fluffy. Add the vanilla paste and egg. Mix until combined. Add the flour mixture and mix until it just comes together.

5. Take 1 to 2 tablespoons of dough and roll into a ball. Place on the prepared baking sheet and lightly press down in the center with your thumb (or a teaspoon) to create an indentation. Repeat until all the dough is used. Place in the refrigerator and allow to chill for at least 2 hours.

6. Preheat the oven to 375°F. Add the strawberry jam into the center of the cookies, making sure it is filled slightly below the top. Place in the oven and bake for 12 to 15 minutes, or until the bottom of the cookies are golden brown.

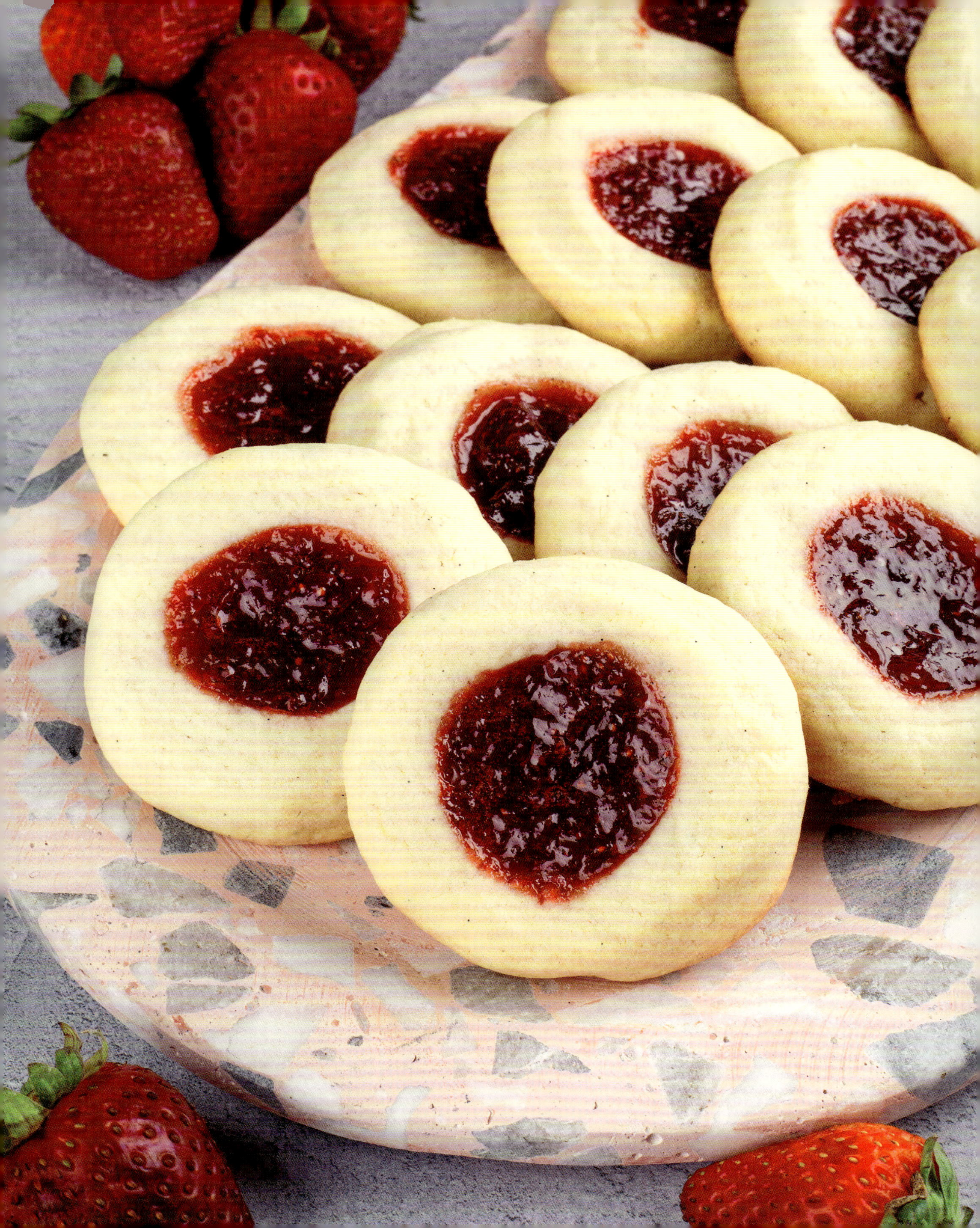

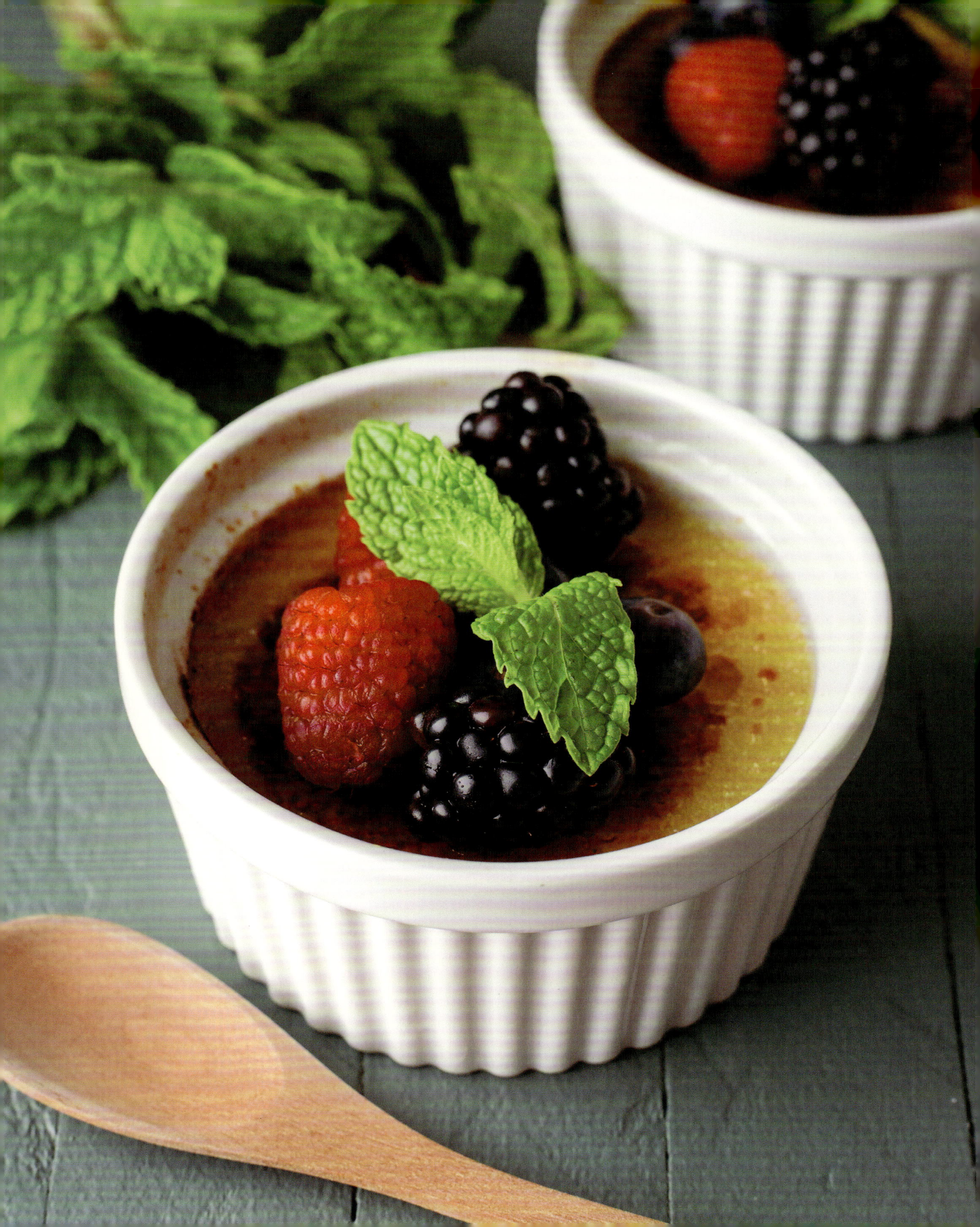

MINT CRÈME BRÛLÉE

DIFFICULTY
Grandmaster

PREP TIME
30 minutes

INACTIVE TIME
3 hours

COOK TIME
1 hour

SERVINGS
6 servings

DIETARY NOTES
Vegetarian, Gluten free

As an apprentice, I studied for a year under Master Chef Shar, who would make crème brûlée at high table feasts. I tried pestering her for the recipe, but she would always reply, "There are some dishes that no one can teach you." Maddening. What was I studying under her for, then? I experimented on my own to work out a passable recipe, but I was still missing some key secret ingredient that made Shar's brûlée sing. For years, I tweaked my recipe until I finally thought to add a ½ ounce of mint. Only then did I discover what Shar had meant. Was my mint crème brûlée the same as Shar's? No, but it was damn good. Fine-tuning the dish to my own taste made it my own—something that I couldn't have done by just copying someone else's. I won't be as cryptic as she was in my recipe, but if you've got the skills to pull off the whisking, folding, and torching of this recipe, I recommend you adjust it further to satisfy your own tastes.

1. Preheat the oven to 325°F.
2. In a medium saucepan, combine the heavy cream, vanilla, mint, and sugar over medium-high heat. Whisk until the sugar has dissolved. Bring to a simmer, reduce the heat to medium, and simmer for 15 minutes.
3. Scrape the vanilla seeds from the pod and return the seeds to the saucepan. Discard the pod and the mint leaves.
4. In a large bowl, combine the salt and egg yolks.
5. Carefully and slowly pour the heated cream into the bowl with the egg yolks while constantly whisking. Split between the six 4-ounce ramekins.
6. Place the ramekins inside a deep baking dish. Fill the dish with water about halfway up the side of the ramekins. Place in the oven and bake for 35 to 45 minutes, or until the edges are set but the centers jiggle slightly and have reached an internal temperature of 175°F. Remove from the oven and take the ramekins out of the baking dish. Let them cool to room temperature. Once completely cooled, place the ramekins in the refrigerator for at least 3 hours.
7. Before serving, sprinkle the top of the crème brûlée with sugar. Use a torch to melt and caramelize the sugar until amber in color. Top with berries and mint.

Mint Crème Brûlée

2 cups heavy cream
1 vanilla bean, halved
½ ounce mint
½ cup sugar
½ teaspoon kosher salt
7 egg yolks

Topping

¼ cup sugar, plus more as needed
¼ cup blueberries
¼ cup raspberries
¼ cup blackberries
Mint leaves

DIFFICULTY
Apprentice

PREP TIME
30 minutes

INACTIVE TIME
12 hours

COOK TIME
5 minutes

SERVINGS
6 servings

DIETARY NOTES
Vegetarian

TROPICAL MOUSSE

This decadent dessert has an intriguing spot in history, dating back to when the first charr, Olma, fled from the Flame Legion of Ascalon, and began a five-year trek to the Sandswept Isles. As Olma established herself in what would become Atholma, she familiarized herself with the ingredients of the environment. It's unclear whether Olma and her tribe of Olmakhans originated tropical mousse, or if they were given the recipe by other isle dwellers. But what is clear is that some quality of the dish—the tart, tangy combination of passion fruit, dragon fruit, and mango, the smoothness of coast-produced condensed milk—changed and boosted Olma's abilities. She became the first Sandshifter, and by sharing this mousse to her community, helped the Olmakhans develop a new and intriguing power.

Mango Mousse

3 mangoes, peeled and seeded
¼ cup passion fruit purée
1 teaspoon agar agar
1½ cups heavy cream
2 tablespoons sweetened condensed milk
2 tablespoons honey

Dragon Fruit Mousse

1 dragon fruit
¼ cup water
½ teaspoon agar agar
1 cup heavy cream
2 tablespoons sweetened condensed milk
2 tablespoons honey

Topping

2 tablespoons Fruit Salad with Mint Garnish (page 57)
Whipped cream

1. In a blender, pulse the mangoes until puréed. Transfer to a medium saucepan and add the passion fruit purée and agar agar. Heat over medium heat and whisk together well. Cook until the agar agar has dissolved and it has come to a light simmer, about 3 minutes. Remove from the heat and allow to cool.

2. While that mixture is cooling, in the bowl of a stand mixer, whip the heavy cream to medium peaks, 5 to 8 minutes.

3. Transfer the mango mixture to a large bowl. Whisk in the sweetened condensed milk and honey until well combined. Fold in the whipped cream until it is well combined and airy. Place in the refrigerator until the dragon fruit mousse is ready.

4. In a blender, pulse the dragon fruit until puréed. Transfer to a saucepan and add the water and agar agar. Heat over medium heat and whisk together well. Cook until the agar agar has dissolved and it has come to a light simmer. Remove from the heat and allow to cool.

5. While that mixture is cooling, in the bowl of a stand mixer, whip the heavy cream to medium peaks, 5 to 8 minutes.

6. Transfer the dragon fruit mixture to a large bowl. Whisk in the sweetened condensed milk and honey until well combined. Fold in the whipped cream until it is well combined and airy.

7. To assemble the tropical mousses, layer the mango and dragon fruit mousse in serving containers. Cover each with plastic wrap and refrigerate overnight before serving.

8. Once the tropical mousses have set, remove the plastic wrap and serve with fruit salad and a dollop of whipped cream.

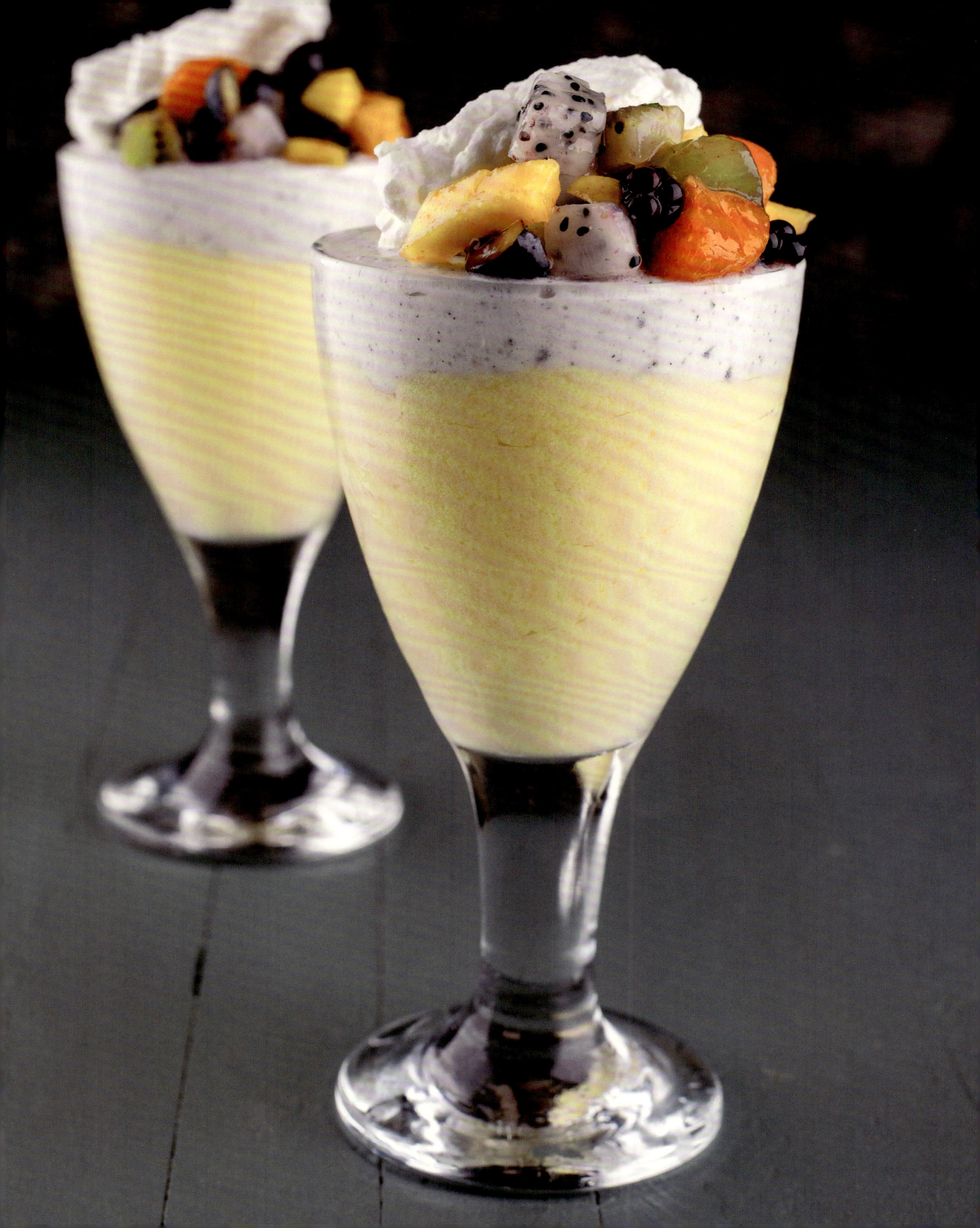

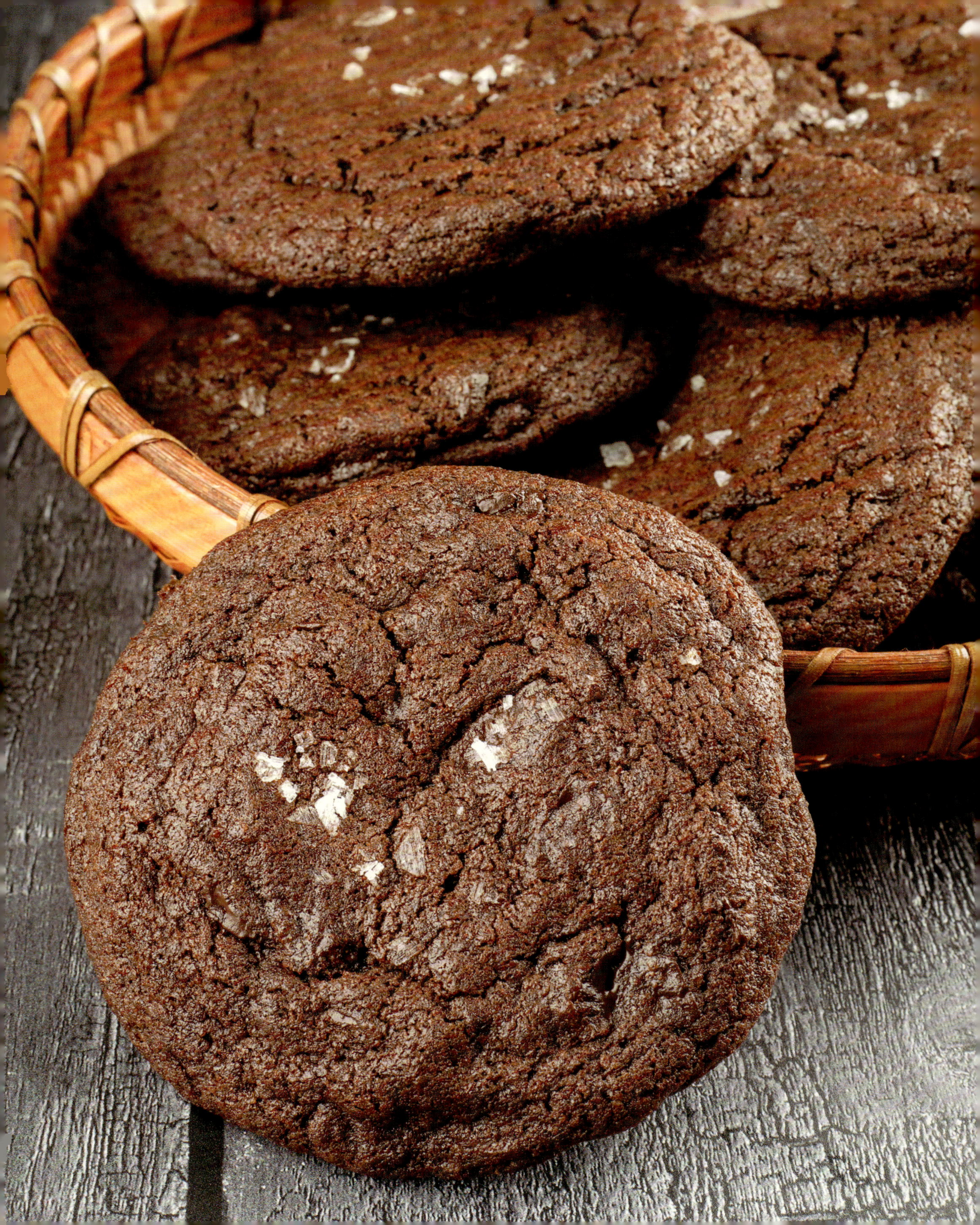

SPICY CHOCOLATE COOKIES

DIFFICULTY
Journeyman

PREP TIME
30 minutes

INACTIVE TIME
8 hours

COOK TIME
17 minutes

SERVINGS
24 cookies

DIETARY NOTES
Vegetarian

This is an original recipe that evokes a particular nostalgia in me. Eating these sweet, spicy cookies when they're warm out of the oven brings me back to playing with my animal wood carvings by the hearth in my grandmother's house. Gran loved to combine sugar and heat, but she was no chef. She used to dip regular chocolate chip cookies into straight chili powder. (I tried it once, and it was overpowering.) To be fair, my gran was a thrillseeker: when she was bored, she would transform into a were-leopard and go fight trolls. I've captured the essence of her daredevil spirit in these much better cookies! Mixing cayenne pepper into the dough mix makes for a much more integrated spice. That pinch of heat melds with the semisweet chunks of melty chocolate to create the perfect cookie for winter nights.

1. In a medium bowl, mix the all-purpose flour, cocoa powder, baking soda, baking powder, salt, cinnamon, and cayenne pepper until well combined. Set aside.

2. In a large bowl, cream the butter until fluffy and pale, about 3 to 5 minutes. Add the brown sugar and granulated sugar and mix until well combined and fluffy, 3 to 4 minutes.

3. Mix in the eggs and yolk, one at a time, until well combined. Whisk in the vanilla.

4. Add the flour mixture and mix until it just comes together. Fold in the dark chocolate pieces.

5. Place parchment paper on a baking sheet. Split the dough into 50 gram (1.75 ounces)–size dough balls and place on the parchment paper. Cover with plastic wrap and let rest in the refrigerator for at least 8 hours, up to a max of 2 days. If you are not baking these cookies yet, place in a freezer-safe resealable bag in the freezer for up to 2 months.

6. Preheat the oven to 375°F. Cover a baking sheet with parchment paper and nonstick spray. Place the cookies on the prepared baking sheet with 2 inches of space between each. Sprinkle the flaky salt. Bake for 15 to 17 minutes, rotating the pan once during baking. Allow to cool completely.

1½ cups all-purpose flour

¾ cup cocoa powder

½ teaspoon baking soda

½ teaspoon baking powder

1 teaspoon kosher salt

1 tablespoon ground cinnamon

½ teaspoon cayenne pepper

1 cup unsalted butter, room temperature

1¼ cups dark brown sugar

½ cup granulated sugar

2 eggs

1 egg yolk

1 teaspoon vanilla extract

8 ounces dark chocolate, chopped

Nonstick spray

Flaky salt, for topping

BLOODSTONE BEARCLAW PASTRY

DIFFICULTY
Adept

PREP TIME
30 minutes

INACTIVE TIME
30 minutes

COOK TIME
15 minutes

SERVINGS
12 pastries

DIETARY NOTES
Vegetarian

I'm a norn with a proud weekly routine and a commitment to enjoy every day as it comes. Which means I celebrate my Thursdays in style with my favorite dessert: bloodstone bearclaw pastries! When I first wrote out this recipe, it had a healthy amount of the titular ingredient: bloodstone dust. Unfortunately for you, I have been informed by Robertus that publishing instructions on how to eat a *technically* "not safe for consumption" substance would get me kicked out of the Durmand Priory. The law leaves no room for innovation. For now, I've substituted the bloodstone filling with a mix of sweet spices that are almost, *almost* as delicious. But if you want to know the real deal, find me on a Thursday.

Bloodstone Filling

3 tablespoons dark brown sugar
2 tablespoons ground cinnamon
2 teaspoons ground star anise
1 teaspoon ground cardamom
1 teaspoon cayenne
Pinch of kosher salt

Assembly

2 puff pastry sheets, thawed
2 tablespoons unsalted butter, melted and cooled
1 egg yolk
1 tablespoon coffee liqueur
2 teaspoons granulated sugar
½ teaspoon ground cinnamon

Glaze

1 tablespoon unsalted butter, melted
½ cup confectioners' sugar
¼ teaspoon cinnamon
Pinch of cayenne pepper
Pinch of kosher salt
1 teaspoon coffee liqueur
2 tablespoons sweetened condensed milk

1. In a small bowl, combine all the ingredients for the filling. Set aside.
2. Prepare a large baking sheet with parchment paper.
3. Take each of the puff pastry sheets and cut into three equally long strips.
4. Take one of the strips and lay it in front of you horizontally. Brush the sheet with butter, leaving a ½-inch border around the edge.
5. Generously top with the filling and lightly press it in. Take the bottom of the puff pastry and tightly roll it up, pinching the ends shut. Cut the roll in half, making two portions.
6. Take one of the portions and cut five slits on one of the edges. Transfer to the prepared baking sheet, making sure to curve the pastry slightly to keep the cuts separated. Make sure not to place the pastries too close to one another, giving them about 1 inch of space around them. Repeat this step with the other half.
7. Repeat steps 4 to 6 with the remaining sheets and filling. You should end up with 12 pastries.
8. Place the baking sheet in the freezer and allow them to rest for 30 minutes.
9. Preheat the oven to 400°F. In a small bowl, whisk together the egg yolk and coffee liqueur. In another small bowl, combine the granulated sugar and cinnamon.
10. Brush each of the pastries with the egg mixture and sprinkle with the sugar mixture. Place in the oven and bake for 12 to 15 minutes, or until golden brown.
11. While the pastries are baking, in another small bowl, whisk together the ingredients for the glaze until smooth.
12. Once the pastries are done baking, allow them to rest for 5 minutes before drizzling the glaze over them.

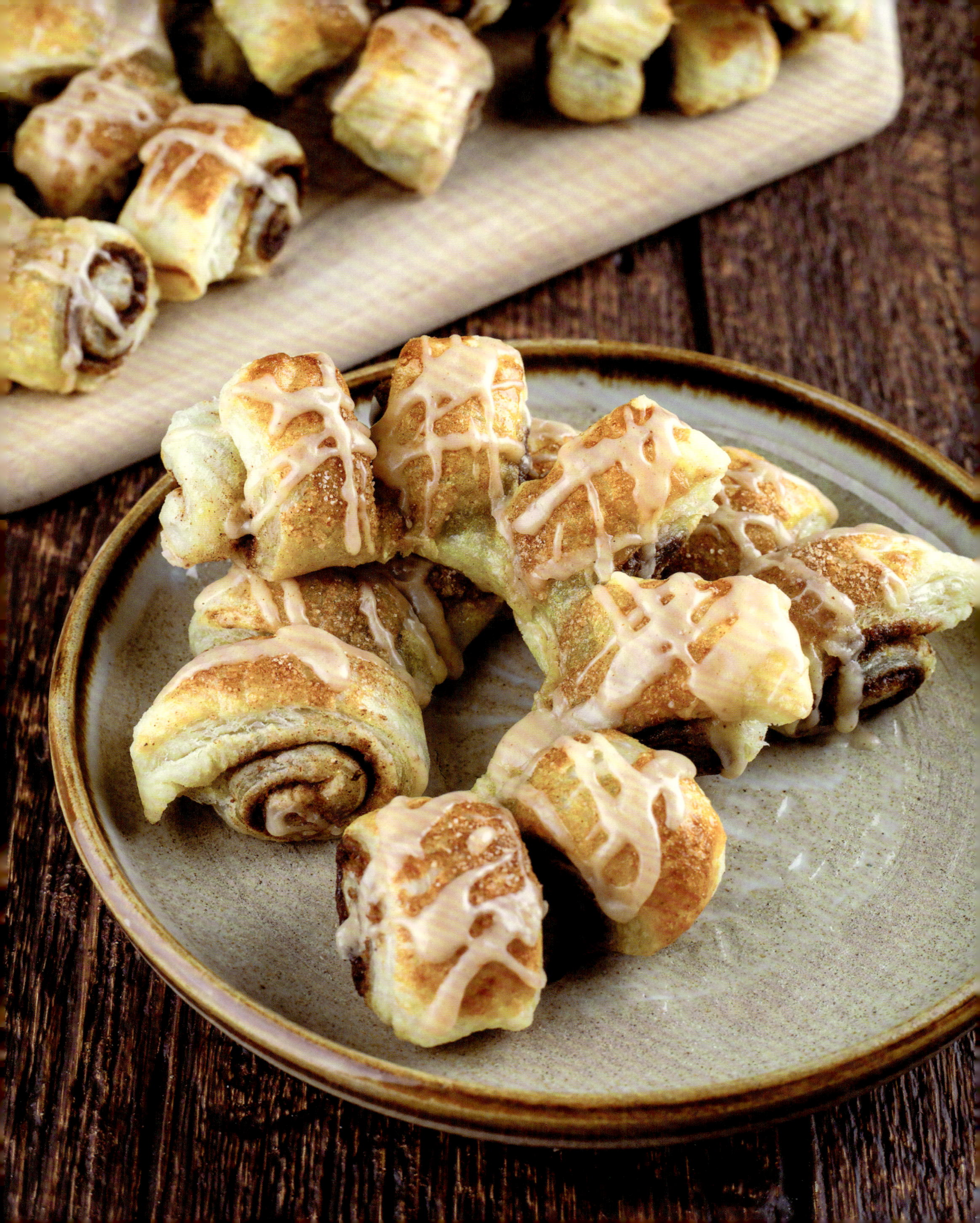

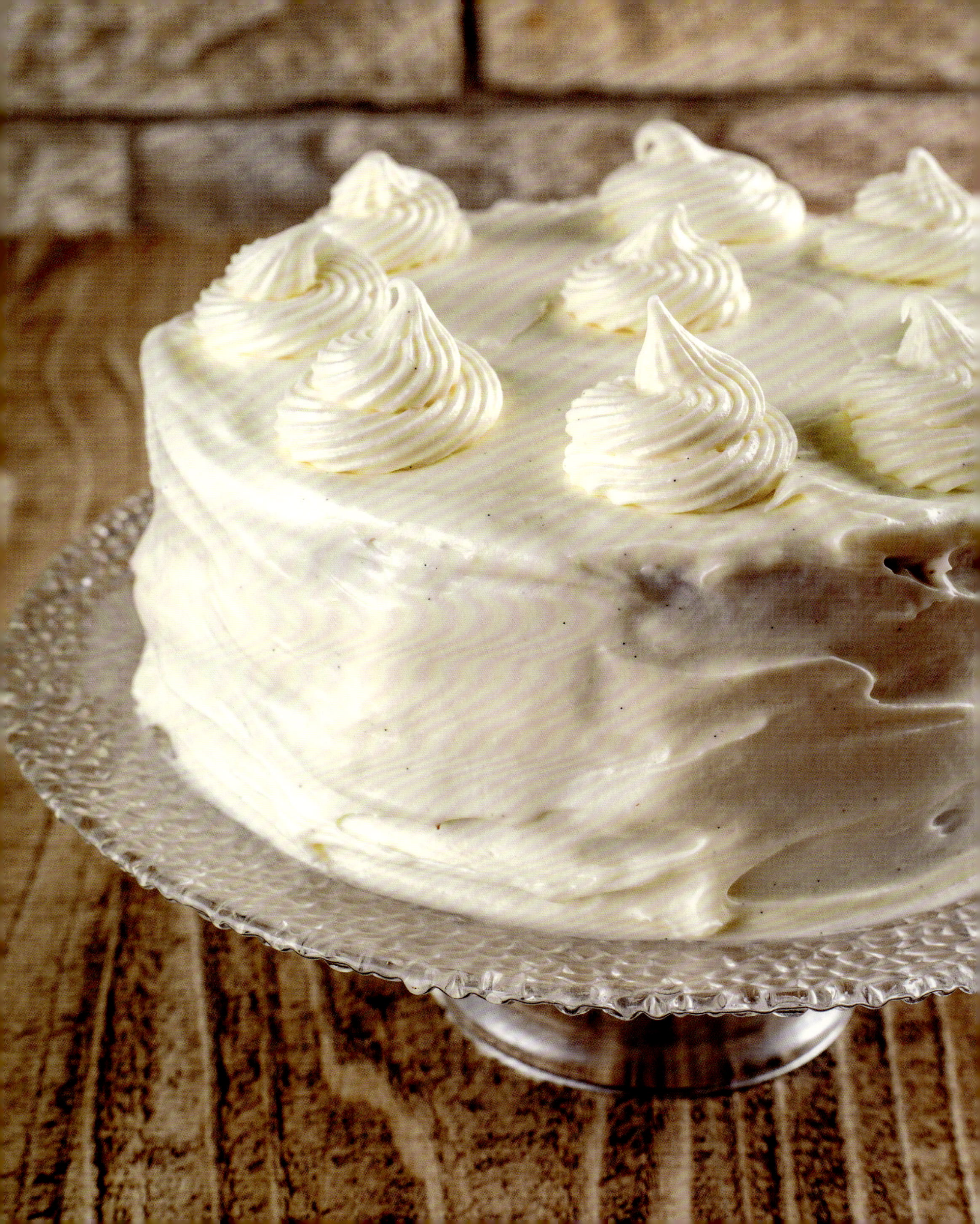

MANDRAGOR ROOT CAKE

DIFFICULTY
Adept

PREP TIME
40 minutes

INACTIVE TIME
2 hours

COOK TIME
40 minutes

SERVINGS
1 cake

DIETARY NOTES
Vegetarian

Every chef knows that the best way to obtain Mandragor Root is by slaying Mandragor beasts. But did you know that the qualities of Mandragor Roots differ between locations? The slithers and imps of Kourna produce roots that hold more water, giving it a smoother texture. Mandragor devils of the charr homelands drop roots with a smoky flavor that my friend Chef Ghoran swears by. Of course, it's not always easy or convenient to pop out and defeat a plant monster, so my recipe includes substitutes that will give you the same great taste: cinnamon, allspice, and cloves to bring that hint of warmth; walnut liqueur for a smooth nuttiness; and molasses for the smooth sweetness that ties the cake together with a moist, tender crumb, all topped with cream cheese frosting to add tang!

1. Preheat the oven to 350°F. Prepare two 8-inch cake pans and spray the inside with nonstick spray. Carefully line each with parchment paper.

2. In a medium bowl, combine the flours, baking soda, ginger, cinnamon, salt, cloves, and allspice and set aside.

3. In a large bowl, combine the butter, brown sugar, and granulated sugar. Mix together until well combined. Add the molasses, walnut liqueur, and egg and egg white. Mix until combined.

4. Add half of the dry ingredients and mix until just combined. Add the yogurt and milk and mix until combined. Finally, fold in the remaining dry ingredients. Be careful not to overwork the batter.

5. Split the batter evenly between the two prepared cake pans. Lift each of the pans and bang lightly on the counter to remove any large air bubbles. Place in the oven and bake for 35 to 40 minutes or until a toothpick test comes out clean.

6. Allow to rest for 5 minutes and then remove from the pan onto a cooling rack. Make sure to remove the parchment paper from the cake and allow them to cool fully, at least an hour.

Cake

Nonstick spray
2 cups all-purpose flour
1 cup cake flour
2½ teaspoons baking soda
1 tablespoon ground ginger
1 teaspoon ground cinnamon
1 teaspoon kosher salt
¾ teaspoon ground cloves
½ teaspoon ground allspice
¾ cup unsalted butter, room temperature
1 cup dark brown sugar
¼ cup granulated sugar
¾ cup unsulphured molasses
2 teaspoons walnut liqueur
1 egg
1 egg white
1 cup Greek yogurt
¾ cup milk

Recipe continued on next page

Cream Cheese Frosting

16 ounces cream cheese, room temperature

¼ cup unsalted butter, room temperature

3 cups confectioners' sugar

1 tablespoon heavy cream

1 teaspoon vanilla paste

Pinch of kosher salt

7. In a large bowl, mix together the cream cheese and butter. Once well mixed, slowly add the confectioners' sugar. Add the heavy cream, salt, and vanilla paste and mix until well combined.

8. Once the cake layers have fully cooled, level both layers by cutting the top bump with a serrated knife. Place one of the layers on your serving plate, cut-side up.

9. Add about ⅓ inch of frosting on top and spread evenly. Top with the other layer of cake, cut-side down.

10. Use the remaining frosting to cover the cake. Let the cake sit covered in the refrigerator for at least 1 hour before cutting into it. The cake can be stored in the refrigerator for up to 4 days.

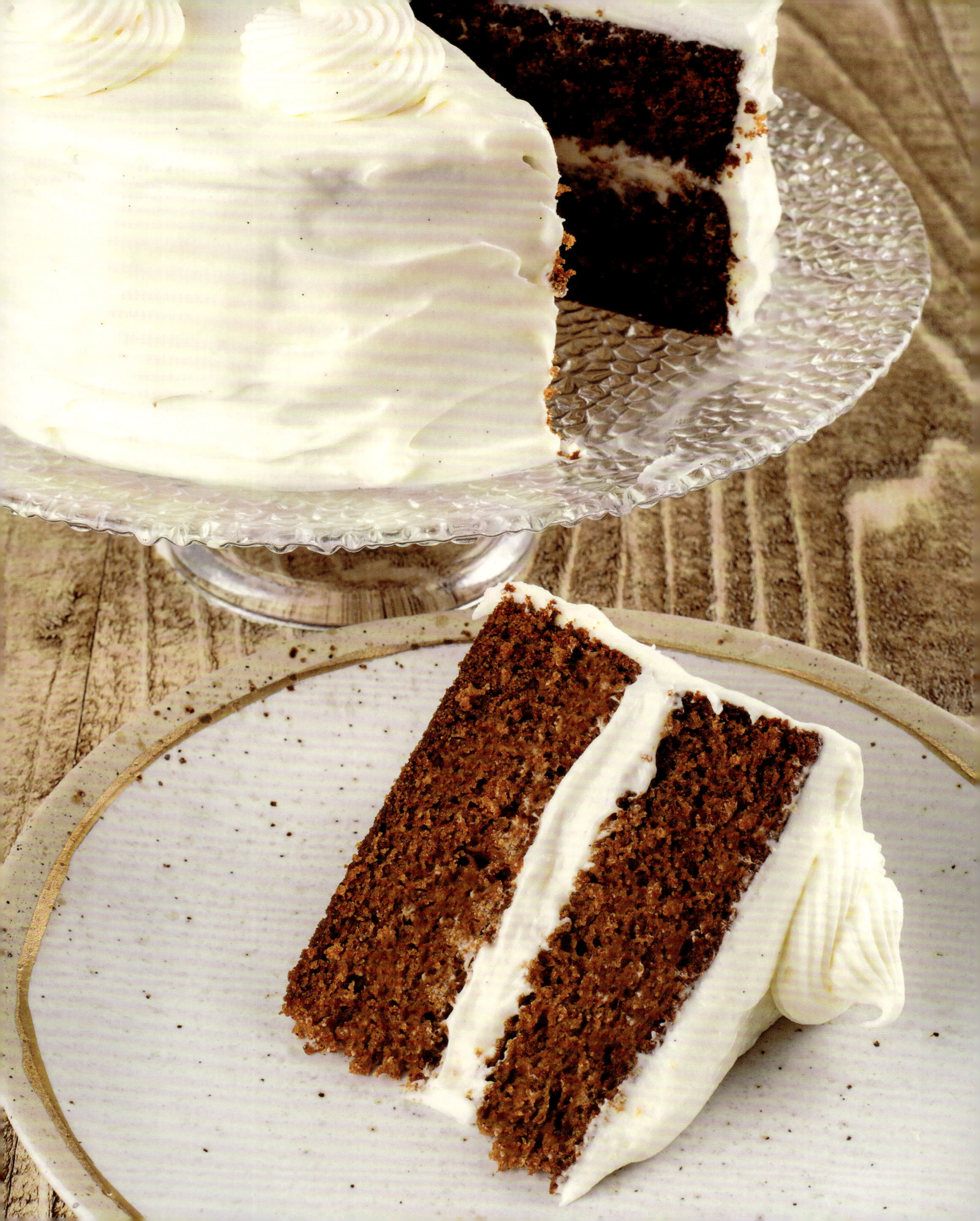

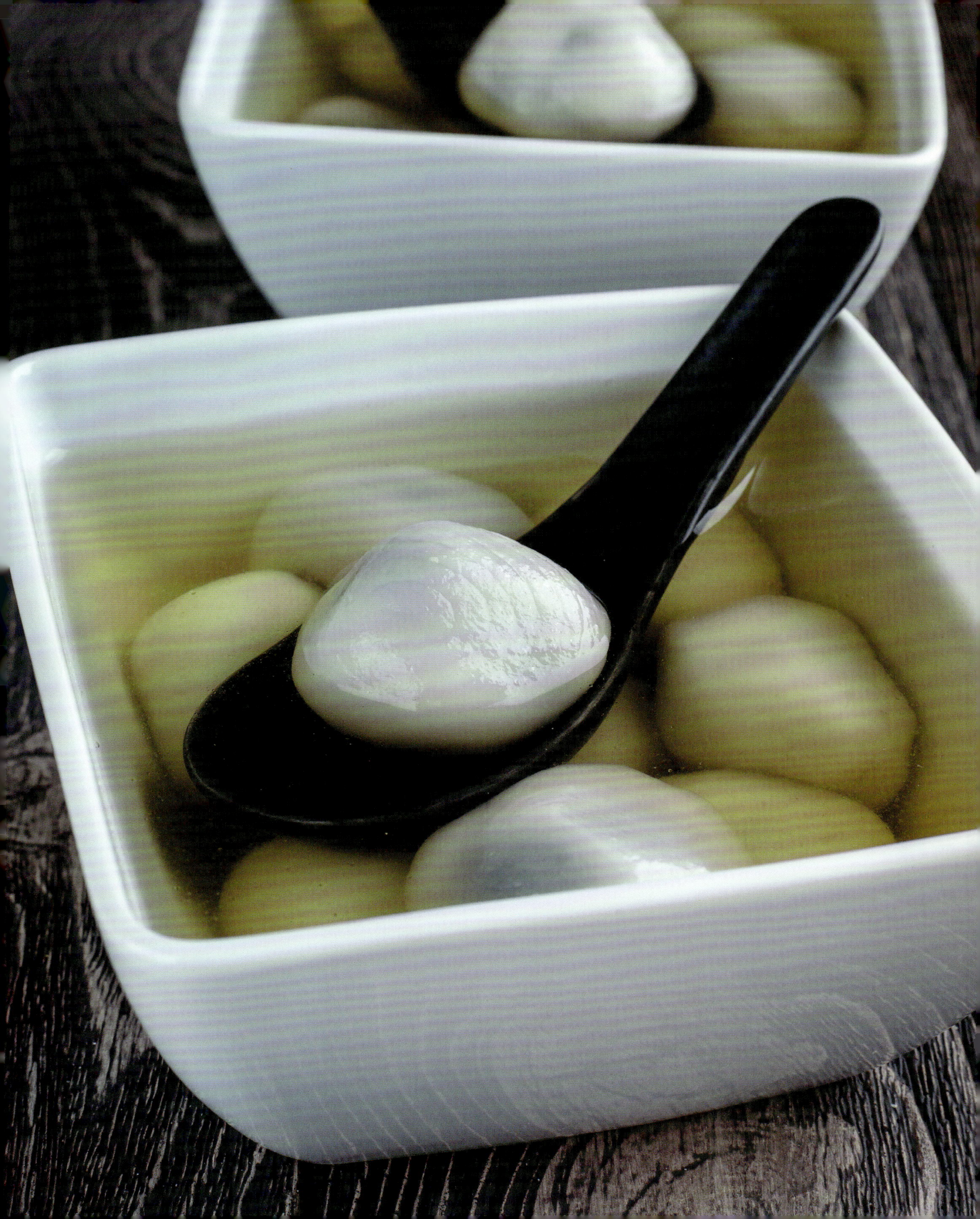

DELICIOUS RICE BALL

The rice used to make this sweet rice ball is grown in paddy fields in the outskirts of New Kaineng City and shipped into the city's marketplace. If you're fortunate enough to visit during the Lunar New Year, make sure to pick up a few lucky red envelopes. You might find delicious rice balls inside! The balls are said to symbolize the harmony and reunion that originated in 510 BE, when warlord Kaing (later known as Kaineng Tah) united the Canthan tribes and founded the empire. Of late, delicious rice balls have gained a non-holiday utility as healers' nourishment of choice. The mild sweetness of the chewy, sticky dough and the semisweet, somewhat nutty filling inside are a welcome prescription for any recovery!

DIFFICULTY
Master

PREP TIME
45 minutes

INACTIVE TIME
1½ hours

COOK TIME
30 minutes

SERVINGS
6 servings

DIETARY NOTES
Vegetarian

---

1. In a medium stainless-steel pan, toast the sesame seeds and peanuts over medium-high heat. Cook until the sesame seeds start to make a popping sound, 3 to 5 minutes.

2. Transfer to a mortar and pestle or food processor, and add the sugar. Grind until grainy and well combined. Add the honey and butter and mix until it is well combined and smooth.
   Note: If you are using a mortar and pestle, transfer the mixture to a small bowl before adding the honey and butter. Mix it in the bowl to combine the honey and butter with the sesame seeds.

3. Transfer to a small bowl, cover and place in the freezer for 30 minutes. Prepare a medium baking sheet with parchment paper.

4. After the filling has chilled, remove from the freezer and split into 1 teaspoon (10 gram)–size spheres (you should end up with about 24 portions). Place on the prepared baking sheet.

5. Place in the freezer for at least an hour, or until you are ready to assemble the dumplings.

6. In a medium saucepan, heat all the soup ingredients over medium-high heat. Bring to a boil and reduce the heat. Stir until the palm sugar has dissolved. Simmer for 25 minutes.

7. Remove and discard the pandan leaf and ginger. Keep the liquid warm until you are ready to serve.

Black Sesame Filling

¾ cup black sesame seeds
¼ cup peanuts
⅓ cup sugar
¼ cup honey
6 tablespoons unsalted butter, room temperature

Soup

3 cups water
1 pandan leaf
6 slices ginger
3 tablespoons palm sugar

Dough

2⅓ cups glutinous rice flour
½ cup boiling water
½ cup cold water

Recipe continued on next page

8. Place the rice flour in a medium bowl. Add the boiling water and mix until most of the flour is hydrated. Slowly pour in the cold water and stir. You may need more or less water. The consistency of the dough should feel like an earlobe. Lightly knead the dough until completely smooth.

9. Cover with a damp towel and allow to rest for 15 minutes.

10. Split into 1½ teaspoon (15 gram)–size portions. Cover with a damp towel to keep these from drying out.

11. To assemble, take one of the dough portions into your hand and spread into a 2-inch disk. Place one of the prepared filling portions in the center and carefully wrap the dough around it and seal. Roll it in your hands to smooth it out into a round portion. Place back under a damp towel until all are formed. Repeat this step until all the dough is used.
    Note: If you are not going to be consuming all these rice balls in one serving, place them in an airtight container and freeze for up to 1 month.

12. Bring a medium pot filled with water to a boil. Add the sesame balls to the water and give it a light stir to make sure they don't stick to the bottom. Wait until the water returns to a boil and then cook for 5 minutes, or until they start to float.
    Note: If heating these rice balls from frozen, it might take slightly longer for them to cook.

13. Add ½ cup of cold water to the pot and then transfer the sesame balls to a bowl with cold water.

14. Transfer to serving bowls and then top with the soup.

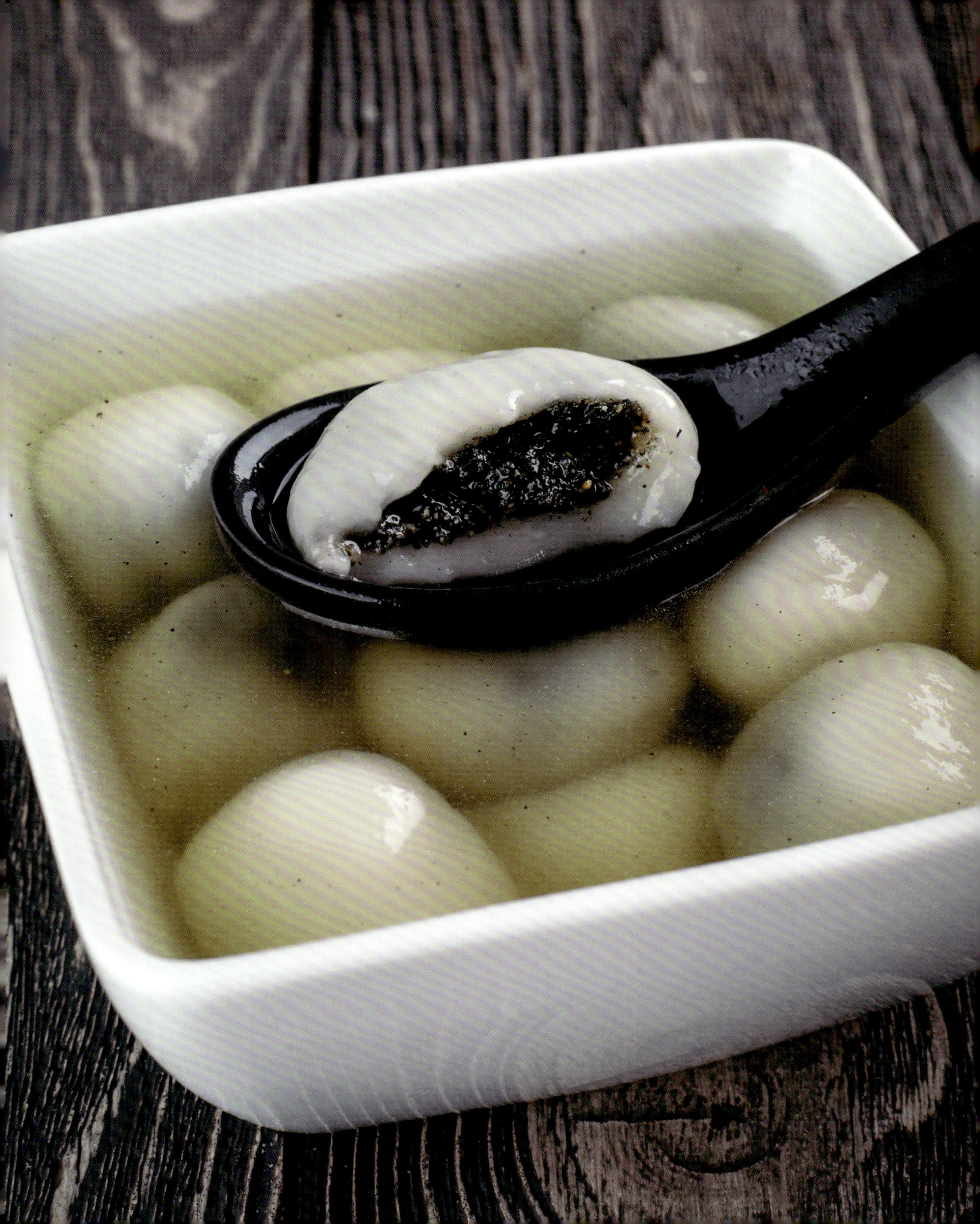

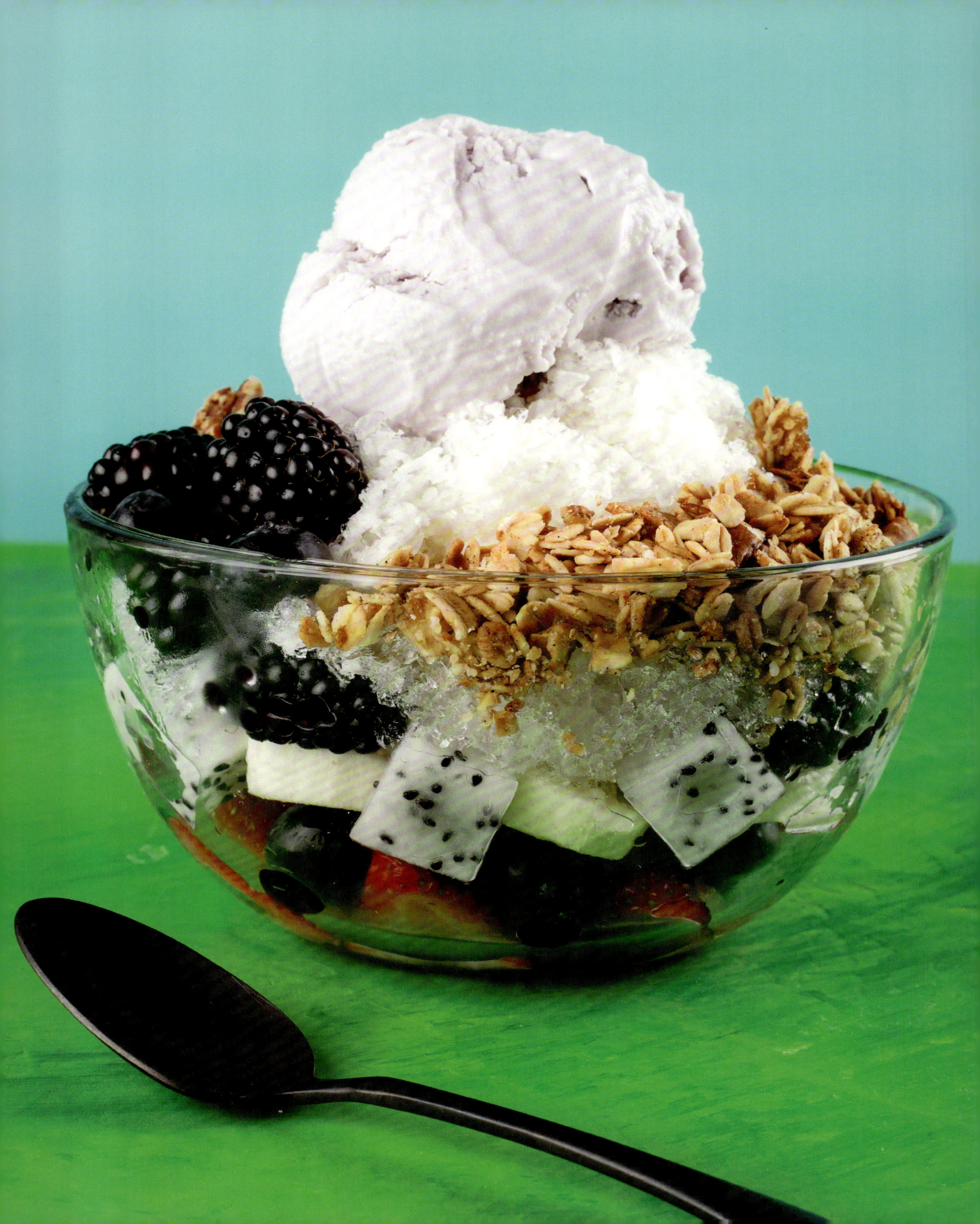

SUPER MIXED PARFAIT

DIFFICULTY
Adept

PREP TIME
45 minutes

INACTIVE TIME
5 hours

COOK TIME
40 minutes

SERVINGS
8 servings

DIETARY NOTES
Vegetarian

I swear by the Spirits, my attempt to obtain this recipe was one of the weirdest experiences I've had. While spending some time in Metrica Province, I heard of a recipe that could only be found at the Super Adventure Festival. I went into Rata Sum not knowing what to expect, and via a strange box I ended up in a bizarre world made up entirely of cubes with a smiling sun! There were other adventurers in this square land that were just as bewildered as me, but we wandered together through the savannah, jungle, and volcano and had a fantastic time. It was only after I'd left that I realized I hadn't even needed to go in to begin with—I was able to buy the recipe from a strange vendor in Rata Sum's Creator's Commons. Thankfully, the dessert itself isn't cubic—it's a mild but delicious ube coconut ice cream with whole rolled oats and brown sugar to top it!

Ube Coconut Ice Cream

14 ounces sweetened condensed coconut milk

14 ounces coconut cream

1 cup ube halaya

1 teaspoon vanilla paste

Pinch of kosher salt

2 cups heavy cream

Coconut Granola

2 cups old-fashioned rolled oats

½ cup coconut flakes

1 cup pecans

¼ cup unsalted butter

¼ cup maple syrup

1 tablespoon dark brown sugar

½ teaspoon ground cardamom

½ teaspoon kosher salt

1 teaspoon vanilla paste

1. In a large bowl, combine the sweetened condensed milk, coconut cream, ube halaya, vanilla paste, and salt. Whisk together until well combined.

2. Place the heavy cream into a bowl of a stand mixer. Mix until the whipped cream forms medium peaks. Transfer to the bowl with everything else. Carefully fold in the whipped cream until it is well combined.

3. Transfer to an airtight container and spread into a smooth even layer. Cover and place in the freezer for at least 5 hours before serving.
Note: Due to the water content in the coconut milk, this ice cream will be a bit difficult to remove from the container. Remove it from the freezer 20 minutes before serving to make scooping a bit easier.

4. Preheat the oven to 350°F. Prepare a baking sheet with a sheet of parchment paper. In a large bowl, combine the rolled oats, coconut flakes, and pecans. Set aside.

5. In a medium saucepan, combine the butter, maple syrup, brown sugar, ground cardamom, salt, and vanilla paste in a saucepan. Place over medium heat and mix together until the butter has melted and the sugar has dissolved, about 3 to 5 minutes. Carefully pour into the large bowl with the oat mixture. Mix together until well combined.

6. Transfer to the baking sheet and spread into a thin layer. Place in the oven and bake for 15 minutes. Stir and bake for another 15 to 20 minutes, or until golden brown. Remove from the oven and let cool for 45 minutes. Once cooled, transfer to an airtight container.

Recipe continued on next page

Additionals
⅓ cup evaporated milk
⅓ cup coconut cream
1 tablespoon sweetened condensed milk
2 cups shaved ice
2 ounces strawberries
2 ounces blueberries
2 ounces blackberries
4 ounces banana
1 ounce coconut flakes
Coconut Granola
Ube Coconut Ice Cream

7. The granola can be stored at room temperature in an airtight container for 10 days and makes enough granola for about eight portions.

8. In a small bowl, whisk together the evaporated milk, coconut cream, and sweetened condensed milk. Set aside.

9. To assemble, place ½ cup of shaved ice at the bottom of a large bowl and then top with the rest of the toppings to your liking. Pour a few tablespoons of the evaporated milk mixture over the ice to flavor. Top with the coconut granola and a scoop of ube coconut ice cream.

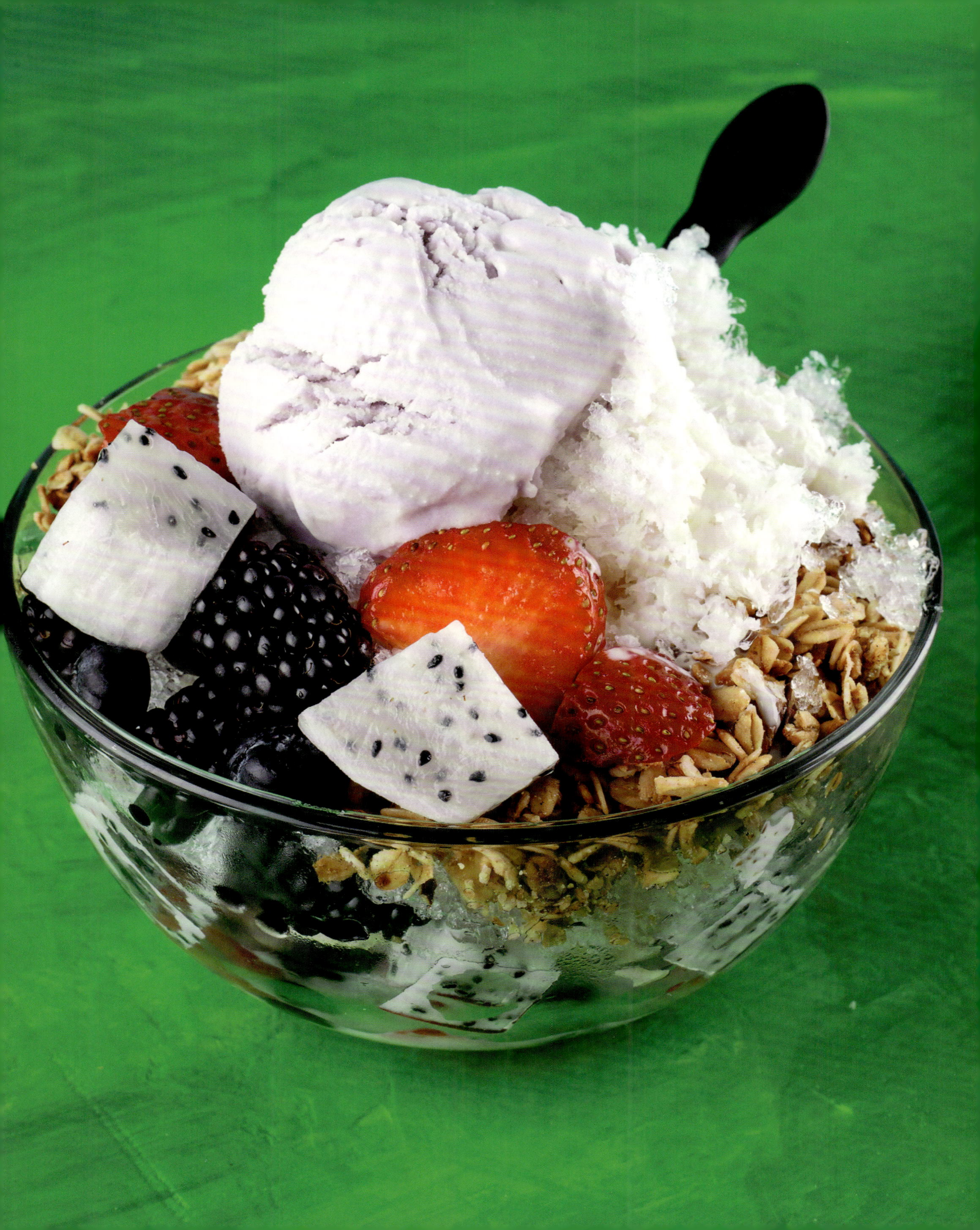

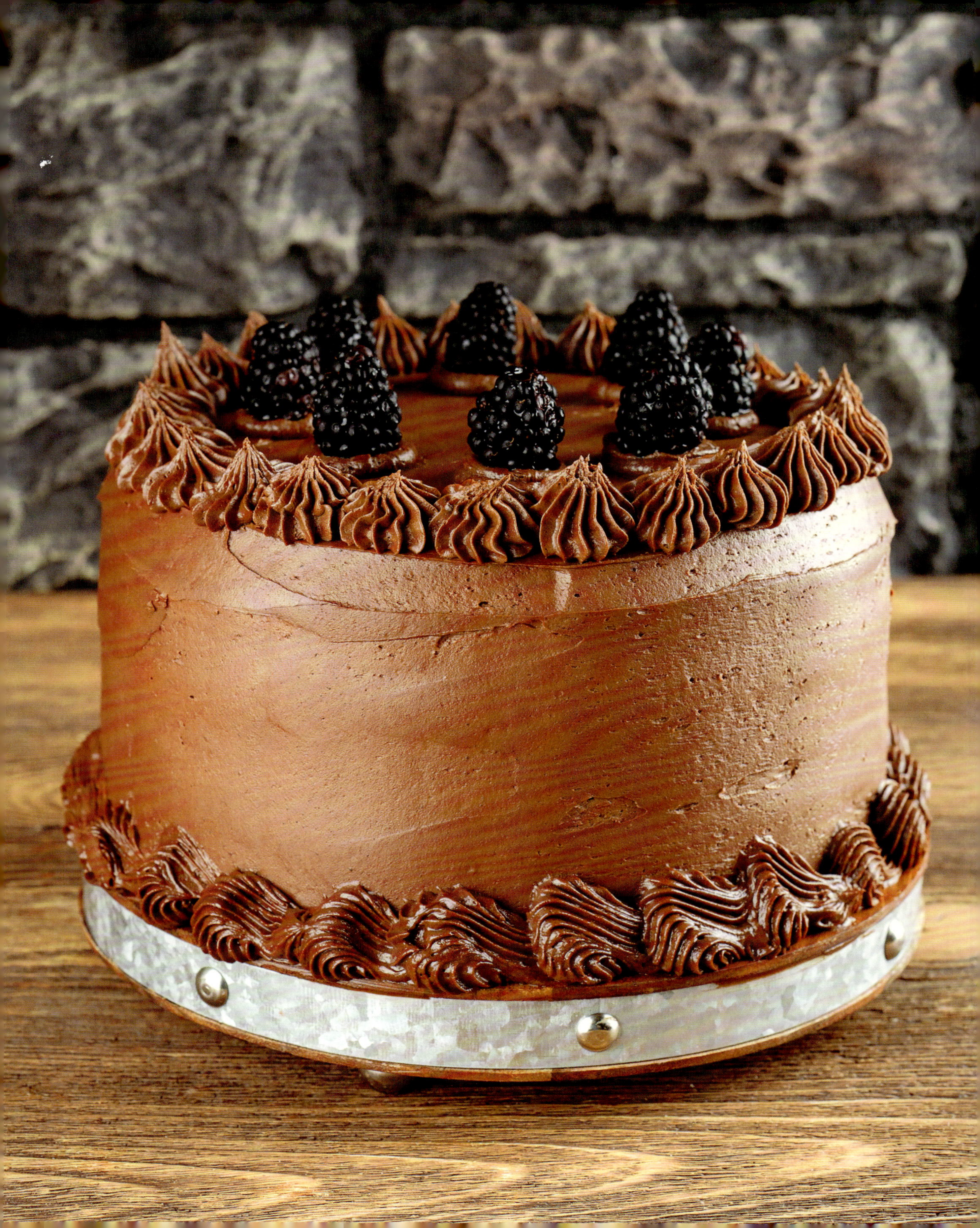

CHOCOLATE OMNOMBERRY CAKE

DIFFICULTY
Master

PREP TIME
2 hours

INACTIVE TIME
12 hours

COOK TIME
1½ hours

SERVINGS
1 cake

DIETARY NOTES
Vegetarian

The Chocolate Omnomberry Cake once served a heroic purpose in the Harathi Hinterlands. I stayed a few nights at a rare settlement where charr and norn were working together to try to stave off the Blood Hill Camps' centaurs that threatened their community. They weren't having much luck. I'd learned that the centaurs had something of a sweet tooth. I baked a few dozens of these delectable cakes—enough that the sweet cocoa scent whirled through the town—and the next time we heard the gallop of hooves thundering toward the settlement, I piled the desserts at the front gates of the town. Who could resist that fruity jelly when it's over-moist, fluffy chocolate? Not the centaurs. While they were pigging—horsing?—out, we climbed the walls and rained a storm of arrows down on them. They've never returned since!

1. To make the jelly: The night before, place all the jelly ingredients in a medium saucepan. Heat over medium-high heat and bring to a boil. Reduce to a simmer and cook for 20 to 25 minutes.

2. Transfer to a blender and pulse until smooth. Pass through a fine-mesh strainer back into the saucepan.

3. Heat back up over medium-high heat and allow to simmer for 15 minutes, until it thickens and reduces slightly.

4. Transfer to an airtight container and allow to cool. Let sit in the refrigerator at least overnight, up to 2 weeks.

5. To make the cake: Preheat the oven to 350°F. Prepare three 8-inch cake pans by spraying the insides with nonstick spray. Carefully line each with parchment paper.

6. In a small bowl, whisk together the cocoa powder, omnomberry jelly, and coffee. Set aside.

7. In a medium bowl, combine the cake flour, baking powder, baking soda, and salt and set aside. In a large bowl, combine the butter, granulated sugar, and brown sugar and mix until smooth and fluffy. Add the eggs and vanilla paste.

8. Add half of the dry ingredients into the large bowl and mix well. Add the sour cream and buttermilk. Mix until smooth. Add the remaining dry ingredients and mix until just combined.

9. Split the batter evenly among the three prepared cake pans. Lift each of the pans and bang lightly on the counter to remove any large air bubbles. Place in the oven and bake for 35 to 40 minutes or until a toothpick test comes out clean.

10. Allow to rest for 5 minutes and then remove from the pan onto a cooling rack. Make sure to remove the parchment paper from the cake and allow them to cool fully, at least an hour of resting time.

Omnomberry Jelly

2 tablespoons lemon juice
¼ cup sugar
5 ounces raspberries
3 ounces blackberries
1 pound cherries, pitted and halved

Chocolate Cake

Nonstick spray
¾ cup cocoa powder
½ cup Omnomberry Jelly
⅔ cup freshly brewed coffee
2½ cups cake flour
2 teaspoons baking powder
1 teaspoon baking soda
1 teaspoon kosher salt
1 cup unsalted butter, room temperature
1 cup granulated sugar
¾ cup light brown sugar
3 eggs
2 teaspoons vanilla paste
1 cup sour cream
1 cup buttermilk

Recipe continued on next page

Omnomberry Filling

8 ounces cream cheese, room temperature

½ cup unsalted butter, room temperature

½ cup Omnomberry Jelly

2 cups confectioners' sugar

Chocolate Frosting

2¼ cups confectioners' sugar

4 tablespoons cocoa powder

1 teaspoon kosher salt

8 ounces cream cheese, room temperature

½ cup unsalted butter, room temperature

9 ounces bittersweet chocolate, melted and cooled

¾ cup sour cream

Assembly

8 blackberries

11. To make the filling: In a large bowl, mix the cream cheese and butter until well combined and fluffy. Add the omnomberry jelly and mix until combined.

12. Finally, whip in the confectioners' sugar in batches until fully combined. Set aside until you are ready to assemble the cake.

13. To make the frosting: In a medium bowl, whisk together the confectioners' sugar, cocoa powder, and salt. Set aside.

14. In a large bowl, mix the cream cheese and butter until well combined and fluffy.

15. Add the melted chocolate and mix until well combined. Add the confectioners' sugar mixture in batches until fully combined. Finally, add the sour cream and mix until combined and fluffy.

16. To assemble: Once the cake layers have fully cooled, level each of the layers by cutting the top bump with a serrated knife. Place one of the layers on your serving plate, cut-side up.
Note: If you'd like to make things a little easier on yourself, wrap the cake with a plastic cake collar to keep the filling from spilling out as you layer it. Simply wrap the first layer with the collar and tape it together to hold it in place.

17. Add about half of the omnomberry filling on top and spread into an even layer.

18. Top with a second layer of cake (either side is fine). Add the remaining omnomberry filling and spread into an even layer. Top with the remaining layer of cake, cut-side down.

19. Prepare a piping bag with a large star decorating tip. Transfer a small portion of the chocolate frosting into the piping bag. Completely cover the cake with the remaining chocolate frosting. To get nice smooth sides, take an offset spatula edge against the side and rotate the cake around.

20. Take the prepared piping bag and squeeze a chocolate edge around the top edge of the cake. Do this again around the bottom edge of the cake.

21. Place eight small dollops of the chocolate frosting on the top of the cake. Take the blackberries and place one on top of each of the dollops. Let the cake sit covered in the refrigerator for at least 1 hour before cutting into it. The cake can be stored in the refrigerator for up to 4 days.

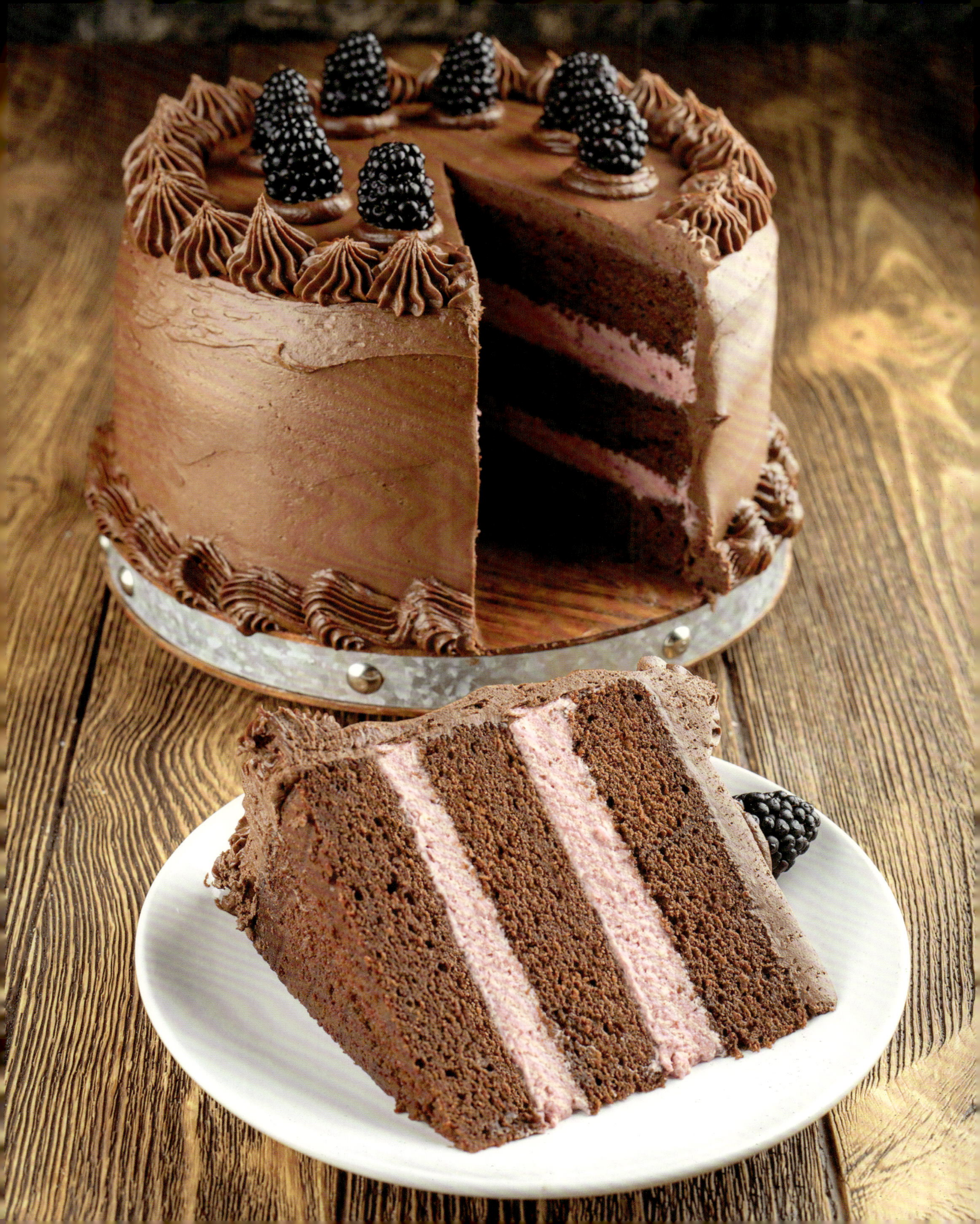

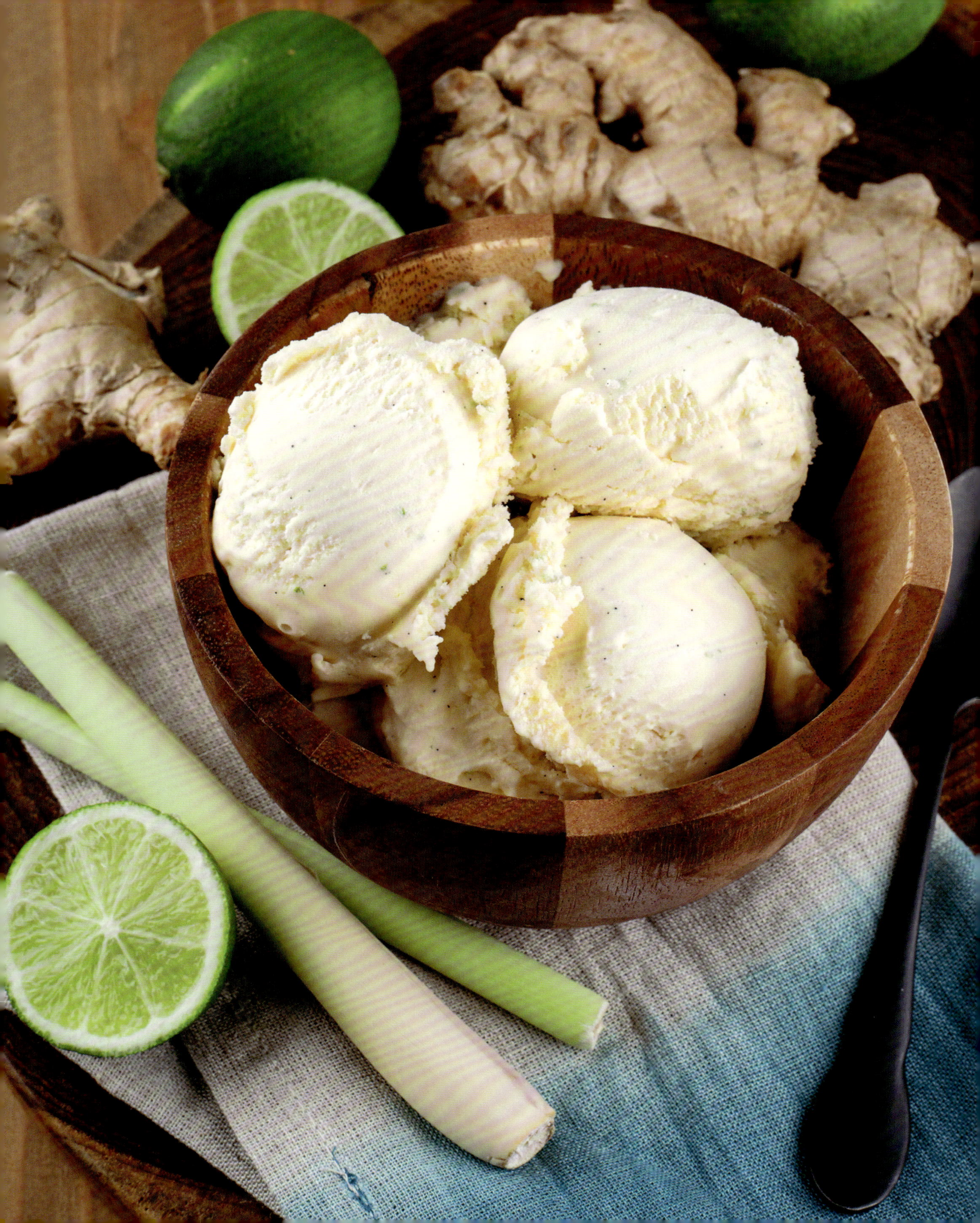

GINGER-LIME ICE CREAM

DIFFICULTY
Adept

PREP TIME
30 minutes

INACTIVE TIME
48 hours

COOK TIME
15 minutes

SERVINGS
8 servings

DIETARY NOTES
Vegetarian

Every dessert expert and gelato master in Divinity's Reach spends time learning how to make this tart, sweet delicacy, as it's said to be a favorite of Queen Jennah's! Rumor mills of the Upper City noticed that whenever her naysayers made political faux pas, envoys of the royal palace happened to buy dessert parlors out of ginger-lime ice cream. It's certainly a delicacy fit for royalty, as guiding the cream through whisking and folding while making sure not to flatten the air out of the concoction requires a measured, elegant hand. But the end product is worth it: The fresh zested lime and ginger is rich and refreshing like nothing else.

1. Two days before you need the ice cream, in a saucepan, combine all the ingredients for the flavored heavy cream. Bring to a boil and reduce the heat and simmer for 15 minutes. Remove from the heat and let cool. Transfer to an airtight container. Place in the refrigerator for at least 8 hours, up to 1 day.

2. In a large bowl, whisk the sweetened condensed milk, grated ginger, lime zest, vanilla, and salt until well combined and set aside.

3. Discard all the bits from the flavored heavy cream. Place the flavored heavy cream and additional heavy cream into a bowl of a stand mixer. Mix until the whipped cream forms medium peaks. Transfer to the bowl with everything else. Carefully fold in the whipped cream until it is well combined.

4. Transfer to an airtight container. Cover and place in the freezer for at least 8 hours before serving.

Flavored Heavy Cream

2 cups heavy cream
1 vanilla bean, split
2 lemongrass stalks
4-inch piece of ginger, sliced
2 limes, sliced

Ginger-Lime Ice Cream

14 ounces sweetened condensed milk
1½ tablespoons ginger, grated
2 tablespoons lime zest
2 teaspoons vanilla extract
Pinch of salt
Flavored Heavy Cream
½ cup heavy cream

BEVERAGES

At the end of the year, after all my jumping around from the jungle to the desert to the islands, my mission was finally over. I got a letter from Gixx, telling me that my next mission was to return to the Priory so my skills could be assessed and a more stationary practice could be set up for me. I was a full-fledged member of the Durmand Priory, and I was on the road to mastery. My travels were over.

I had a short break before I was due at the monastery, so I went home to the Shiverpeak Mountains. Nothing had changed except for me—so infinitely stronger, wiser, full to the brim with knowledge. A few days in, I took myself down to the pub and met up with my friends, boasting to them about all I'd accomplished. I was in the middle of telling them how I'd single-handedly dished out entrées to save the Priory from a champion troll when my friend Magda challenged me: "If you know so much, how do you make that drink in your mug?"

I looked down at the stein of buttered spirits in my hand. By the Spirits, I had no idea how to make it! My boast stopped mid-word. I was a fool, an idiot—I hadn't spent too much time learning to make drinks in my year of travel. And come to think of it, I still needed to learn more Canthan cuisine . . . and I hadn't fully absorbed the food of Divinity's Reach. There was still so much I didn't know! The thought invigorated me. The next morning, I left for the Priory with a plan—how much convincing would Chef Robertus need to take my training on the road again?

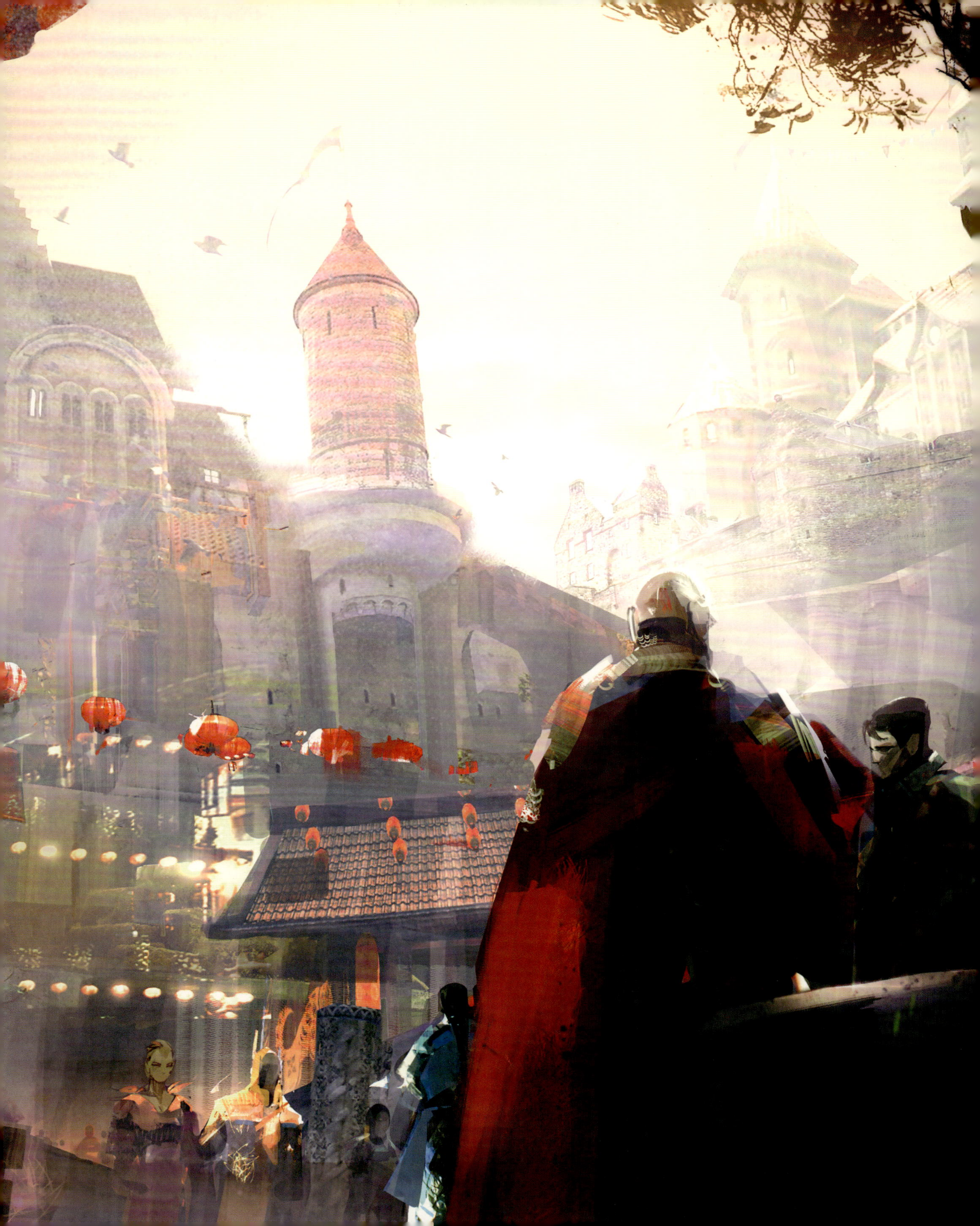

DIFFICULTY
Journeyman

PREP TIME
20 minutes

INACTIVE TIME
12 hours

COOK TIME
10 minutes

SERVINGS
1 serving

DIETARY NOTES
Vegetarian

BUTTERED SPIRITS

It's a crime to celebrate Wintersday without Buttered Spirits! I can't imagine winter holidays without a stein in hand. My best memories are colored by this drink: sitting around the hearth, warmed by the irresistible scents of cinnamon and dark rum, cooking up a feast in the kitchen with family, sharing a pint with friends or spending a treasured evening alone with a mug of paradise in hand. It's made with brown sugar for a comforting sweetness and balanced out with ginger and cloves for a fun edge. Rumor is that if you leave some out after everyone's gone to bed, Toymaker Tixx may show up and leave you a present!

Butter Base
½ cup unsalted butter, room temperature
⅓ cup dark brown sugar
1 teaspoon ground cinnamon
½ teaspoon ground ginger
½ teaspoon allspice
½ teaspoon grated nutmeg
¼ teaspoon ground star anise
Pinch of ground cloves
Pinch of kosher salt

Spiced Syrup
½ cup dark brown sugar
½ cup water
1 cinnamon stick
3 green cardamom pods
2 allspice berries
1 star anise
1 clove

Per Drink
Hot water
2 tablespoons Butter Base
½ ounce Spiced Syrup
2 ounces dark rum
¼ ounce heavy cream
Whipped cream
Grated nutmeg

1. To make the base: In a bowl, mix all the ingredients until well combined. Transfer the mixture onto a sheet of plastic wrap and form into a log. Wrap completely in the plastic wrap.

2. Refrigerate for at least 2 hours before using. Can be stored in the refrigerator for up to 2 weeks. This butter base makes enough for six servings.

3. To make the syrup: In a saucepan, whisk together the sugar and water over medium-high heat. Once the sugar dissolves, add the cinnamon, cardamom, allspice, star anise, and cloves and bring to a simmer. Reduce the heat to medium-low and simmer for 10 minutes. Remove from the heat and let cool.

4. Strain into an airtight container. Allow to cool to room temperature. Store in the refrigerator for at least 12 hours and up to 2 weeks. This makes enough for six servings.

5. To assemble: Fill a serving glass with hot water to heat up the glass. Discard the water. Place the butter base, spiced syrup, dark rum, and heavy cream in the cup. Fill up halfway with hot water and mix until the butter has melted.

6. Add enough water to fill the glass. Top with whipped cream and a generous sprinkling of grated nutmeg.
Note: The size of your glass determines how potent your drink will be. For a stronger punch, use an 8-ounce heat-resistant cup. For a slightly less potent drink, use a 16-ounce cup. Make sure to add the hot water slowly.

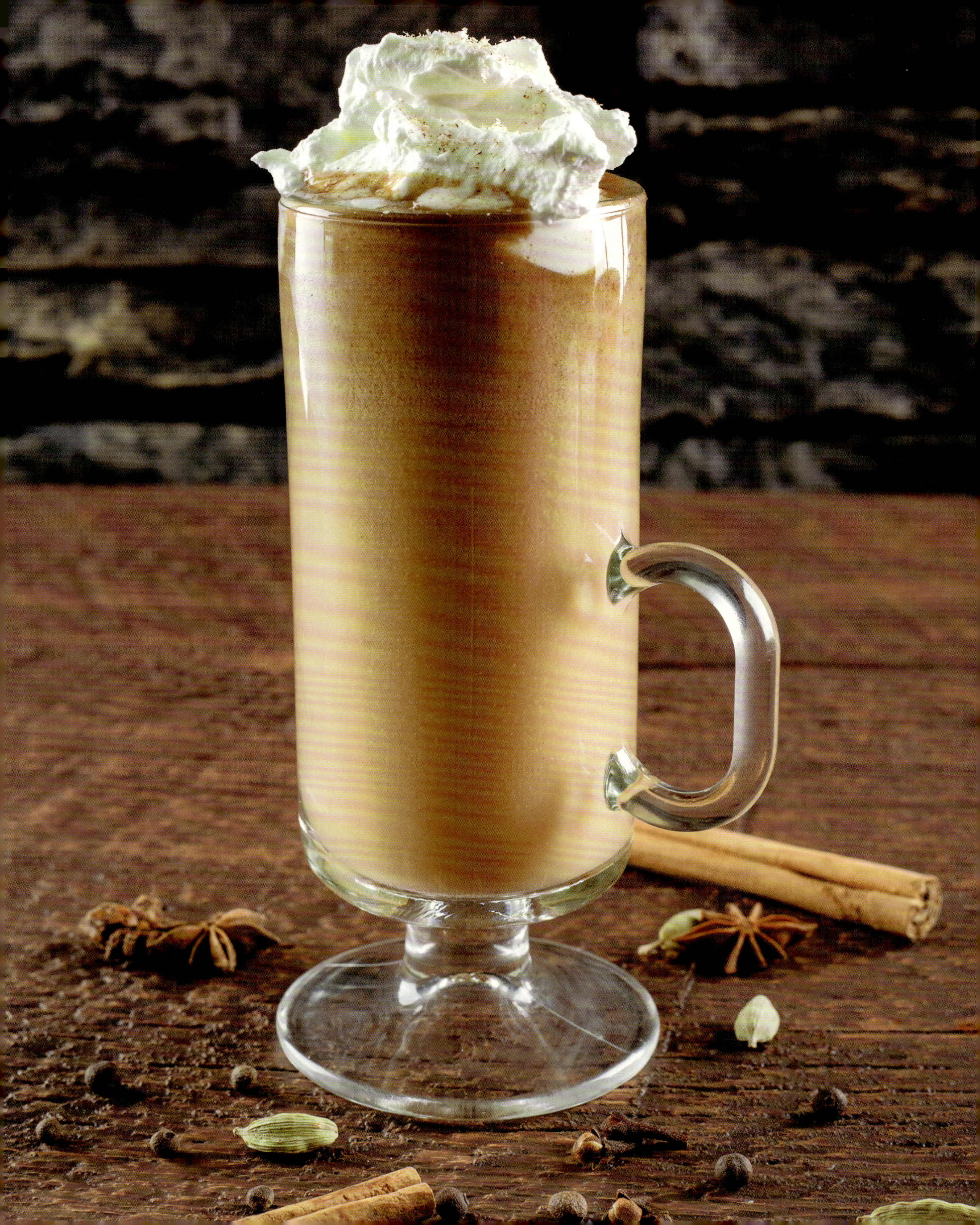

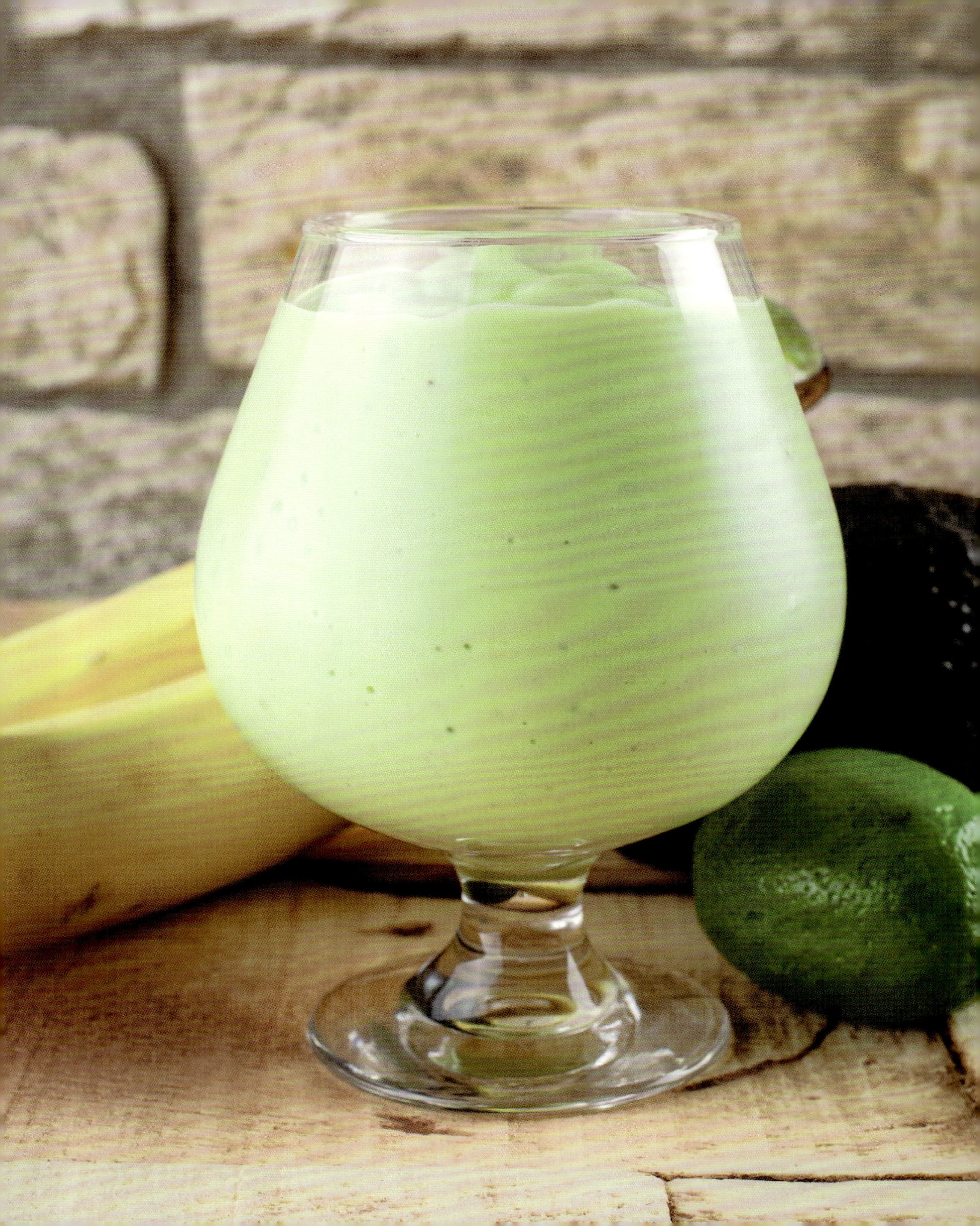

AVOCADO SMOOTHIE

DIFFICULTY
Novice

PREP TIME
10 minutes

SERVINGS
2 servings

DIETARY NOTES
Vegetarian

This rich, buttery smoothie is a healthier dessert option than ice cream while being just as tasty. The blend of coconut milk, salt, and avocado produces a sweet, cold drink with a beautiful aftertaste. The thick, filling texture couldn't be more refreshing! I've heard that Avocado Smoothies are a choice drink among asuran scholars of the College of Synergetics—you can find them chugging green smoothie after green smoothie when their research is up for review. They claim that avocado improves memory and focus. Could be true. I mostly think they just like how good it tastes.

1. In a blender, pulse the avocado, bananas, ginger, lime juice and zest, coconut milk, salt, and honey until smooth. Add the ice and pulse until the ice is crushed. **Note:** Drink this as soon as it is made because the avocado will start to oxidize and brown.

1 avocado
2 bananas
1 teaspoon ginger, grated
Juice and zest of 1 lime
¾ cup coconut milk
Pinch of salt
3 tablespoons honey
1½ cups ice

DIFFICULTY
Journeyman

PREP TIME
5 minutes

COOK TIME
5 minutes

SERVINGS
1 serving

DIETARY NOTES
Vegetarian

BLOODSTONE COFFEE

"For the millionth time, there are no culinary applications for bloodstone dust." If I had a coin for every time Robertus has said that to me, I'd have . . . more money to fund my bloodstone dust experiments! So far, Bloodstone Coffee is the most successful of my trial recipes. This blazing pick-me-up is evidence for the potential of bloodstone dust in cooking: The cayenne and anise blend the power of bloodstone smoothly in with the ground coffee bean. The wafting aroma of the brew, sharp and smoky, rouses the brain. This version has been pared down to be easier on the stomach, but true connoisseurs know where the fun is at!

⅛ teaspoon ground cinnamon
⅛ teaspoons ground cardamom
⅛ teaspoon ground cayenne
⅛ teaspoon ground star anise
1 to 2 tablespoons sweetened condensed milk
14 grams ground coffee
200 grams water, just off boiling

Equipment
Coffee phin
Kitchen scale

1. In a mug, whisk together the cinnamon, cardamom, cayenne, star anise, and sweetened condensed milk. Using a coffee grinder, grind the coffee into a medium grind.

2. Place the coffee phin on the glass and pour the coffee inside. Tighten the metal plate on top of the coffee until it compacts the coffee down, then loosen about a half rotation.
   Note: Make sure not to tighten it too much. If the coffee grounds are too compact, the water won't pass through, and you will over-extract the coffee.

3. Add 30 grams of boiling water to the filter and wait about 20 seconds. Add the rest of the water to bring the total water added to 200 grams. Add the metal cap to the top of the phin and wait for the water to pass through.
   Note: The goal is to have all your water move through the filter in about 3 to 5 minutes. The cap on the filter keeps heat in the brewing chamber, but it helps to occasionally remove it and see how much water has passed to get down the timing. If your water finishes too quickly, tightening the metal plate on the coffee or using a finer grind can lengthen the process. If it takes too long, try doing the opposite.

4. Once the water is done, remove the filter and whisk to mix with the sweetened condensed milk.

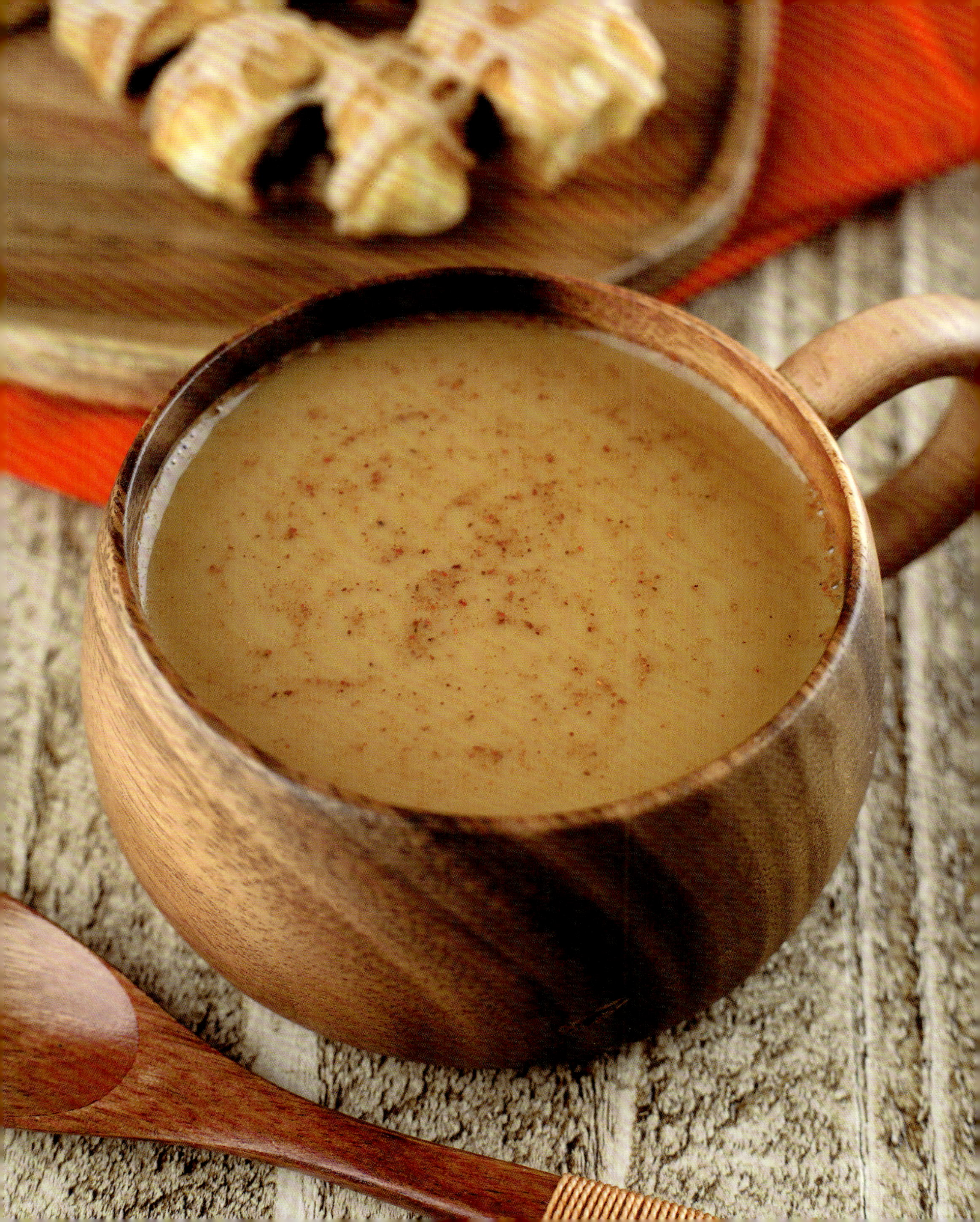

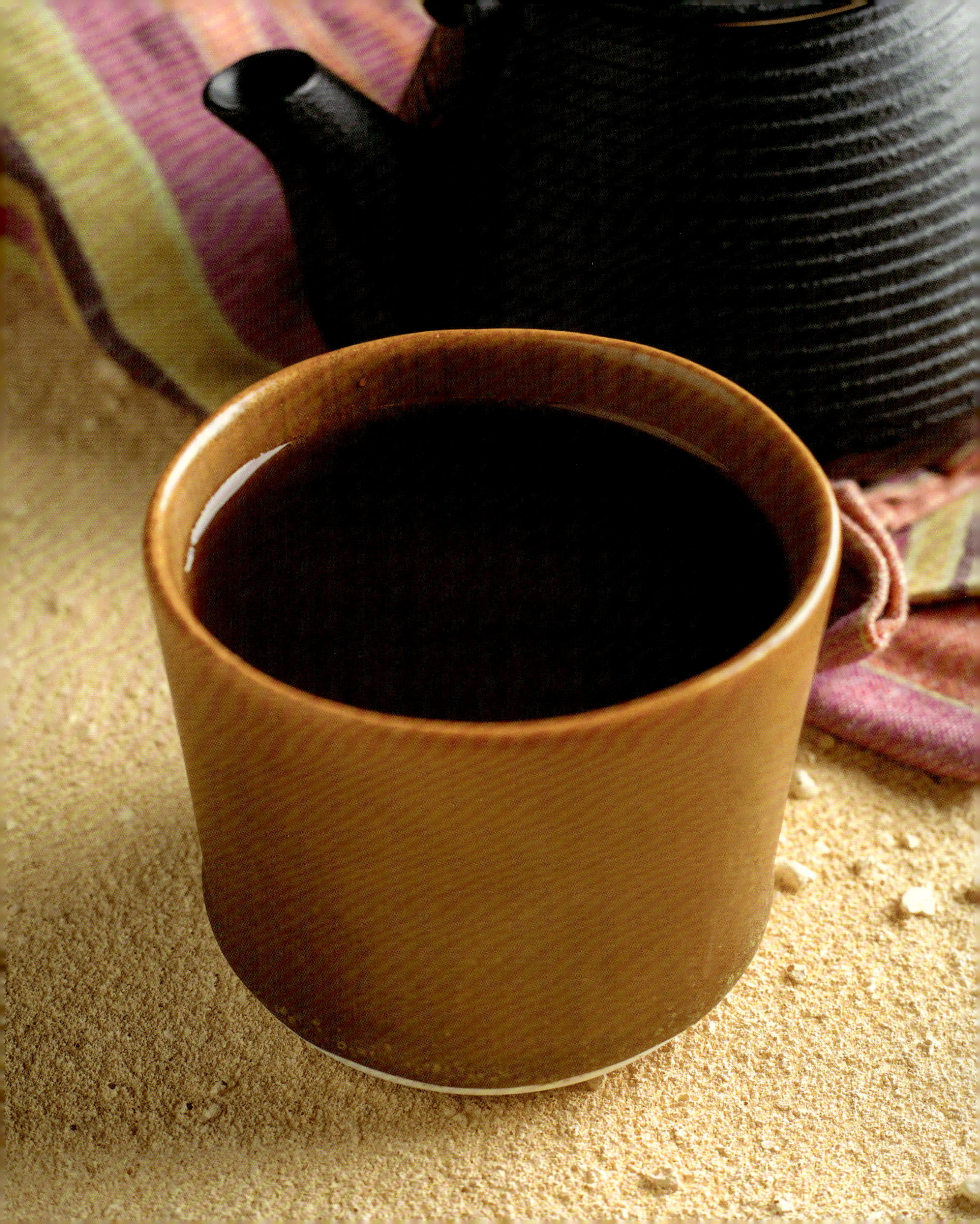

PITCHER OF DESERT-SPICED COFFEE

DIFFICULTY
Adept

PREP TIME
15 minutes

COOK TIME
25 minutes

SERVINGS
2 cups coffee

DIETARY NOTES
Vegan, Gluten free

While roaming the Crystal Desert, my band of travelers took a brief rest at a small oasis. I walked a ways away to scout our next heading when a small, mousy head popped up behind a sand dune. It was a skritt—she seemed just as startled to see me as I was to see her! She scampered off, dropping a scrap of paper with a recipe for Desert-Spiced Coffee on it. Well, well! One of my favorite activities is trying out mysterious recipes of dubious origin. I had picked up a bag of coffee beans at Amnoon Bazaar, so before we left the oasis I brewed a pot. The aroma was unlike any coffee I've had before. The warm tones of cinnamon and the earthy scent of cardamom transported me to a transcendent plane! The strong tastes of cumin and coriander swirled together in the brew and danced on my tongue. It was to die for—though I'm glad I didn't have to fight that caffeinated skritt!

1. In a medium saucepan, heat all the ingredients over medium-high heat and bring to a boil. Reduce the heat and simmer for 20 minutes.
   Note: As the water simmers, it will reduce the total. You should end up with at least as much water needed for a serving.
2. Place the ground coffee into a French press. Pour the spiced water over the coffee and let sit for 5 minutes.
3. Stir the top of the coffee with a spoon, then let sit for at least 5 more minutes.
4. Push down the French press plunger only until it reaches the top of the coffee sitting on the bottom of the French press. Pour into mugs and serve.

Spiced Water
3 cups water
1 cinnamon stick
3 green cardamom pods
1 teaspoon coriander seeds
½ teaspoon cumin seeds
¼ teaspoon black peppercorns
Pinch of kosher salt

French Press Serving
25 grams ground coffee
375 grams Spiced Water, 200°F

Equipment
Kitchen scale
French press

DIFFICULTY
Apprentice

PREP TIME
30 minutes

INACTIVE TIME
12 hours

COOK TIME
45 minutes

SERVINGS
1 serving

DIETARY NOTES
Vegan, Gluten free

MYSTERY TONIC

The first time I drank a Mystery Tonic—what I was sure was an exaggerated title—I suddenly poofed into a cloud of smoke. When I reappeared, my drinking buddies were all hooting and hollering at my bright pink feathers and shiny beak! I was the best-looking pink moa in the bar. Shortly after that, I transformed into a fire imp, then a boar, then an ooze! I was forced to admit that the Mystery Tonic is aptly named. Its funky magical properties are reflected in its intriguing cerulean butterfly pea color and the inviting citrus of lemongrass. Plus, I can promise you that learning how to make this version of the tonic will transform you into something grand: a more skilled mixologist!

Lemongrass Simple Syrup

½ cup sugar

½ cup water

2 lemongrass stalks

2 drops light blue food coloring (optional)

Tea Per Serving

1½ cups water

3 slices lotus root

2 slices ginger

6 dried butterfly pea flowers

1 to 2 tablespoons Lemongrass Simple Syrup

1. In a medium saucepan, whisk together the sugar and water and place over medium-high heat. Once the sugar dissolves, add the lemongrass and bring to a simmer. Reduce the heat to medium-low and simmer for 25 minutes. Remove from the heat and let cool.

2. Strain into an airtight container. Add the food coloring (if using) and mix in. Allow to cool to room temperature. Store in the refrigerator for at least 12 hours and up to 2 weeks. This makes about 10 servings worth of syrup for the tonic.

3. In a small pot, heat the water, lotus root, and ginger over medium-high heat and bring to a boil. Reduce the heat and simmer for 20 minutes.

4. Add the butterfly pea flowers and lemongrass simple syrup. Steep for 6 minutes. Strain and serve.

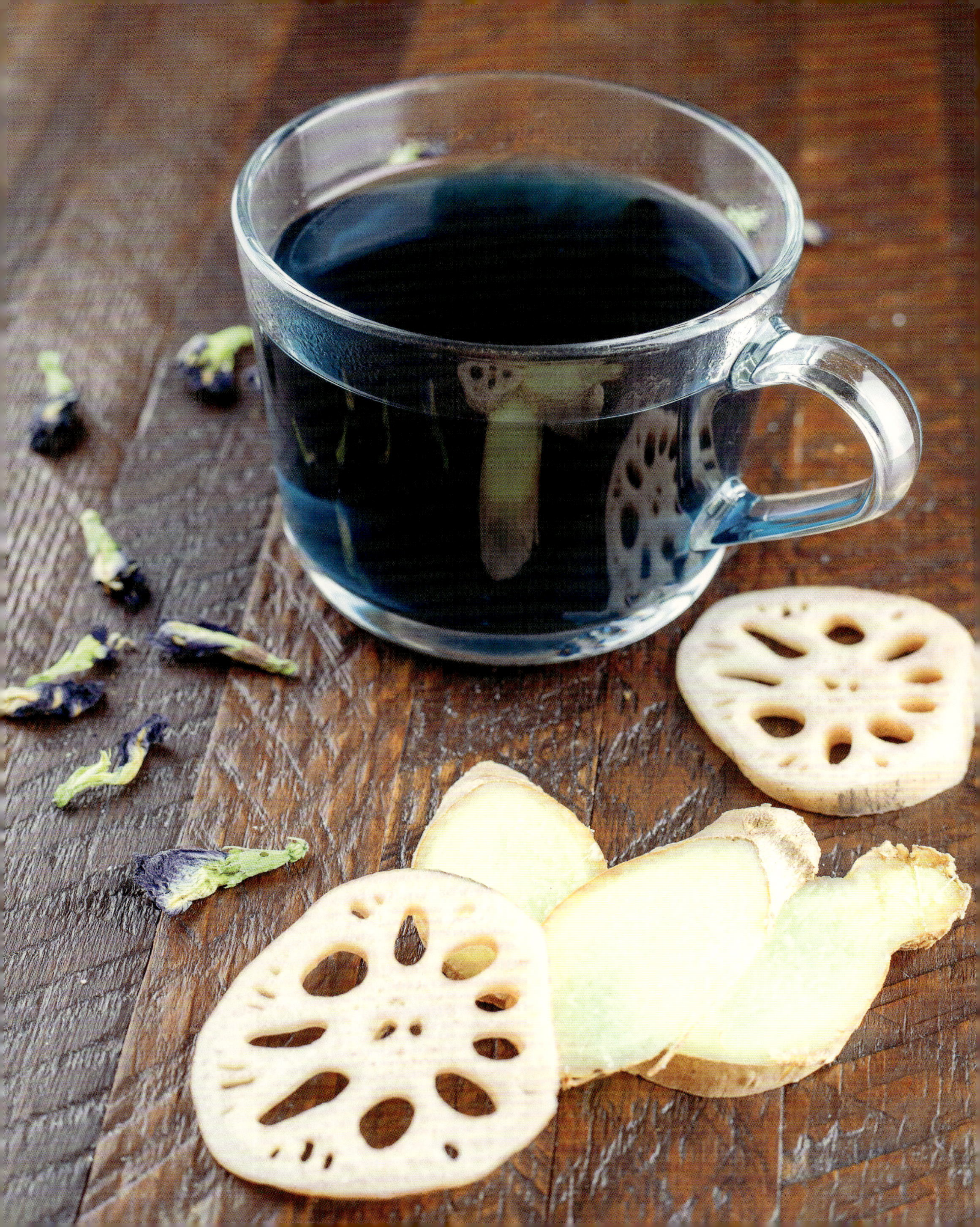

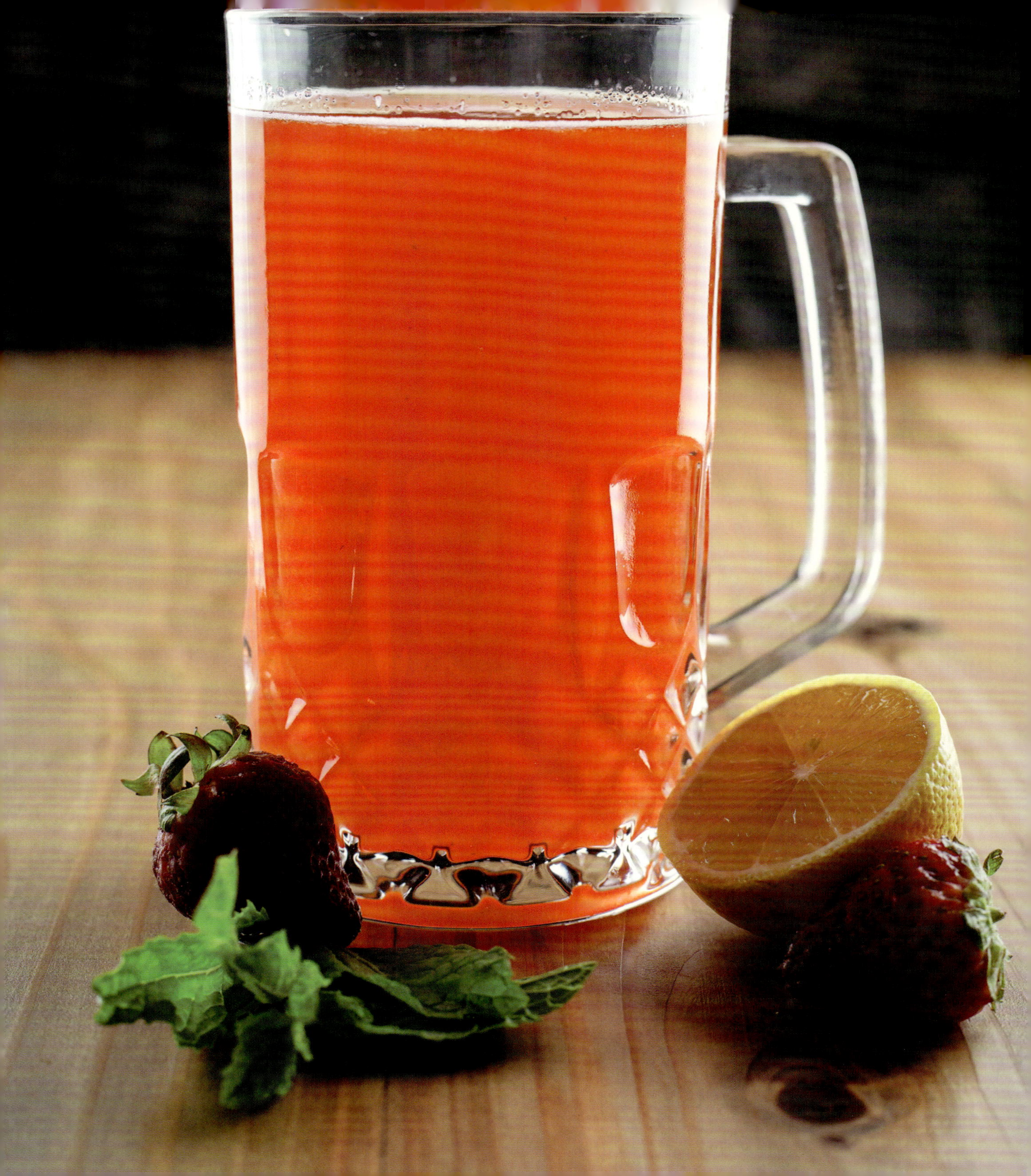

CELEBRATORY DRINK

DIFFICULTY
Adept

PREP TIME
30 minutes

INACTIVE TIME
12 hours

COOK TIME
20 minutes

SERVINGS
6 servings

DIETARY NOTES
Vegan

Celebratory Drink was named and popularized under good old King Doric, the first king of the united kingdoms of Tyria. King Doric shipped fresh strawberries in from the Cereboth Canyons and spread this recipe far and wide. The elderflower lemonade was an immediate hit, particularly in Lion's Arch where strawberries were close at hand. Today, the story of Celebratory Drink's origin has faded from widespread consciousness, but the people of Lion's Arch still raise this drink to celebrate.

1. In a medium saucepan, mix together the sugar and water over medium-high heat and bring to a simmer. Once the sugar dissolves, add the strawberries and reduce the heat to low. Simmer for 20 minutes.
2. Remove from the heat and smash the strawberries. Transfer through a fine-mesh strainer to a large pitcher.
3. Add the lemon juice to the pitcher. Add 2 cups of water. If it is too strong, add another cup or two of water to your liking. Cover and place in the refrigerator overnight to chill before serving.
4. In a cocktail shaker, muddle the strawberries, mint, and lemon. Add ice and the elderflower liqueur. Cover the shaker and shake vigorously for 20 seconds.
5. Pour through a mesh strainer into a large stein. Add the mead and strawberry lemonade and give it a light mix before serving.

Strawberry Lemonade

1½ cups sugar
1½ cups water
½ pound strawberries
2 cups lemon juice
2 to 4 cups water

Per Stein of Celebratory Drink

2 strawberries, hulled and quartered
1 mint sprig
1 lemon slice
1 ounce elderflower liqueur
7 ounces mead
10 ounces Strawberry Lemonade

DIFFICULTY
Initiate

PREP TIME
5 minutes

SERVINGS
1 serving

DIETARY NOTES
Vegetarian

ELIXIR OF HEROES

Here's another drink that's been mixed in celebration—and by some very prominent names! It's said that Logan Thackeray whipped up a batch of these cocktails at a raucous guild party after Zhaitan's defeat. As Queen Jennah's champion, he was well acquainted with the virtues of Ginger-Lime Ice Cream (page 165) and allegedly rhapsodized about them to the rest of his guild with such animation that they gathered up the ingredients together. It's funny to imagine Rytlock Brimstone and Eir Stegalkin crowded around a bowl of cream, waiting for the drink to come together like a bunch of drunkards in a pub. But it's not hard to imagine how much they must have enjoyed this—the bubbly sweet champagne meeting the tart lime! The way the ice cream works so smoothly with the vodka! In my opinion, anyone who makes this deserves the title "hero."

---

1 ounce vodka

1 ounce lime juice

2 scoops Ginger-Lime Ice Cream (page 165)

6 ounces champagne

2 lime slices, for garnish

1. In a large serving glass, combine the vodka and lime juice. Add the ginger-lime ice cream. Slowly pour in the champagne. Give it a light mix. Garnish the cup with lime slices. Serve with a spoon.

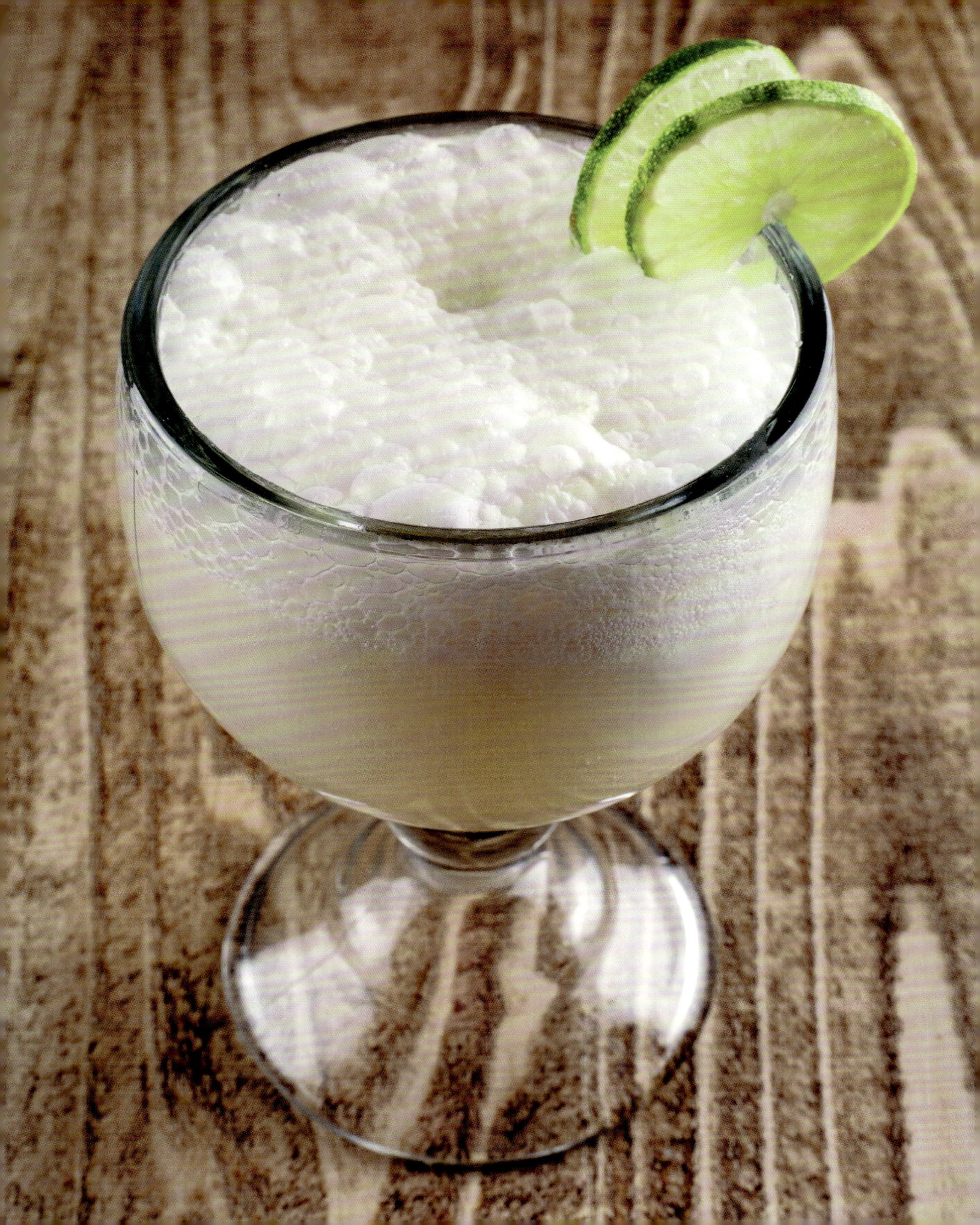

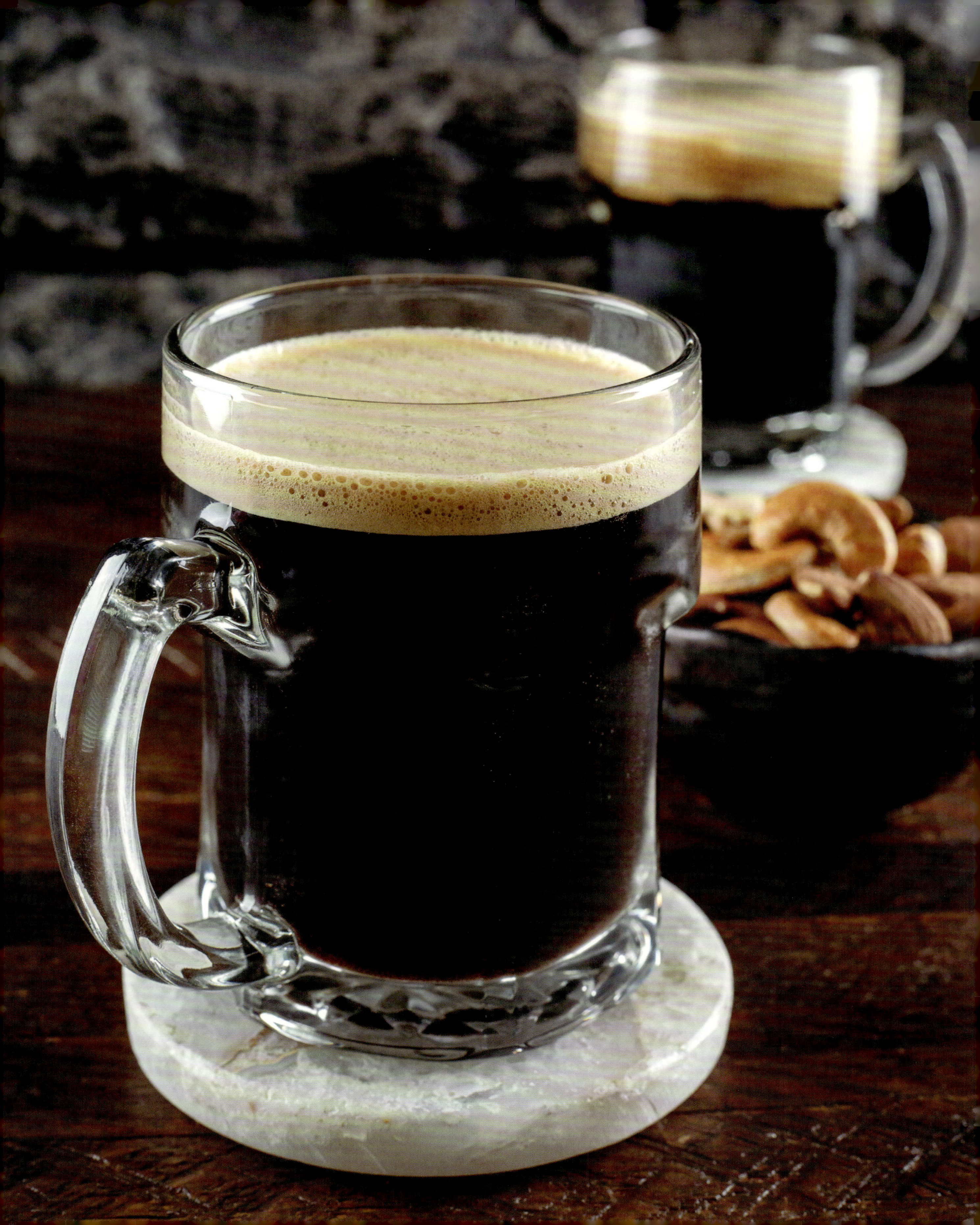

BELCHER'S BLUFF

DIFFICULTY
Initiate

PREP TIME
5 minutes

SERVINGS
1 drink

DIETARY NOTES
Vegan

If you've spent any time in a pub, you know Belcher's Bluff as an infamous drinking game where the loser has to drink this "interesting" concoction. Belcher's Bluff is usually played with raw omnomberry juice—at worst it's completely inedible, and at best it's sour enough to have your brain leaking from your ears. Worry not, my friend, because the preparation for my version of the cocktail allows it to be digestible AND to achieve sweet-and-sour fruity flavors that work in tandem! Chilling the cocktail while you shake it will negate the sourness, and the espresso and caffeinated elements will definitely have you energized. Next bar night, you'll want to keep bluffing for hours!

1. Place the ice cubes in a cocktail shaker. Add the remaining ingredients, cover, and shake for about 5 seconds.
   Note: Make sure to hold the top of the cocktail shaker and not to shake too much. If your stout has a high level of carbonation, it could cause too much pressure to build and pop the top off.
2. Strain into a chilled glass and serve.

3 ice cubes
8 ounces imperial stout
1 ounce bourbon
½ ounce coffee liqueur
½ ounce simple syrup
1 shot espresso
2 dashes chocolate bitters
Pinch of kosher salt

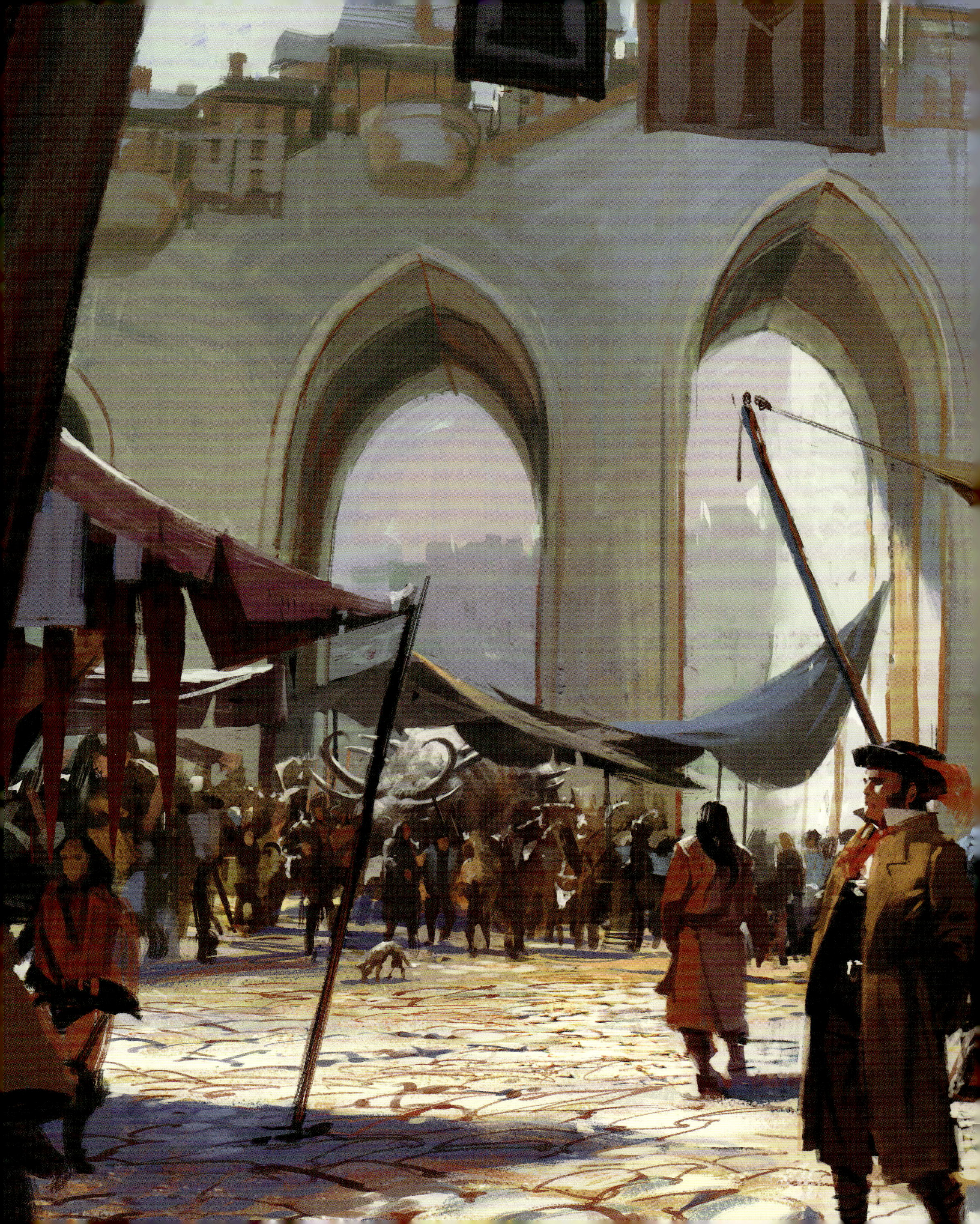

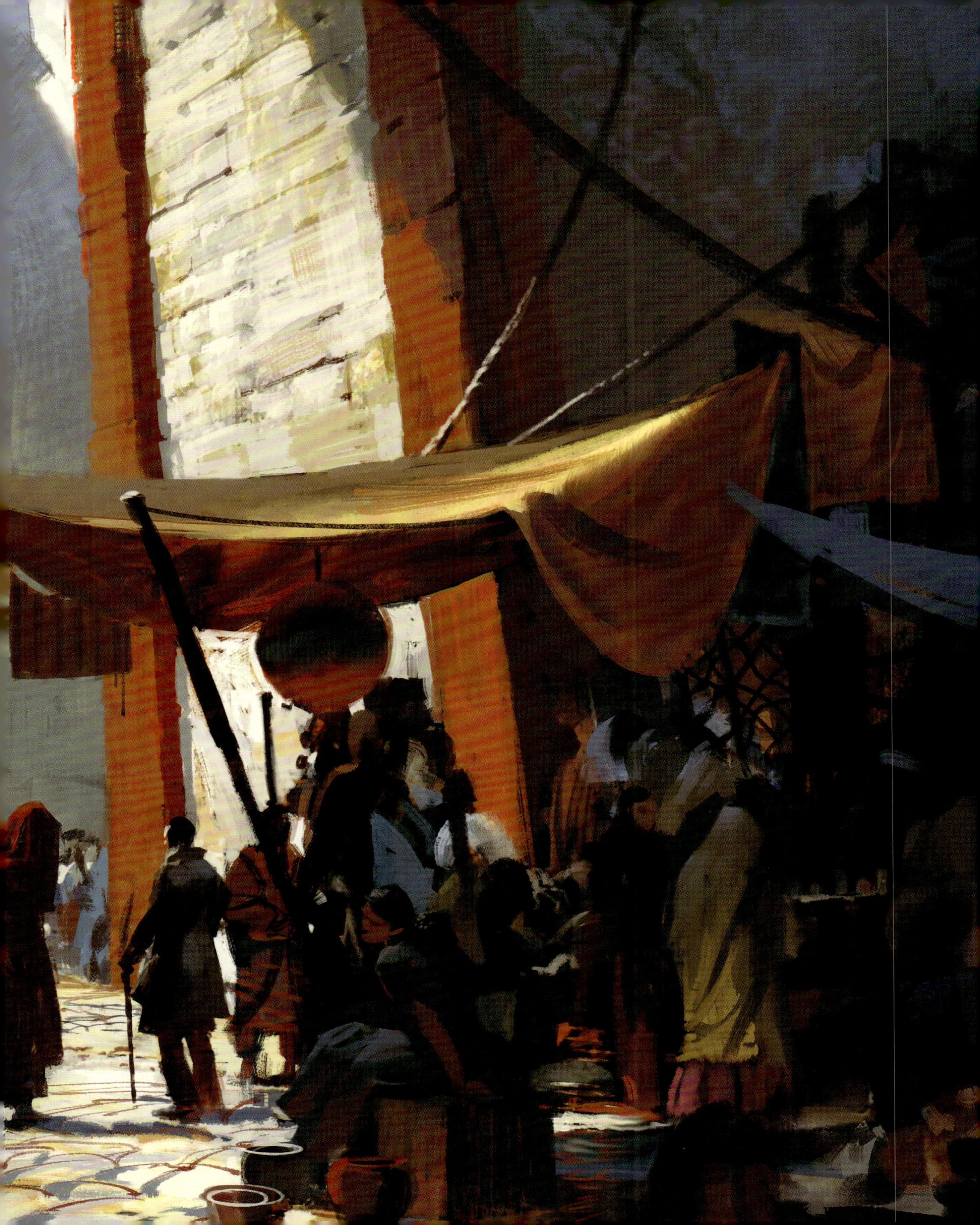

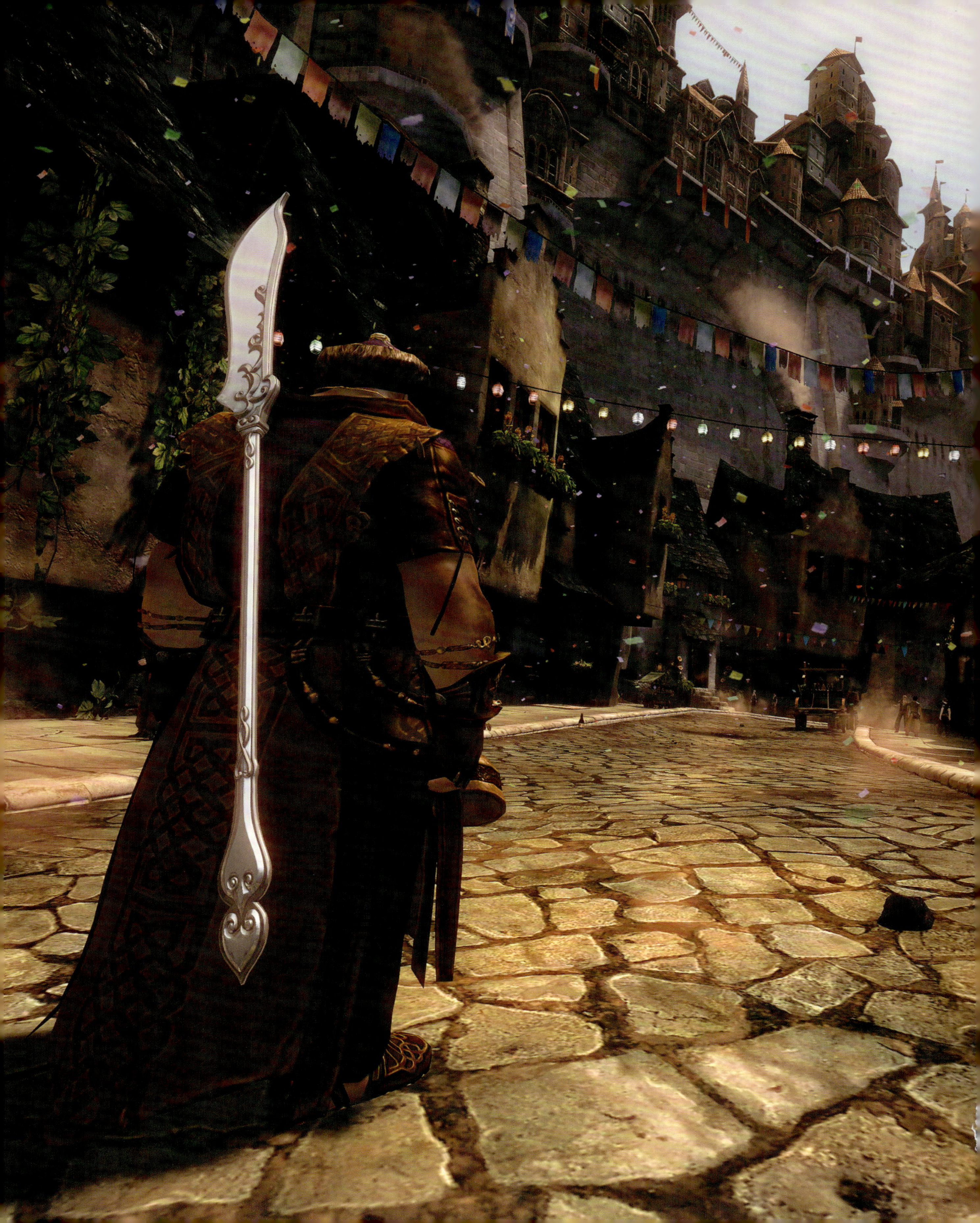

CONCLUSION

After my year of travel, I returned to the Durmand Priory to begin my formal training at the hands of Chef Robertus. I came into his kitchen with sharpened knives, ready to combat whatever first culinary challenge he threw at me. He did have a test prepared—but it wasn't one that relied on my cooking skills. It was just one question: "What drives your passion as a chef?"

I felt like I'd been knocked on the head with a bloody bludgeon! He had me completely stumped. Why *did* I like cooking? My first thought was the sense of warm triumph I got when doling out good food to people who appreciate it. But that was wrong. That wasn't why I had chosen to toil over the stove when other young norn were training with axes or spears. No warm, fuzzy feelings had made me leave the Shiverpeaks to pursue the Priory. Those sentiments had come later for me. No, I'd started cooking because I had a hunger for growth. I wanted to learn more. To become the great master I knew I could be! To fulfill my potential.

And guess what? That same potential lies within you. Now you have everything you need to start your culinary journey. You can use my recipes to cook up feasts for your family and dazzle your friends' taste buds. You can even leave a crumb or two for your enemies! But your journey doesn't need to end within the confines of this book. After you've mastered every recipe here, you should go off and hunt down more. Let your passion and potential drive you to greater heights!

And if you ever run into Chef Robertus, you can give him your own answer.

DIFFICULTY INDEX

NOVICE
- Bowl of Hummus
- Poultry Stock
- Red Meat Stock
- Vegetable Stock
- Mashed Potatoes
- Avocado Smoothie

INITIATE
- Cup of Lotus Fries
- Cheesy Cassava Roll
- Zucchini Bread
- Feast of Coleslaw
- Fruit Salad with Mint Garnish
- Potato and Leek Soup
- Tomato Soup
- Meaty Asparagus Skewer
- Elixir of Heroes
- Belcher's Bluff

APPRENTICE
- Saffron Stuffed Mushrooms
- Chili Pepper Popper
- Lake Doric Mussels
- Flatbread
- Salad à la Consortium
- Valravn Stew
- Spiced Mashed Yams
- Spicy Marinated Mushrooms
- Eztlitl Stuffing
- Jerk Poultry
- Poultry Piccata
- Tropical Mousse
- Mystery Tonic

JOURNEYMAN
- Spicy Moa Wings
- Mint-Pear Cured Meat Flatbread
- Zephyrite Fish Jerky
- Koi Cake
- Crispy Fish Pancakes
- Rosemary Bread
- Ascalonian Salad
- Feast of Bean Salad
- Fancy Creamy Mushroom Soup
- Butternut Squash Soup
- Grilled Plantains with Passion Fruit Sauce
- Fishy Rice Bowl
- Lemongrass Mussel Pasta
- Spicy Chocolate Cookies
- Buttered Spirits
- Bloodstone Coffee

ADEPT
- Red-Lentil Saobosa
- Kimchi Tofu Stew
- Carne Khan Chili
- Savory Spinach and Poultry Soup
- Feast of Meatball Dinner
- Peppercorn-Spiced Coq Au Vin
- Filet of Rosemary-Roasted Meat
- Beef Rendang
- Strawberry Cookies
- Bloodstone Bearclaw Pastry
- Mandragor Root Cake
- Super Mixed Parfait
- Ginger-Lime Ice Cream
- Pitcher of Desert-Spiced Coffee
- Celebratory Drink

MASTER
- Cinnamon Toast
- Mushroom and Asparagus Risotto
- Sugar Rib Roast
- Fancy Veggie Pizza
- Meaty Rice Bowl
- Peach Pie
- Delicious Rice Ball
- Chocolate Omnomberry Cake

GRANDMASTER
- Salsa Eggs Benedict
- Mint Crème Brûlée

ABOUT THE AUTHORS

VICTORIA ROSENTHAL launched her blog, *Pixelated Provisions*, in 2012 to combine her lifelong passions for video games and food by re-creating consumables found in many of her favorite games. When she isn't experimenting in the kitchen and dreaming up new recipes, she spends time with her husband and corgi hiking, playing video games, and enjoying the latest new restaurants. Victoria is also the author of *Fallout: The Vault Dweller's Official Cookbook*, *Destiny: The Official Cookbook*, and *Pokémon: My Pokémon Cookbook*.

ERIN KWONG is a writer and narrative designer of video games, board games, and everything in between. She is a lifelong fan of playable stories and enjoys subjecting her loved ones to playing with her. In her spare time, she directs the local ballet company in her hometown of Rockville, Maryland.

CONVERSION CHARTS

VOLUMES

US	METRIC
⅕ teaspoon (tsp)	1 ml
1 teaspoon (tsp)	5 ml
1 tablespoon (tbsp)	15 ml
1 fluid ounce (fl. oz.)	30 ml
⅕ cup	50 ml
¼ cup	60 ml
⅓ cup	80 ml
3.4 fluid ounces (fl. oz.)	100 ml
½ cup	120 ml
⅔ cup	160 ml
¾ cup	180 ml
1 cup	240 ml
1 pint (2 cups)	480 ml
1 quart (4 cups)	.95 liter

TEMPERATURES

FAHRENHEIT	CELSIUS
200°	93.3°
212°	100°
250°	120°
275°	135°
300°	150°
325°	165°
350°	177°
400°	205°
425°	220°
450°	233°
475°	245°
500°	260°

WEIGHT

US	METRIC
0.5 ounce (oz.)	14 grams (g)
1 ounce (oz.)	28 gram (g)
¼ pound (lb.)	113 gram (g)
⅓ pound (lb.)	151 grams (g)
½ pound (lb.)	227 grams (g)
1 pound (lb.)	454 grams (g)

INSIGHT EDITIONS

PO Box 3088
San Rafael, CA 94912
www.insighteditions.com

Find us on Facebook: www.facebook.com/InsightEditions
Follow us on Instagram: @insighteditions

Published by Insight Editions, San Rafael, California, in 2025.
No part of this book may be reproduced in any form without written permission from the publisher.
Library of Congress Cataloging-in-Publication Data available.
ISBN: 979-8-88663-868-4

Publisher: Raoul Goff
SVP, Group Publisher: Vanessa Lopez
VP, Creative: Chrissy Kwasnik
VP, Manufacturing: Alix Nicholaeff
Publishing Director: Mike Degler
Art Director: Catherine San Juan
Junior Designer: Samuel Louie
Editorial Director: Jennifer Sims
Senior Editor: Eric Geron
Editorial Assistant: Jeff Chiarelli
Managing Editor: Nora Milman
Production Manager: Deena Hashem
Strategic Production Planner: Lina s Palma-Temena

Photography by Victoria Rosenthal
Text by Victoria Rosenthal and Erin Kwong

ROOTS of PEACE   REPLANTED PAPER

Insight Editions, in association with Roots of Peace, will plant two trees for each tree used in the manufacturing of this book. Roots of Peace is an internationally renowned humanitarian organization dedicated to eradicating land mines worldwide and converting war-torn lands into productive farms.

Manufactured in China by Insight Editions
10 9 8 7 6 5 4 3 2 1

ArenaNet

Head of Marketing: Lis Cardy
Director of Events and Partnerships: Katy Radelich
Senior Brand Manager: Pedro Cano
Studio Narrative Director: Bobby Stein
GW2 Art Director: Aaron Coberly
User Interface Lead: Duncan Kay
Special Thanks: Carol Stein

©2009–2025 ArenaNet, LLC. All rights reserved. Guild Wars, Guild Wars 2, ArenaNet, NCSOFT, the NC Logo, and all associated logos and designs are trademarks or registered trademarks of NCSOFT Corporation. All other trademarks are the property of their respective owners.